UNEXPECTED CONSEQUENCES

The Diaconate Renewed

SUSANNE WATSON EPTING

Morehouse Publishing
NEW YORK

Morehouse Publishing, 19 East 34th Street, New York, NY 10016

Morehouse Publishing is an imprint of Church Publishing Incorporated.

www.churchpublishing.org

Cover design by Laurie Klein Westhafer

Typeset by Denise Hoff

Library of Congress Cataloging-in-Publication Data

Epting, Susanne Watson. Unexpected consequences : the diaconate renewed / Susanne Watson Epting.

pages cm

Includes bibliographical references.

ISBN 978-0-8192-2979-3 (pbk.)—ISBN 978-0-8192-2980-9 (ebook) 1. Deacons—Episcopal Church. I. Title.

BX5967.5.E68 2015 262'.14373—dc23

2014046404

Printed in the United States of America

Contents

Preface   v

**1 Creating a New Vision; Setting the Stage for a
    Renewed Order**   1
    Six Long Years   4
    Imagining New Possibilities, Reenvisioning the Church   7
    Influences, Asides, and *Lex Orandi, Lex Credendi*   11

2 Waves and Ways of Being   17
    Riding the Waves   17

3 Shaped by a New Prayer Book   35
    The Total Ministry of the Church   39

4 Shaped by Living—The Fifth Wave as a Decade of Definition   47

5 Living in the Fifth Wave—Wading into a Sixth   61
    From Definition to Interpretation   61

6 The Sixth Wave—Interpretation and Prophetic Voice   79

**7 Wading More Deeply into the Seventh Wave—Up to Our
    Waists Integrating All We've Learned**   97
    Theological Education for the Anglican Communion (TEAC)   99
    The Constable Fund Grant for a Partnership Project
    between the Office for Ministry Development and the
    North American Association for the Diaconate   103
    Principles Common to Quality Deacon Formation Programs   108
    Proclaiming Education for All (PEALL)   110
    The Diaconate and Called to Common Mission   113
    Changing Assignments in Diocesan Contexts and New
    Relationships with Church-Wide Offices   118

8   Seven Waves and Room for More   **123**
   Interpretation, Integration, Ebbing, Flowing, and
   Unexpected Consequences   123
   Baptismal Identity   125
   On Engaging the *Diakonia* of All Believers   127
   The Diaconate as Adaptable and Contextual   132
   The Importance of Diaconal Community   141
   Unexpected but Critical—The Charge to Be Interpreters   148

9   Are We There Yet?   **155**
   Thoughts about Educational Content and Process . . .   156
   Promotion of Both the Diaconate and the *Diakonia* of
   All Believers   159
   New Models of Ministry   161
   Diaconal Spirituality   162
   Attention to Youth and Young Adults   164

Postscript   171

Acknowledgments   173

Appendix One: Deacons Are in the Picture   175

Appendix Two: Citizens of the World—Servants of Christ   183

Appendix Three: Principles of Orderly Exchange   193

Notes   195

Preface

The title of this book comes from two places. The first is from a conversation twenty years ago about the then still new Book of Common Prayer. Even though we had lived with the 1979 Prayer Book for some fifteen years, it still seemed new. Sitting at a table with colleagues, I remember someone saying, "You know when the authors of this prayer book finished, and the book was adopted, they said that there would be some surprises. And they said we'd just have to live with the new book and discover them."

The second place "unexpected consequences" cropped up was in a statement I wrote jointly with C. Christopher Epting, bishop and then presiding bishop's Deputy for Ecumenical and Interreligious Relations. The statement was prepared for a conference on the diaconate held in Stuttgart, Germany, in November of 2003. In preparation for the meeting, Epting's office was to send a summary on the state of the diaconate in The Episcopal Church. As we wrote that statement, we went through all the ordination vows and charges, and gave a brief summary of their meaning and implications. When we reached the charge to "interpret to the Church the needs, concerns, and hopes of the world," we included this:

> This prophetic and interpretive role of the deacon may well be
> an unanticipated result of the restoration of the order in today's
> world. In fact, this area for all its strength is sometimes a point
> of tension. For while the deacon can point the way toward mis-
> sion and the building of the church, it is also the deacon who
> sometimes must ask the church to **dismantle** those things that
> get in the way of mission and care for others, inviting her to
> recreate herself as a servant structure.

Fast-forward ten years to the spring of 2013, and the conception of this book. I had been asked to do a review of the waves of the diaconate in

The Episcopal Church for the annual gathering of formation directors and archdeacons, sponsored by the Association for Episcopal Deacons. Part of the motivation for that request was that, in some dioceses, the deacon community included individuals who had been trained in the "third wave" to be sacramental and pastoral assistants. Others had been trained out of a model that came during the first decade or so after the 1979 Prayer Book was adopted. This model was oriented more toward having a "servant ministry" outside the church. Still others were trained a little later, when it became important to empower and engage all our parishioners in diaconal ministry. And so it went.

As I prepared for the presentation, I realized that I had experienced all of those models and that there was an important history to be recorded about the contemporary diaconate in The Episcopal Church.

Ormonde Plater has written a definitive volume on the diaconate in *Many Servants*. In it, he describes four waves of the diaconate in The Episcopal Church. He also offers much more on the history of the diaconate, the training of deacons, and the care and feeding of them. Here I have reviewed and retold the story; however, this is not a primer or a "how-to" book for deacons. It is the history of a movement, an Order in the contemporary church, and, I hope, a testimony to the power of living more deeply into the words and theology of our prayer book.

I have continued to use the metaphor of "waves" to describe the ebbs, flows, and shifts as deacons have claimed the vision the church has articulated and called them to. It makes this all a little messy. It's sometimes hard to see where one wave ends and another begins. Often, they swirl together. There is nothing cut and dried about how we have matured. However, under the fourth, fifth, sixth, and seventh waves, the foundation remains the ordination service in the Book of Common Prayer, along with the Baptismal Covenant. It is impossible to separate them.

For some, the unexpected consequences might seem more logical than unexpected. For those who began with a prayer book vision, but no experience, I suspect there will be some surprises. We will find that the waves are marked by transition, definition, interpretation, and integration. Underneath it all, we hold the Baptismal Covenant, and the total ministry of the church, as the most critical to understand and embrace.

It is my hope that this volume will serve not only to preserve history but to highlight the foundation on which we might move in creative new ways.

Susanne Watson Epting
The Feast of David Pendleton Oakerhater, 2014

CHAPTER 1

Creating a New Vision; Setting the Stage for a Renewed Order

It's been said that history doesn't look like history when you're living through it; it just "looks confusing and messy, and it always feels uncomfortable."[1] Perhaps that's one reason why, unless our personality is somewhat analytical, we don't often think about how we are living history. In The Episcopal Church our attention to history is thwarted, from time to time, by the fact that we focus so much on what we call the "triennial," a three-year cycle of General Conventions at which we set new priorities, recommit to old ones, forget the ones we already set, or wonder why we set any at all.

Perhaps we don't attend to history because no one ever made it relevant or exciting. That's somewhat ironic given that, as church folk, we tell and retell the stories of people of faith, throughout the ages, as part of our rhythm of communal life. In the midst of them, we don't realize that the stories we're living now, the patterns we are establishing, the changes we are making, the generation-to-generation legacies we are leaving, are not so unlike the history that Moses and the Israelites were making during their generation of exile. A lot happened in that forty years in the wilderness. In fact, a lot has happened in the last forty years in The Episcopal Church. Indeed as we consider the diaconate in this church, the last forty years are critical to our understanding and development of the Order.

It thus becomes important to reckon with the history we've been a part of making. History here, as it relates to the contemporary story of deacons, and to the diaconal ministry of all believers, begins just after the approval of our current Book of Common Prayer (hereafter BCP 1979). Of course, I find this part of church history remarkable because it's the part of the church's history that I've lived. I've never lived with any other version of the Book of Common Prayer, so I assumed from the beginning (my beginning in The Episcopal Church being in 1977 when the book was already in pews for trial use), that the theology set forward in our current prayer book is what we all believed. What I didn't realize, for many years, is that it has taken the church a while to live into this theology and the changes this version of the prayer book brought us. The diaconate is part of that. In fact, the church's understanding of her own servant nature is part of that.

Only now am I coming to recognize the ways in which I was personally (along with many others) caught up in making history as I journeyed, nudged by the Spirit, toward the life and work of a deacon and the meaning of a long-ignored Order in the Church. While I offer this interpretation of history from my own point of view, there are many others who have been making it and living it in their own ways.

I was thirty-one years old when a supportive vicar spoke to the bishop about my becoming a deacon. The year was 1980—just a year into the "official" use of the BCP 1979. I had struggled with the ordination of women and, though I supported it, it called me to move beyond tradition in a way that surprised me. Looking back, I suspect the struggle was less about ordaining women and more about patriarchal models of leadership. As more and more women were ordained to the priesthood, I would be uplifted by new models, new images, and new possibilities. However, at the time, someone suggested that since I wasn't sure about ordination to the priesthood, maybe I should look at being a deacon. I had no idea what a deacon was, but when I looked at the ordination service, everything about it resonated with me. It wasn't any longer about women's ordination, but about which Order captured my soul. And because I was a new Episcopalian, unaware of the significance that the Order was being reenvisioned, I simply had no idea that this was such a novel and unexplored option in The Episcopal Church. It's taken me nearly twenty-five years to recognize how significant that was and, I suspect, the church may still be living into that—into what came with the liturgical and theological revisions incorporated into the BCP 1979.

In 1980 the bishop didn't tell me no. Nor did he tell me yes. He told me that the church had undertaken a six-year study to examine what the diaconate should be in its new incarnation.[2] He offered to send me to a conference at Notre Dame on the diaconate, and suggested that I report back and keep him informed. What I experienced there is, quite likely, what carried me through the next eight years of waiting.

Those in attendance were history makers. They'd already been part of research on the diaconate, shaping the prayer book, and offering statements on why they thought this distinctive Order important, even necessary. They were leaders in thinking about the "total ministry of the church." While they envisioned a distinctive diaconate, it was always in relationship to all other ministry, and especially so as the church claimed a new and deep commitment to develop "lay ministry." But before I say more about that gathering, it's important to return to the beginning of the six-year study the church had already undertaken.

A report of a 1978 survey said:

> At its 1977 meeting in Port St. Lucie, Florida, the House of Bishops asked the Council for the Development of Ministry to undertake an empirical study of the Diaconate in the Episcopal Church in the United States. The study was underway when the house met in Kansas City in 1978. The charge was then enlarged to ask not just for data on the diaconate, but for analysis and recommendations from the Council.
>
> During the past two years the Council has designed and executed the survey, analyzed the results, and appointed a special committee to prepare recommendations. While committee members often disagreed and debated the issues, in the end they found they could come to a common mind and submit this report for the consideration of the House. This consensus is evident in the following agreed statement:
>
> Upon reflection on the report of the findings of the survey, the committee agrees that the primary issue of concern is the servant (diaconal) nature of the church. Questions directly related to the order of deacons are secondary to the primary issue.
>
> The study has demonstrated to us that there is an obvious gap between the experience of the Diaconate as it appears in the study, and a vision of the Diaconate expressed by a majority of diocesan Commissions on Ministry and bishops.
>
> The doctrine of diaconal ministry as expressed in the Ordinal of the Proposed Book of Common Prayer and the description of actual diaconal ministry as portrayed in the Study point to a disparity between the reality of the diaconate as it is now practiced and the ideal expressed. We believe that some change will be necessary if the permanent Diaconate is to live out more clearly the understanding of the Church as the servant (diaconal) people of God.
>
> Though some amongst us think that the permanent Diaconate might be discontinued, others feel that it has validity but should be enhanced. Given the realities of the study and the opinions identified therein, we all believe that the new directions called for in the study should be evaluated and this evaluation should be presented not later than 1985 at General Convention.

> The report has demonstrated the need to explore new forms of ministry which express the servant ministry of the Church. . . .
>
> The disparity between the vision of a diaconal ministry of servanthood and the actuality of a diaconate which is often seen—and often sees itself—as a minor order of priesthood understandably evokes the apparently conflicting responses reported in the survey: 94% of all respondents feel that the church should have a vital diaconate, yet only 18% of the participatory bishops have plans to ordain permanent deacons.
>
> The survey makes it obvious that there is reluctance on the part of many to continue support of the diaconate in its present form. At the same time, there is a great interest in developing a Diaconate which would be distinctive from and yet enhancing of the ministry of the other clergy and of the laity.[3]

It's taken me many years to fully appreciate why the bishop in my diocese wanted to wait until the six-year study was complete. Here I was in 1980, only two years after "some amongst us" thought the permanent diaconate should be discontinued. And yet, the church had just adopted a prayer book which included a new vision of the diaconate. How like Episcopalians!

While the diaconate has a long history, beginning with the earliest church, and while there had been many discussions about renewing it for the contemporary times, The Episcopal Church simply did not have a history with the new vision offered in the prayer book. Thus, it was easy to conclude that, for a time, there was no common understanding of this Order. Since then, however, many deacons and others who believe in diaconal ministry have more clearly defined that vision.

It is that defining journey that we will explore here. How did we get from "some amongst us" believing that we should do away with the diaconate to an order that is vibrant and vital?

Six Long Years

After the empirical study conducted in 1978 and the presentation of its subsequent analysis to the House of Bishops, the 1979 General Convention "directed the Council for the Development of Ministry to begin to implement the recommendations contained in their report and to be prepared to make a presentation on the results at the 1985 General Convention."[4] The next step was for the Council to call a Consultation on the Diaconate in May of 1980.

Thirty-one dioceses (about a third of the dioceses in the church at that time) were represented at the consultation. We learn from their report that

> the first task of the consultation was to define *servant ministry*, a term entering the consciousness of many people, at least in regard to the Episcopal diaconate, for the first time. Once arrived at, the definition quickly became the focal point of all the discussions that followed. This was their definition of the servant ministry:
>
> Servant ministry is the sacrificial work of the baptized community in which we share *Christ's presence and activity of making whole* by our response to and advocacy for those in need. This work includes identifying and proclaiming to individuals, institutions, and authorities the needs of the world.[5]

It was through this lens that those attending the consultation would look at the selection and deployment of deacons, appropriate training, supervision, and the effects of the diaconate on other ministries.

The consultation spent no small amount of time in reiterating and clarifying that "in order to select people for the servant ministry of the diaconate there had to be a clear idea on the part of the persons selecting as well as on the part of the aspirants to the diaconate what the role of the deacon was actually to be."[6]

It is important to note here that at the time these studies were undertaken, the role of deacons in the church had been primarily as pastoral and liturgical assistants. In the servant ministry definition shared by the Consultation, we begin to see the importance of the "baptized community." It was a remarkable thing that the church was looking at the relevance of an Order in relationship to the whole people of God. It would also be remarkable should the church do that with all other Orders! The important thing, however, is that the diaconate was not reenvisioned in a vacuum.

Recall the church of that time was deeply committed to the development of lay ministry, now what we simply call "ministry." Over time we would come to see that this careful definition of the diaconate, albeit at times painfully slow, would serve us well in recognizing the role of deacons in developing ministry in and with others, owning a primarily baptismal identity, and pushing the church to deal with her tendency toward clericalism.

We would also come to realize that, while these initial attempts to define a role, the training for it, the best ways to deploy those serving in it, and how best to tell the church about it, those definitions were being offered by people who had never lived in that role. This will be important to keep in mind as we observe the further unfolding of the definition of the ministry, and the living of it.

The culmination of the church's six-year review of the diaconate would come with one more study, conducted between 1981 and 1984, of eight dioceses engaged in the renewal of the diaconate (Albany, California, Central Florida, Hawaii, Michigan, Nevada, Pittsburgh, and Spokane). With this study we begin to see questions about the diaconate that have now evolved into patterns, qualities—questions not to be solved with a definitive answer but with a flexibility of living—and a conscious recognition of the importance of being contextual and adaptable.

The study of the eight dioceses addressed:

- the purposes and benefits of ordaining persons to the diaconate, including thoughts on the deacon as symbol of servant ministry, the meaning of ordination, the deacon's role in the liturgy, the deacon as enabler of lay ministry;
- the hierarchy of orders, including whether deacons should have a distinctive and equal ministry, factors that hinder that equality with other orders, canonical requirements regarding authority, differences in education between priests and deacons, the part-time status of nonstipendiary deacons compared with the full-time status of the stipendiary priest;
- issues in the training and deployment of deacons, including how deacons might be similarly or differently trained than priests, whether they should stay in their home congregations, or whether they should be moved, ministry assignments in general;
- equality in the relative value among orders, including establishing collegial relations between priest, supervisor, and deacon, the relationship with the bishop, and developing distinctive ministries;
- and finally an assessment of the overall impact of the participating dioceses' diaconate program on the understanding of the Order and of deacons in these dioceses on the ministry of their congregations.[7]

We discover that overall the diaconate is growing and seen positively. And yet we read in the foreword to the document, "In spite of current enthusiasm all should not be viewed as in order. From those surveyed, it is clear that there is no consistent or necessarily coherent vision of what the diaconate should be, specifically what is distinctive about what the deacon is to do to be an effective sacramental sign of our common ministry of servanthood in Christ."[8]

Once again we return to a key concept. All of the study, all of the questions, all of the issues about training, deployment, authority, relationship—all of these—were ways of defining an Order that would enable the church to engage with the *diakonia* of all believers—to be a servant church.

Often the church tends more to institutional concerns created by new ideas than it does to spiritual ones. In fairness, those institutional concerns can come to make up the important infrastructure that will undergird glorious new possibilities, but without holding the practical spiritual living of the idea in tension with our constitution and canons, we risk rather brittle interpretations of what the living, breathing, changing, growing, imagining body of Christ really is. Without the positive and practical, that infrastructure can be used to control instead of to free us with support. Therefore, it's important to consider what other initiatives were taking place at the same time as these church-sponsored studies.

Imagining New Possibilities, Reenvisioning the Church

At the same time the six-year study was taking place, a movement was growing. While my first exposure to that movement was at Notre Dame in 1981, that meeting was actually the second gathering of reformers committed to the renewal of the diaconate.

In 1979 a three-day meeting on "The Diaconate . . . A Unique Place in the Total Ministry" was sponsored by the National Centre for the Diaconate and Associated Parishes, Inc., with the help of the Episcopal Dioceses of Central Florida, Indianapolis, Louisiana, Minnesota, Nevada, Pittsburgh, and Western Massachusetts. The program was held in liaison with the Episcopal Church Council for the Development of Ministry, though it is not clear that the Council was an actual sponsor or financial contributor. They were conducting studies of their own.

The final press release reported that "despite the difficulties caused by the United Airlines strike and the gasoline crisis, about 165 persons from all over the United States and Canada attended a successful major conference on the diaconate. . . . There was also Lutheran, Methodist and Roman Catholic representation."[9]

While the studies requested by the House of Bishops and others were important, the attendance of so many at this conference, from such a variety of locations, was testimony to the persistence of those committed to the renewal of the diaconate. It was also an opportunity for many who

were curious to learn about historical, theological, liturgical, and ministerial aspects of the Order.

Three things stand out as especially significant to the future evolution
of deacons in The Episcopal Church. The first is that the gathering was a
good mix of scholarly, spiritual, and practical approaches to this ministry.
The second is that deacons participated—in the presentation of a major
paper, in liturgy planning and participation. Third, the title of the conference and the intention of its planners reflected a very important concept
of the time, that is, the total ministry of the church. These gatherings were
not held simply to reenvision the diaconate for its own sake. (Indeed total
ministry language had been used in some of the church-sponsored studies
already discussed. The implication was that there was a shift occurring,
away from the community gathering around a minister, to a community
gathered around a table and a font, becoming ministering communities.)
It is heartening to remember that the church once thought about "total
ministry" as something other than a method of survival for small congregations and small dioceses. At that time small dioceses and small congregations were leading the way in examining how to live a theology newly
articulated in the revised prayer book—partly through local formation and
team ministry. But in the context of these gatherings about the diaconate,
the total ministry of the church meant just that—the whole church.

The church, as a body, was beginning to live into a renewed ecclesiology where baptism was not only the initiation into the church, but the
first call to ministry. The role of the baptizing community was not just to
receive the newly baptized, but to nurture them. And with the advent of
the Eucharist as the primary Sunday service, the community's identity was
becoming one of gathering around the table, sharing the meal, sharing as
liturgical ministers, being sustained in new ways because of the regularity
of the Eucharist and the public nature and call of baptism.

Keeping in mind that this was the context for the initial, but ongoing conversations about the diaconate, and thus the servant nature of the church,
the words of one of the presenters in that first gathering at Notre Dame
capture the spirit of that mutuality. Deacon Phina Borgeson, ordained to
the diaconate in 1974 before women's ordination to the priesthood was possible, but when liturgical reform was bringing a renewed understanding of
the diaconate, spoke clearly in her keynote address as she remarked:

> My interest in the diaconate, both general and personal, began
> with a revelatory moment centered on the words . . . "to inter-
> pret to the Church the needs, concerns and hopes of the world."
> After theologizing about the diaconate for some time, I ques-
> tion whether this activity might not be a luxury which we can

ill afford. At a variety of meetings and continuing education endeavors in the last year, I have heard a message repeated: it is time for Christians to do some serious rethinking of our faith. The world has changed, and the expression of the truth of our faith must change too. In classical terms, what is called for is a new apologetic. In my terms, the task is one of renewed vigor in mutual interpretation. While we have been busy theologizing about the diaconate and in-house concerns, the need for a diaconal theology has overtaken us. Part of our service from Church to world is the service of mutual interpretation. It is a necessary component of the mission for which the Church exists.

Let us hope that a renewed interest in the diaconate, and theological reflection on the diaconate, will help to equip us for the interpretive tasks of the Church's diaconal ministry. Not only a re-emphasis on servanthood, but a relating of servanthood to modern images would be a place to begin. Certainly the recognition that all of our ministries are interrelated and that each has diffuse boundaries, for all are derived from the one ministry of Christ, is a way to begin refreshing our theology. The recognition of mutuality in practice demands mutuality in theologizing. The realization that deacons do not do all our servant work, but are necessary to bring it into focus, should enable us to get about that work with a more consistent vision. The vision must include both a more active proclaiming of the Gospel and a more sensitive listening to the world.[10]

Borgeson's words from that gathering serve us as well today as they did in 1979. As we take a further look at how we got here from there, they will serve as a helpful reminder of the importance of mutuality in ministry—on all kinds of levels.

There would be one more conference at Notre Dame that paralleled the years of the church-wide study. Held in May 1984, articles about the conference tell us that again the theme was "Deacons in the Total Ministry of the Church." The Very Rev. Durstan McDonald, dean of the Seminary of the Southwest, provided the two-part keynote.

Dean McDonald would address an issue that to this day I believe has not satisfactorily been resolved. It may never be. Grounding his remarks in the context of the ministry of all the baptized, he speculated:

I wouldn't be a bit surprised that if, on an unconscious but intuitive level, the revived diaconate raises fears because there is an intuitive perception that to revive the diaconate will have revolutionary implications about the way we think about lay ministry now. It will revise and recast the language and thought of many people who understand already the importance of the total ministry of the laity.[11]

I believe that the speaker hinted at an unresolved issue. It is not only about how we understand the diaconate, but how we understand all the orders, not so much in relationship to each other as in relationship to the whole people of God. It is as important to understand the presbyterate in relation to the total ministry of the church as it is the diaconate. That work has not been done.

Dean McDonald suggested a number of distinctions that might be considered, including revisiting the term "pastoral," and the difference between pastoral and diaconal functions. He suggested, in agreement with Associated Parishes (frequently a partner with the Centre for the Diaconate in sponsoring these conferences), that the church do away with the transitional diaconate. He made other controversial recommendations about doing away with collars and titles for deacons, but only because of the privilege already associated with them, primarily as it related to the presbyterate.

Along with these recommendations and within the context of the ministry of all the baptized, Dean McDonald never wavered from recognizing the two major charges given by the church to deacons. He remarked:

> Concerning the diaconate itself, let me applaud the emphasis of your Centre on a special ministry of servanthood, as an icon, and as a sign of the servanthood of the whole people of God, lay and ordained. The focus on the dual function of the deacon serving the poor and the weak in the name of Christ on the one hand, and on the other, interpreting the needs, the concerns, and the hopes of the world, has potential for removing and revisioning pastoral ministry and lay ministry alike. The acid test, of course, is whether our practice matches our rhetoric. Whether we fall into the trap of worrying about our status or whether in the words of that marvelous sermon by Bishop Bigliardi, whether we are icons to be looked through, rather than to be looked at, icons of Christ's servanthood to the world and icons of the poor to the church.[12]

Dean McDonald recognized, most effectively, the place of the diaconate in an ordered church, one that had only just begun to live into a prayer book theology that strengthened, in great measure, the role of all the baptized, the priesthood of all believers, and the servant nature of the church.

Influences, Asides, and *Lex Orandi, Lex Credendi*

During the years that I was waiting for the church-wide study to be completed, there were not multiple resources to read about the diaconate—at least none that were easily accessible. Interestingly, the very month after the vicar of my little congregation had gone to see the bishop on my behalf, I accepted a position working as an administrative assistant for five campus ministers. They represented three denominations sharing space at the Wesley Foundation in our community. One of the first volumes I discovered on the book shelf in the student lounge was *The Diaconate Now*. Edited by Richard T. Nolan, an Episcopal priest teaching at Hartford seminary, the book was published in 1968. Nolan's introduction to the book reads:

> In 1963 a bishop of the Episcopal Church laid his hands on my head and said, "Take thou authority to execute the Office of a Deacon in the Church of God committed unto thee; In the Name of the Father, and of the Son, and of the Holy Ghost. Amen." Three days later began my month's supply ministry in a parish whose rector was on vacation. Except for a Sunday supply priest, I was quite on my own for all practical purposes. As a matter of curiosity, I took up the Book of Common Prayer to see again what specific functions I had as a deacon; academic theory and ordination promise had suddenly acquired a jolting dimension of existential reality! Finding listed some tasks I felt unprepared for, and some that perhaps were not to be done, I ministered as I could for the four weeks.
>
> When I returned to the final months of my sojourn as a master in the Choir School of the Cathedral Church of St. John the Divine, New York, I sought to satisfy my lingering curiosity about the diaconate, a curiosity now safely academic. . . .
>
> Neither persons nor books I sought out furnished unanimity on the tasks for the contemporary deacon. Thus, with the encouragement from some senior clergy, I set out to gather essays about the diaconate from some perceptive Christians.[13]

Nolan's experience was common to many like him, and points to how congregations understood the diaconate as well. A deacon was someone who was a priest in training, and often would be with the parish for only a short time. In an attempt to more clearly define the diaconate, his book includes essays on its historical perspective, in Protestantism, in the Roman Catholic Church, in the Orthodox Church, in Anglicanism, in the Church of South India. It also includes an essay on deaconesses and one on the future of the diaconate.

Nolan's book is important to mention here because he was speaking about the diaconate as it was envisioned in the 1928 Book of Common Prayer. Someone was asking questions, even then, and the revised prayer book has now articulated a clear vision.

That book is what I had to go on—along with the ordination service in the prayer book, until later that year when I was able to secure a copy, fresh off the press, of James Barnett's *The Diaconate: A Full and Equal Order* (1981). Soon to follow the next year was John Booty's *The Servant Church*. However, it would be another ten years before the first printing of Deacon Ormonde Plater's *Many Servants*, the first resource with stories of real deacons, their history, their recruitment, deployment, care, and feeding.

I suspect that many others were in similar circumstances. We had little bits of things. Scholars were able to trace the diaconate historically. Church studies were able to describe some possibilities, but were constrained by not having lived the vision, while the church hierarchy looked for canons and training programs and answers to what it might mean to be a servant church. In the meantime, many of us simply went about the business of living the questions and defining the Order.

On a personal level, James Barnett's book was most important to me. Tracing the diaconate throughout the church's history, considering the theology behind it, suggesting it as a full and equal Order, offering ideas about training, deployment, liturgical roles, it was a significant offering to the church. For this deacon, however, there was no paragraph more important than Barnett's very first one in the book:

> The principle of the diaconate as an office and function in the Church is rooted in the nature of the Church itself as it was originally founded and lived in the pre-Nicene world. The first principle of that Church as it came into being was that it was *laos*, the people of God. The Church was called into being by God and made a "chosen race, a royal priesthood, a holy nation, God's own people."[14] All were *laos*. There was no word to distinguish, in the sense of today, between clergy and laity. The clergy were laity along with others who belonged to the people of God.[15]

His next paragraph continues, "It is here that we must begin if we are to clarify our understanding of the Church's ministry, because we must first rethink our theology of the Church itself."[16]

As I've looked back at this deep influence, I've become aware that with the revision of the Book of Common Prayer, the church was doing just that. The diaconate happened to be caught between a church that was not just reenvisioning an Order, but was reenvisioning itself. It was living into the Eucharist as the primary service of the gathered community, as well as into the centrality of baptism, baptism as public, as the first call to ministry, and into a community who shared and spoke covenant language.

In fact, in the same year that Barnett's book about the diaconate was published, so was a volume entitled *Worship Points the Way: A Celebration of the Life and Work of Massey H. Shepherd, Jr.* Shepherd, known throughout the Church for his *Oxford American Prayer Book Commentary* on the 1928 Book of Common Prayer, his volume in the Church's Teaching Series, *The Worship of the* Church, and for his leadership in the Associated Parishes and on the Standing Liturgical Commission, he is honored in this book by a distinguished and ecumenical group of former students, professional colleagues, and friends." In the essay contributed by Urban T. Holmes, III, on "Education for Liturgy," we read:

> It is evident that Episcopalians as a whole are not clear about what has happened. The renewal movement in the 1970's, apart from the liturgical renewal often reflects a nostalgia for a classical theology which many theologians know has not been viable for almost two hundred years. The 1979 Book of Common Prayer is a product of a corporate, differentiated theological mind, which is not totally congruent with many of the inherited formularies of the last few centuries. This reality must soon "come home to roost" in one way or another.
>
> In other words, the revision itself was the product of an awakening, a newly educated theological consciousness. Now it becomes a *source* for a much broader awakening through participation and reflection upon the meaning of the participation. For those of us that believe that the theological emphases of the 1979 book are appropriate for people in the late twentieth and early twenty-first centuries this is a splendid opportunity. It is why we do not see the choice between 1928 and 1979 as a matter of taste. It is more a question of truth for our time. Two standard Books of Common Prayer would be theologically naïve, to put it kindly. The task that lies before us is to show how in fact

> *lex orandi* is *lex credendi* and to rewrite our theology books in the
> light of our liturgy. This can be a tricky process.[17]

Without rehearsing the arguments about liturgical renewal, or the
fullness of the theological changes the "new" prayer book encompassed,
the important thing to recognize is that this was a remarkable period of
change, discovery, definition, and redefinition. The diaconate was not the
only new thing, but that its reenvisioning took place in this climate is significant, both in how easily it was accepted—or not, and how mutually it
was defined—or not. The baptismal theology pointed right at what Barnett
had described about the pre-Nicene church and, in the end the church was
determining how she would live into a baptismal theology that mimicked
the early church and contextualized and updated a way of believing for
the times in which we were living.

As a result, I often repeat a beloved mentor's words. "It is no small thing
that the renewal of the diaconate and the renewed understanding of baptism occurred at the same time."

I believe it has had a deep effect on how the diaconate has come to be.
Deacons often see themselves, not just as doers of diaconal ministry, but
developers of diaconal ministry in others.

As an aside, having become a member of The Episcopal Church in 1977,
my introduction to the church included a congregation steeped in spirituality and renewal, along with a new prayer book, and another steeped in a
vision of mission and justice, the ministry of the baptized, and liturgy as
the work of the people.

My understanding of ministry was intuitively and practically grounded
in baptism and in community as organic; not gathered around a minister,
but around Christ, with opportunities blessed and strengthened in being
part of Christ's body in the world. I see now that I have been privileged
to taste a radical equality that many have longed for, or have worked to
create, but not as many have experienced. Having tasted that vision, the
reality of the radical equality that comes with baptism, I become impatient
with the power dynamics of a church that is often more institutional than
organic, more concerned about structure as control, rather than as support.

And finally, we return to *lex orandi, lex credendi*. We believe what we
pray. Praying shapes believing.

Many years ago, I was sitting at a table with colleagues at a board
meeting of the North American Association for the Diaconate (now known
as the Association for Episcopal Deacons).

Someone commented that the authors of the revised Book of Common
Prayer suggested that there would be surprises as we continued to use it.
I recently tried to remember and track down the person who made that

remark. While I was unsuccessful, I did end up having a lovely correspondence with the Rev. Dr. Louis Weil. Most recently he taught at the Church Divinity School of the Pacific, prior to that at Nashotah House, and he has served several terms on the Standing Commission for Liturgy and Music.

When I asked if he could remember anyone talking about these "prayer book surprises," this is how he responded.

> I have mulled a good bit. I can think of things I have said along that line, but I am pretty sure that I have never attended a NAAD meeting. But that does not necessarily mean that something like this wasn't quoted by a former student—they do that a lot, which is fine except for when (as has happened) the "quotation" is 180 degrees opposite to what I said. As to this quotation, which I see may also have been attributed to Boone (Porter), I suspect that all of us in the field of liturgy have said comments similar to that. What I do remember clearly is that when the 1979 Book of Common Prayer became official, I commented to a class of students at Nashotah House (that was still the "good old days!") that it would take us fifty years to live into the implications of the new book. That is still true. It amazes me how much the 1979 book is still "read" through the prism of 1928—but I stick to my guns, as I once heard Paul Tillich say.
>
> My point was that the reshaping of a mentality—any mentality, and certainly a liturgical mentality—is a very slow process because this operates at a very deep level—not at the cognitive level where we are inclined to think it operates. Piety is in our gut—and often shapes our attitudes at an unconscious level. So "reshaping," that is shattering. I know that in the midst of my doctoral studies in Paris, some of the historical material finally hit me between the eyes: this was no longer an academic matter, it was threatening my piety—my God this is serious!
>
> This does not help you with the origins of the phrase you mention, but I do think that among us "seniors" in the field, there was an enormous common sense that emerged, and it certainly transcended the ecumenical boundaries. That also was threatening to some people, still is, especially for people heavily invested in the institutional structures.[18]

It would take us fifty years to live into the implications of a new prayer book. As of this writing, it is has been thirty-five years. The diaconate was just one of the manifestations of a shift in theology, an old Order for a new world. And if we consider that the church-sponsored studies maintained that the primary issue was about the meaning of a servant church and not just the diaconate, the implications may be even more remarkable.

Over the course of the next several chapters we'll see just how deacons have lived into the words they pray and that the church prays with them as they make their vows and accept their charges.

Waves and Ways of Being

Riding the Waves

In *Many Servants*, Deacon Ormonde Plater effectively describes the first four waves of the diaconate in the Episcopal Church. Plater built on the work of Jay Lowery, an Episcopal priest who directed the Centre for the Diaconate in the late 1970s and early 1980s. The Centre was established when the Central House of Deaconesses closed in Chicago, and was deeply involved in organizing the conferences at Notre Dame, conducting studies, and generally advocating for the renewal of the diaconate.

Just as Plater built on Lowery's work, so I build on Plater's. A cursory review of the first three waves delineates three expressions of the diaconate in the Episcopal Church. It is important to keep in mind the idea that, as Plater writes, "these categories are not neatly exclusive; to a large extent they overlap. But they demonstrate that the order of deacons has developed and changed as the church has responded to the needs of the world in different historical circumstances."[1]

The First Wave

Missionary or indigenous deacons who served from the 1840s through the 1930s were the first wave. Perhaps the most well-known of that period was David Pendleton Oakerhater. Once a Cheyenne war chief, Oakerhater served in the Cheyenne nation in Oklahoma in the late nineteenth century. Other deacons of that era served in a variety of remote areas, or with distinctive populations, generally on their own. They were responsible for both the spiritual and physical needs of their congregations and engaged heavily in preaching, teaching, and pastoral care. In fact, with the exception of presiding at the Eucharist, their ministries closely resembled those of priests.

The Second Wave

The second wave of the diaconate was that of deaconesses. In the Episcopal Church they served from 1885 to 1970. The ministry was modeled after the deaconess institutes which started in the 1830s with Theodor Fliedner, a Lutheran pastor in Germany. There was interest in establishing such communities in the Episcopal Church in the United States starting in the 1840s. However, it would take until 1889 before canons were established to provide for this particular expression of the diaconate.

In her essay in *The Diaconate Now,* Deaconess Mary Truesdell provides a glimpse into the vision some had for this important ministry. Understanding the early vision for deaconesses and how their communities grew will provide an appreciation for the debt of gratitude deacons owe them today.

As Truesdell shares the history, it was Bishop Cobbs of Alabama who had one of the first clear visions of what deaconesses could mean in the church. She writes:

> He planned a cathedral to be built in Montgomery with a group of institutions around it, including a house for deacons who were to do missionary work and assist in pastoral ministrations, and a house for deaconesses who were to teach and take care of the sick and poor. . . . The plan never materialized, probably because of the immanence of the Civil War.[2]

However, even though there was not canonical provision, Bishop Cobbs's successor, Bishop Wilmer, set apart deaconesses in Alabama in 1885. Likewise, Bishop Henry Codman Potter of New York did the same in 1887.

It is helpful to remember something of what was happening in the country during these years. Especially in the South, reconstruction after the Civil War had taken place. Various tribes of indigenous people were struggling after having been moved from the eastern part of the country. Railroads were being built. New industries were being developed. There were labor issues, health issues, education issues. And in the midst of that period just after Reconstruction and up to the First World War, there was a social gospel movement. It was no wonder that deaconesses were needed and affirmed.

Truesdell writes:

> After the Episcopal Church had officially recognized the revival of the ancient office with the passage of the deaconess canon in

1889, there was considerable interest and enthusiasm. Schools for training were started in various parts of the country—at San Francisco, New Orleans, Minneapolis, Philadelphia, New York, Berkeley, and Chicago. Several hundred women were trained and "set apart" into the office of deaconess, and quietly and humbly served in various capacities to the glory of God. Some were teachers, some nurses, some headed institutions for the care of children or the aged, some served in church settlement houses and in parochial work. In many lands, in many places, in the city, in the lonely country, with the rich, the poor, the delinquent, the troubled, deaconesses have labored . . . for Christ and his Church.[3]

While many of the schools for deaconesses were short-lived, lacking in financial resources, the schools in Philadelphia, New York, and Berkeley would continue for some time.

We learn from Truesdell, however, that the New York Training School for Deaconesses was the last of the diocesan schools. Even though it had been forced to close at one point, the deaconesses raised enough money to reopen it. Unfortunately because of an agreement with the Diocese of New York, the building in which they were housed was needed for diocesan work and so it was surrendered. (However, it is important to note here that today, the archives kept on the property of the Diocese of New York include important documents from that deaconess community.)

In 1953, Bishop Conkling of Chicago called a group together to discuss a solution, resulting in the establishment of the Central House for Deaconesses in Chicago. When Truesdell was writing her essay in 1968, the Central House was still in existence, but would eventually change into the Centre for the Diaconate in 1974. There was not the same need for the training center after the canons were changed in 1970, eliminating the office of deaconess and making everyone—both men and women—deacons.

As of this writing Sister Priscilla Jean Wright of the Community of the Transfiguration, now a deacon (because of the change in canons in 1970), is the last living deacon to have entered church service as a deaconess. On June 18, 2014, Sister Priscilla celebrated fifty years of service in the diaconate. In a news release celebrating her forty-fifth anniversary, Deacon Phina Borgeson wrote:

When Wright, teaching school in Southern California almost fifty years ago, began discerning, there were basically three choices for women who felt called to dedicate their lives to full time work in the church. They could enter life in a religious community, pursue certification as a professional church worker, or become a deaconess.

Wright, influenced by Deaconess Evelyn Ashcroft, who had served in the Philippines during World War II, chose to enter diaconal ministry. . . . Wright met with her bishop, took a psychological exam and was quickly off for the Central House for Deaconesses in Chicago.

Sister Priscilla recounted that the senior class at Seabury-Western Theological Seminary, where she was a student in the Masters in Christian Education program, "made themselves very tedious, if not obnoxious."

After completing her studies, she was set apart as a deaconess by Bishop Bloy at the Cathedral of St. Paul in Los Angeles on June 18, 1964.

Sister Priscilla served the Navajo people in Arizona and New Mexico. She later joined the Community of the Transfiguration.

With the change in canons in 1970, authorizing the ordination of women to the diaconate, deaconesses automatically became deacons. Shortly after that Sister Priscilla attended the General Theological Seminary and received a Master of Divinity Degree.

Sister Priscilla served for many years in the Dominican Republic where the Community of the Transfiguration had a ministry with children living in poverty, overseeing a school, clinic, and church.[4]

Knowing Sister Priscilla personally has been a great joy. It is amazing to consider her participation in multiple waves of the diaconate and a religious community as well!

The Third Wave

The next identifiable wave of the diaconate, the third wave, is that of perpetual deacons. These deacons were male and they served from 1952 to 1970. There would be some overlap between these deacons and those who were ordained after 1979. In fact, these are the deacons who were serving when the church-sponsored studies about a new kind of diaconate began. These faithful men served in a more pastoral role, more like curates, when the church was trying to articulate a vision of the diaconate more like that of the early church. Thus there was tension between what people were imagining as a new kind of deacon and the perpetual deacons who had been asked by the church, post – World War II, to be very different.

As we look back, we see that after World War II, the church experienced significant growth. The diaconate was restored in the form of perpetual deacons, primarily to serve as pastoral and sacramental assistants. One might conclude that these deacons were defined more by their relationship to the presbyterate than anything else. In fact, in the 1928 Book of Common Prayer, the bishop says to the deacon ordinand: "It appertaineth to the Office of a Deacon, in the Church where he shall be appointed to serve, to assist the Priest in Divine Service, and specially when he ministereth the Holy Communion, and to help him in the distribution thereof; and to read Holy Scriptures and Homilies in the Church; and to instruct the youth in the Catechism; in the absence of the Priest to baptize infants; and to preach, if he be admitted thereto by the Bishop. And furthermore, it is his Office, where provision is so made, to search for the sick, poor, and impotent people of the Parish, that they may be relieved with the alms of the Parishioners, or others."[5]

In the final collect of this ordination service, the bishop goes on to pray that God make these deacons to be "modest, humble, and constant in their Ministration, to have a ready will to observe all spiritual Discipline; that they, having always the testimony of a good conscience, and continuing ever stable and strong in thy Son Christ, may so well behave themselves in this inferior Office, that they may be found worthy to be called unto the higher Ministries in thy Church."[6]

Clearly the priesthood was a higher office, the episcopate higher still. And the diaconate was defined in relationship to that hierarchy.

In 1952 the canons specified that a man who wished to be a deacon would do so "without relinquishing his secular occupation and with no intention of seeking advancement to the Priesthood" (Canon 34, Section 9).

It is interesting to note that men could become priests at age twenty-four, but could not be perpetual deacons until they were at least thirty-two. One assumes this was to ensure he was appropriately ensconced in secular employment and settled in a parish.

Not unlike the missionary deacons of the nineteenth century, perpetual deacons served almost like curates. They shared with the priests in pastoral visits at home, in the hospitals, and with shut-ins. They assisted in the liturgy and often performed what were known as "Deacons' Masses," that is, communion from the reserve sacrament. In a growing church, a postwar baby boom, as well as an economic boom, these men provided leadership, assistance, and stability. What's more, they were free labor.

Plater tells us that there were 517 perpetual deacons ordained during the years the canon was in effect (1952–1970). Having served primarily as pastoral assistants, some of these deacons had a difficult time when the vision of the diaconate changed with the BCP 1979. And many people who were aspiring deacons after the revised prayer book was introduced had caught the vision of a renewed diaconate and sometimes had difficulty understanding the perpetual deacons.

Many bishops involved in church-wide studies and questionnaires were partly reluctant to ordain new deacons because they no longer saw the need for perpetual deacons and wanted to be clear about this new vision. However, it is ironic that some deacons who were ordained after 1970 still functioned in primarily pastoral roles. It would take some time before bishops and commissions on ministry would take the time to educate themselves about how the renewed diaconate was being defined.

I find one of the most important paragraphs in Plater's *Many Servants* the one that expresses appreciation for the perpetual deacons. While each of the first two waves of deacons lasted roughly ninety years, perpetual deacons were canonically authorized for less than twenty. They were formed from the 1928 Prayer Book, often misunderstood after the BCP revision, and essentially left to find their own place in the church's new way of thinking. Plater writes:

> So let us honor the perpetual deacons. For almost two decades, maybe longer, the church needed them and ordained them. Most of them ministered with dedication and did not aspire to "higher office." They loved the church they served, the people they served, the altar they served. But the need for them had passed.[7]

I believe that the same could be said about each wave of the diaconate. The Order has seen many changes throughout history. It is adaptable. By and large the capacity to change is good. But let us take time to honor each wave, each defined by the church's needs in a changing world.

The Fourth Wave—The "Real" Transitional Diaconate

Lest we think this is a clean and linear history, it's important, once again, to acknowledge that there was overlap between the waves. Just as ocean waves roll forward, they also trickle into waves that have gone before and recede back into waves newly headed for shore. So it has been with the waves of the diaconate. Plater calls the 1970s a transitional time. He describes the fourth wave of the diaconate in the Episcopal Church by using the term "contemporary deacons." He defines the wave as beginning in 1971 and brings the fourth wave up to the present day. We will identify other waves within the last forty years, further clarifying how deacons have been and are being defined, and how critical their place is in today's church.

The 1970s were indeed a transitional time. While it would be confusing to call it a time of the "transitional diaconate," that is in fact what it was. Indeed, I believe that the 1970s and part of the 1980s were something of a fourth wave in and of themselves.

While deaconesses had become deacons in 1970, whether they wanted to or not, they took their way of being and serving into an Order where men had been serving primarily in pastoral and liturgical roles. This was no small thing. In fact, this was a time of transition that is well recorded in the minute book of the Central House of Deaconesses in Chicago. While many know stories about individual deaconesses, the influence of the larger deaconess community in transitioning to a new vision of the diaconate is less well known. Retelling their story here encourages us to recognize both the adaptable and flexible nature of the Order, as well as the work, sacrifice, and adjustment needed by some remarkable women and those who supported them.

We recall that it was Deaconess Mary Truesdell who wrote a chapter in Richard Nolan's *The Diaconate Now* published in 1968. It was that same deaconess who served as secretary for the board of the Central House. Her name would be signed in the minute book from the first meeting in 1953 until the 20th annual meeting of the board in 1973. Later Deaconess Truesdell would continue to serve as a member of the Board of Trustees for the National Centre for the Diaconate, and later still, as an honorary trustee. She had a big picture view of the deaconess community across the church and that knowledge would serve to guide and influence the order during the time of great transition in the 1970s.

As early as October of 1969, Deaconess Frances Zielinski, the deaconess in charge of the Central House, began asking at board meetings whether if the canons were changed to incorporate deaconesses into the diaconate, the Central House would be needed.

In that discussion the consensus was that the Central House "serves as a focal point for Candidate information and guidance, and also for publicity aimed at the Church at large; serves as a much needed center for the widely scattered members of the Order; augments the theological study in seminaries with information, inspiration, and guidance in matters peculiar to the Deaconess vocation and ministry; meets a real need and would continue to do so for many years to come."[8]

Deaconess Zielinski asked the question again in March of the following year, just before the General Convention of 1970. Bishop Burrill answered, "The Deaconess Office is recognized as an Order of Ministry with a function. This necessitates a place for a *specific* training. Really in seminaries there is no place for training 'non-stipendiary deacons.' In a place for the training of priests, they are really 'second-class citizens.'"[9]

At the post – General Convention board meeting later that year, Deaconess Zielinski reported:

> The 63rd General Convention accepted the Resolution of Lambeth 1968, "That those made deaconesses by the laying on of hands, with appropriate prayers be declared to be within the diaconate." Along with this acceptance, the Convention adopted a new Canon "ON WOMEN AND THE DIACONATE" to replace Canon 50. This clarification of status may well be a turning point and brings up questions: (a) Should The Central House for Deaconesses continue as at present? (b) Should there be an expansion of our ministry to include the whole diaconate? (c) Is our present name misleading as "Deaconess" is no longer the canonical title.[10]

Six months later, in April 1971, a special committee affirmed that the Central House could still have a role in counseling those studying for the diaconate, assist in defining roles for women in ministry, and continue to serve as a headquarters for deacons.

But there were other issues. Deaconess Zielinski reported that "there has been a feeling of frustration, perhaps of disappointment, as the acceptance of women in the diaconate has been slow in many dioceses. Perhaps too much was hoped for too soon. There is frustration because of lack of jobs. . . . The woman, though in the diaconate, is usually the most vulnerable member of the staff when budgets must be reduced. Should our ministry have new expressions of service? Or is the priesthood for women the answer?"[11]

Even though the church was moving steadily toward liturgical reform, and the canons had encouraged a new style of deacon, the blending was not without difficulties. Who would provide jobs for deaconesses, who would pay their pensions now that the canons had changed, what would the real purpose of the Central House be in this configuration—these were all questions that would take time to answer.

Despite all these questions, the deaconesses moved forward, keeping the health and possibilities of the Order in mind. They took an active part in arranging conferences on the diaconate, the first in 1973. As reported in the minutes of the meeting in April 16, 1974, the conference identified concerns which included: "a need to clarify the theology of the diaconate and to explore new and creative uses in roles other than parish assistant; a need for national guidelines, with local adaptations, for the training of deacons; a need for a national organization; the concern about disenfranchisement in national and diocesan conventions if deacons had no vote or representation; a need for deacon representation on boards, councils and programs of the church; the relationship between seminaries and the diaconate."[12]

The deaconesses and their friends on the board of the Central House developed a strategy to prepare papers on the diaconate, to work toward canonical change and clarification, to assist in sending out questionnaires for the study of the diaconate, to encourage seminaries to include the diaconate in their training programs and to continue to sponsor conferences.

Finally the name of the Central House was changed to the National Centre for the Diaconate, a new board configured, and a new chapter launched.

Indeed the church-wide community of deacons owes these deaconesses a great debt. We have benefitted from their collective actions in ways that aren't often acknowledged. While many of them were forward thinkers and eager to contribute to a new vision of the diaconate, closing down the Central House, distributing assets, and leading the way for a deacons' association that would continue to define and strengthen deacons across the church—all these contributions were significant as a new vision of the diaconate emerged, ever so steadily.

There was more evidence of transition, sometimes confusion, certainly different streams of the diaconate that would take time to integrate into a clearly recognizable whole.

While the church moved steadily toward liturgical reform and renewing the diaconate, from 1970 on, women who could not be ordained to the priesthood were often ordained to the diaconate. While some of them even had good relationships with the Central House, their intention was not to be a new kind of deacon, but to be ready for the time the church saw fit to ordain them to the priesthood. There were also men during this decade who used the new canon to enable themselves to become priests.[13]

In the meantime, even though the canons had done away with perpetual deacons, many who had been ordained pre-1970 continued to be faithful to what their understanding and the church's needs demanded of them. For example, Deacon Ed Horton, ordained in 1969, served faithfully in several capacities. In personal correspondence, I was privileged to learn some of his story. He shared:

> I have been a deacon for forty-five years (ordained February 25, 1969), with an interesting variety of activities during that time. I started out in the Diocese of California. I was then serving on active duty with the Navy. Two years later we moved to Albuquerque, NM, still on Navy duty, and served at St. John's Cathedral, where I was the first perpetual deacon they had had. I was

not particularly aware of the current canon; I just did what the deacon was supposed to do.

Two years later, in 1973, I retired from the Navy and we migrated to Papua New Guinea, where I served with Wycliffe Bible Translators, a Protestant, nondenominational, international mission organization as a teacher and administrator in the high school the mission operated for children of missionaries. . . .

Shortly after we got there, the bishop (Diocese of New Guinea, Province of Queensland, Anglican Church of Australia) visited me and asked if I would serve the Anglican congregations in the local area, who did not have a resident priest. That was the beginning of a real twenty-five-year adventure. . . .

In 1999 we came back to the States . . . and settled in Orlando, Florida. I served there with St. Mary's of the Angels . . . and later at St. Andrew's, Downers Grove, Illinois. After a few years, my old age finally caught up with me, and I am now unable to stand up on my feet long enough to do the things a deacon does. So I helped train another man in the congregation who then was ordained and took over the job.[14]

So at the same time Deacon Horton continued to serve faithfully with one understanding of the diaconate, Sister Priscilla was teaching in Arizona and New Mexico, and other deaconesses-become-deacons were trying to make a faithful transition. At the same time that women were awaiting approval for ordination to the priesthood, and men were being ordained to the priesthood by using the new deacon canon, the church was reenvisioning a whole new way for deacons to be! In his book, Plater shares several stories of individual deacons during that time.

While doing research about this transition time, I discovered other stories. In personal correspondence, Frederick Erickson, former archdeacon of the Diocese of Los Angeles, shared what it was like to be preparing for ordination in the 1970s, as well as experiences about the understanding of the diaconate from place to place during those years. He wrote:

I've been thinking about your question about the understanding of the diaconate during the "in-between time" of the 1970s before the 1979 Prayer Book was printed.

As I recall, the service used at my ordination was the 1979 one, then available for use on a trial basis. I was ordained by Bishop John Burgess (on behalf of Bishop James Montgomery because I was then canonically resident in Chicago) at the Church of St. John the Evangelist in Boston, on June 14, 1975.

I had been sent forward for postulancy in the winter of 1970 from a mission congregation on the West Side of Chicago—St. Andrew's. It is still there hanging on with a tiny congregation and an unpaid worker-priest. I had been attending there since 1964 when I began doing youth work at a West Side YMCA and was a volunteer in Dr. King's Southern Christian Leadership Conference "Northern Initiative." I was also involved in the founding of an Alinsky-inspired community organization in the Lawndale neighborhood. The congregation of St. Andrew's was, at that time, all African American and the priest was white. His name was Grant Gallup. Grant was a remarkable man—wonderfully articulate, a radical, involved in the freedom movement (he marched in Selma with Malcolm Boyd), then became one of the founders of Integrity, read the emerging liberation theology, and eventually, after early retirement, went to Managua, Nicaragua, where he started a house of study and hospitality for North Americans interested in learning more about what was happening in Central America. Grant's wonderful and slightly crazy notes on preaching the three-year lectionary cycle, called "Homily Grits," are still available on Louie Crew's website. I learned a lot from the devotion of people from the congregation of St. Andrew's and was honored when they asked me to become a member of the Bishop's Committee.

Before 1964 I had been a music student at Northwestern. After a few years of working in Lawndale I went back to Northwestern and got a PhD in a then-new field, anthropology of education, with special interest in urban education, issues of language, culture, race, ethnicity, and what we now call "educational justice." While I was in the doctoral program I met Fred Hampton, the Black Panther leader who was murdered by the cops a couple of years after he was introduced to me as the president of the Youth NAACP in Maywood, Illinois.

My point here is that I did a lot of the deacon-like justice-engaged work before I was ordained. (I'm not unique in that, but after ordination I was, for a number of years, more a liturgical deacon than an outreach ministry deacon.) I received the PhD in 1969 and a year later began study toward ordination as a "permanent deacon." I had a job teaching urban education at the then-new University of Illinois, Chicago.

Thinking back now, I'm not sure that Grant's (my rector's) conception of the diaconate wasn't somewhat in the "liturgical deacon" mode. He adopted the trial rites for "renewed liturgy" as soon as they came out, but as I recall, all he said to me at the time was, "The Roman Church is rediscovering the diaconate as a lifelong ministry, and now we're going to try it in the Episcopal Church in Chicago—would you be interested?" When my newly married wife and I spoke briefly about it with Bishop Burrill, he didn't say anything about what was distinctive about permanent deaconing, nor did the psychiatrist I went to for a psychological exam. His single question to me was, "What books did you like to read as a child?" I said, "*Treasure Island*, *Kidnapped*, books about castles and knights, *Huckleberry Finn*, and *The Hobbit*." (My mother was a children's librarian.) He said, "That's fine." End of psychological exam.

I was in the first class of those preparing to be ordained as permanent deacons in the Diocese of Chicago.

The Saturday courses for prospective deacons at Seabury-Western Theological Seminary didn't address what was distinctive about the diaconate. We had one topic in the morning and another in the afternoon. For a while the pair was church history in the morning and pastoral theology in the afternoon. Both were excellent academically and the historian, Jules Moreau, emphasized the way in which the late ancient Church and the medieval Church became the equivalent of the U.S. Departments of Health and Human Services combined with the Department of Education. As someone who was churchy and a history buff, I remember being amazed at how the medieval Church was so thoroughly involved in "corporal acts of mercy," and at the time of Henry VIII's separation from Rome, the Church controlled one-third of the arable land in England— one third of all the capital.

But nothing was said about the roles of deacons in all that (except for mention that Thomas Becket was a deacon until two days before he was consecrated as Archbishop of Canterbury). The classes were condensed versions of standard seminary courses (we've seen that a lot since, haven't we?), focusing on preparation for the priesthood. Since many in the class didn't have college degrees, they found the academic content hard to grasp. We've seen that since also.

In the pastoral theology course, the emphasis was on principles for counseling penitents in confession and some on

Christian ethics. I remember a discussion on whether or not the U.S. should have bombed Nagasaki and Hiroshima. If the intentions were good (to save American lives), did that justify the action? The teacher noted that if you looked at this act from the perspective of intention, it was not formally a sin. It could be thought of as having the matter of sin, but not the form. After several of us in the class had opined, one of the class members said quietly that he had been the pilot (or copilot) of the Enola Gay. That was a conversation stopper. While I had registered at age eighteen as a conscientious objector, I have never forgotten that moment, as a turning point in realizing that things concerning ethics and justice are not as simple as they may seem at first glance.

I finished theological study at Episcopal Divinity School after I moved to Boston with one course in New Testament, one in Old Testament, and an independent reading course in liturgy. Again, no particular emphasis on deacons and what they do. I took the Diocese of Chicago's canonical exams (for priests) in January 1975—the first year the GOEs were offered, but Chicago thought their exams were more rigorous than the GOE, and they were indeed. Again, no questions focusing on the diaconate. At the end of the oral exam, held at General Seminary, I was told by Chicago's chair of the board of examining chaplains that I had done better in the written exams than most of the MDiv seminary students, but nothing was said in particular about the diaconate.

After my ordination in June I served primarily as a liturgical deacon at the Church of St. John the Evangelist in downtown Boston. In January of 1977, two-thirds of that congregation, the priest in charge, who was a Cowley Father, the curate, and the entire novitiate at the monastery left to become Roman Catholics, in protest over the ordination of women, approved at the 1976 General Convention. The superior of the Cowley Fathers and I took up the pieces at St. John's Church.

There were no permanent deacons in the Diocese of Massachusetts at that time, and so I had no one to talk to about being a deacon. But I had taken very seriously the ordination charge to "interpret to the Church the needs, concerns, and hopes of the world." My preaching emphasized that and we created a group of lay Eucharistic ministers who visited shut-ins. I was an advisor/chaplain to that group.

In 1979 I had moved to Michigan State University and became an assistant in the campus ministry there. I assisted in the liturgy, taught, encouraging the ministry of all the baptized, preached (often focusing on something about "the world"), and eventually taught a church and society course through the Whitaker School of Theology and was asked to join their board as a deacon. I worked together wonderfully with the chaplain, but you could say that what I was doing then as deacon was distinct from priesthood more in emphasis than in anything diaconal.

There were lots of deacons in the Diocese of Michigan and I met some of them. By then the 1979 Prayer Book words were gaining currency. Deacons were not simply apprentice priests, but they also were not simply social workers with a collar. As a social scientist and educator I was developing a "prophetic" ministry of social analysis and social action, but not doing so deliberately as diaconal ministry. It was only later as I met and became friends with Joanne Leslie, my successor as archdeacon in Los Angeles, that I began to realize that all along my secular career as an academic and its concerns for fostering "educational justice" had been an integral part of my diaconate. But in the early 1980s that had not occurred to me. My mentor from Chicago, Grant Gallup, said at the time he thought the diaconate was truly a "New Testament" ministry—deacons deliberately giving up the careerism—that tempted and obsessed many priests. And I read the pamphlets from the North American Association for the Diaconate and remember being very excited by the published sermon of Maylanne Whittall (now Maylanne Maybee), with the image of going upstream to see who was throwing the drowning people into the river instead of just pulling the drowning out, downstream.

However, all that was years after I'd been in formation for ordination and had years as an ordained deacon.

Frankly, from 1970 to 1979 or so, I got almost no messages from the Church about what a lifetime role as a deacon might be. And it was only when academic life took me to Philadelphia that I fully joined and helped to build a diocesan community of deacons, as I did after 1999 in Los Angeles. At this point, I think I've learned a lot, but much of it, by necessity, was self-taught.[15]

Despite the confusing times, a vision not-yet-emerged, a church transitioning into the use of a new prayer book, there were individuals that had a clear hope, if not a clear picture, of the possibilities that could come with a renewed diaconate. Bishop William Folwell, res., of Central Florida was one such person. Deacons of the "new order" were ordained in that diocese as early as 1975 because of his belief in that new vision. In personal correspondence, Bishop Folwell reflected on his thinking in the 1970s. He wrote:

> In thinking this over, and going back over many of my convention addresses, the majority of what I have available is based mostly on memory.
>
> When I became bishop in 1970 we had about five vocational deacons in the diocese. One taught school, the others (I believe) were retired. Their primary duties as deacons were liturgical and visits to parishioners in hospital. I, early on, began to believe that the Order of Deacon had been almost lost sight of throughout the church. I first went to the BCP to see what was said there about the diaconate. I also checked the New Testament, which wasn't much help as far as contemporary thought and experience is concerned. . . .
>
> This Order was perhaps the most evolutionary of the three Orders of our tradition. I became concerned that we might lose this Order completely if we did not give it a legitimate place in both worship and service. To that end I began taking it seriously and looked into our understanding and practice at the time. In the end I went to the BCP (at that time we were using one of the Trial Liturgies, but it was basically the same as the adopted Prayer Book we have used since 1979).
>
> The Catechism says "The ministry of a deacon is to represent Christ and his Church, particularly as a servant of those in need; and to assist bishops and priests in the proclamation of the Gospel and the administration of the sacraments" (BCP, 856).
>
> The service of Ordination of a Deacon says: "In the name of Jesus Christ, you are to serve all people, particularly the poor, the weak, the sick and the lonely . . . and to make Christ and his redemptive love known, by your word and example, to those among whom you live, and work, and worship. You are to interpret to the Church the needs, concerns, and hopes of the world" (BCP, 543).
>
> I thought these two ministrations (assisting in worship, **and** interpreting to the Church the needs of the world) were ideal for those of us in Central Florida, considering we were within one of the fastest growing areas of the nation. So I began to

stress this ministry in preaching, teaching, and writing. It also became the basis for establishing the Institute of Christian Education. We had very good response. I remember so well ordaining fifteen new deacons at the Cathedral (I think it was 1975 or so). That was exciting. As the years went on there were more and more, until by my retirement there were fifty deacons serving.

As I look back on all this, I remember becoming concerned that the "assisting the Bishop and Priests in . . ." was becoming the norm. It bothered me that "to interpret to the Church the needs, concerns and hopes of the world" did not seem to be happening very much. . . .

In fairness, we had one man who was a lineman for the power company, several public school teachers, at least two physicians, who started a prison ministry, and I had no real knowledge of just how much they proclaimed the Gospel, but their very ordained ministry was itself a proclamation, and I never gave up my full support of this ministry.

(Incidentally, we have a deacon at our parish here. He is still the Chief Program Officer of the town Rescue Mission. He is our best preacher, bringing lots of humanity into his sermons!)[16]

Clearly in some dioceses bishops and others were doing their best to live into something new in the total ministry of the church. In fact, the Institute for Christian Studies still exists in the Diocese of Central Florida. The website of the diocese tells us:

> The "Lay Institute" was founded in 1973 by a group of committed Episcopalians. The Church in Central Florida was experiencing renewal, people of the diocese were seeking sound teaching, and a revival of the ancient order of the vocational diaconate was taking place. Individuals seeking to become deacons needed to be prepared for that ministry. Today the mission of the ICS is the same: to provide adult Christian education and training for any interested person, training for aspirants to the diaconate, and continuing education for clergy.[17]

The need for the Institute in Central Florida pointed toward trends all around the church. It is essential to remember that the total ministry of the church, the centrality of baptism as both initiation rite and first call to ministry, and the Eucharist as the primary Sunday service, along with renewal movements and cultural shifts, was the context for the renewal of the diaconate. With so many models of deacons and deaconesses and a whole church in transition, it was no wonder that there was such a need for conferences and consultations, academic papers and practical testimony. It is for these reasons that I consider the period from 1970 to the mid-1980s as a fourth wave of the diaconate in The Episcopal Church.

Shaped by a New Prayer Book

If the fourth wave of the diaconate in The Episcopal Church can be defined as one of transition, I believe the fifth wave can be identified as one of "definition."

In the studies conducted on a church-wide basis from 1979 to 1985, the questions that were addressed and the new questions that were raised would be asked for several years. It would be up to those living the ministry as deacons, along with those who supported them, to provide more definitive answers.

The fact is those who had the power to choose or not choose, train or not train, deploy or not deploy deacons, for the most part, simply had not lived nor experienced the vision of diaconal ministry set forth in the 1979 Book of Common Prayer.

The church would turn to its best scholars to define historical aspects of the Order—to chart its existence in a variety of forms, from the earliest church, and to make a case—or not—for its contemporary renewal.

But with the recently revised prayer book, the church had already assumed, at a certain level, a new vision—not just of the servant nature of Christ's ministry as lived out the lives of deacons, but of the servant nature of Christ's body—the church. It is with these circumstances we ground most deeply in the link between the renewal of the diaconate and the restoration of baptism to its proper place: public, communal, initiatory, calling, affirming. And it is with these circumstances that perhaps we begin to grow into unexpected consequences.

There is no stronger evidence of the ways in which the diaconate was growing, both in numbers and in understanding than the newsletters and publications of the National Centre for the Diaconate, and its successor, the North American Association for the Diaconate.

While I believe that a fifth wave was emerging from the time the church officially began its use of the 1979 Book of Common Prayer, we must note again that all the waves of the diaconate were neither linear nor strictly chronological. They washed into each other. Just as the fourth wave was one of transition, the emerging fifth wave in the 1980s had one foot in the transition and another in new visions and definitions.

There are two themes that are integral parts of what we might call a fifth wave. I would plead with the reader not to forget them. I believe the first theme is most important and will carry us, in many ways, to the present, and into unexpected consequences. That theme is **the total ministry of the church**. This language was used in the early reports of the church-wide studies on whether the diaconate should exist, how it should exist, and why it should exist. Church Center staff and members of the Council for the Development of Ministry used the term frequently, not only in relation to the diaconate, but as the church grew more fully into greater lay participation in the liturgy, along with the affirmation of baptism as the first call to ministry. If we hold this in tension with Louis Weil's prediction that it would take the church at least fifty years to live into the implications of the 1979 Book of Common Prayer, we discover, once again, that the diaconate was being redefined with a new vision of the church in mind. One wonders whether this new vision, this baptismal ecclesiology, has become as clearly defined as the diaconate. (One could argue that some dioceses articulate this clearly in their common life. However, it is seldom that we see the structures of the church organized around the radical equality of baptism.)

The Centre's newsletters remind us that all three conferences at Notre Dame included the idea of the total ministry of the church either in their theme title, or in the subject matter of the conference.

The second theme that is important to acknowledge, and in some ways must be held in tension with the first, is that of **"servant ministry."** Commissions on Ministry and others responsible for ordination processes would often focus on an individual's understanding of the word "servant." Most would ask every aspirant, "What is your diaconal ministry?" Seldom were there questions about how the aspirant would invite the community into ministry. And even less often were there questions about how the aspiring deacon might develop diaconal ministry with others, affirming and equipping others. The emphasis was on the individual more than that person's relationship with the congregation and how deacons would serve as living reminders of the diaconal ministry to which we are all called at baptism.

The danger here was that some people came to think about deacons as ones who performed outreach ministry, thus letting everyone else off the hook. It also led to a fairly dualistic way of thinking, with people often describing presbyters as having an "in-house" ministry and deacons having an "out-house" ministry. This was over simple as we'll discover in further reviewing the growth and maturing of the diaconate. It not only let presbyters off the hook when it came to diaconal ministry, sometimes it discouraged deacons from an appropriate kind of teaching, preaching, and equipping of saints inside the church's walls that comes with the charge to interpret to the church. While it was a step toward helping the church understand distinctive ministries, the more dualistic description could either promote a peaceful coexistence between presbyter and deacon because the presbyter wouldn't feel threatened by activity outside the church's walls, or it was such a bifurcation that it didn't encourage the building of good partnerships or include the whole community in a common diaconal vision.

All this points toward the fact that, at least for a while, individual ministries of service were the primary focus—and requirement—for those who were choosing and approving aspirants for the diaconate. I've sometimes referred to this as the "what-is-your-diaconal-ministry-syndrome." What the "deciders" were looking for were answers like "prison ministry," or "the free medical clinic," or "maintaining the food pantry at our church." What they did not expect to hear was, "My diaconal ministry is to serve as an interpreter, helping the church understand the needs, concerns, and hopes of the whole world. It is to expand the meaning of our baptismal covenant, especially in striving for justice and peace and respecting the dignity of every human being (BCP, 305). Doing those things may take me to different places at different times. Though I've had experience with _____, there may be a time that something else is more important to the congregation and to the community. I am asked to listen and to read the signs, and to help others attend to the needs of the world as well."

It would take several more years before Commissions and others were able to see the ways in which deacons didn't simply "assist" in the liturgy, but their role reflected who the church had asked them to be as leaders of a servant church. They would often "attend" rather than assist, bringing the integrity of their distinctive ministry to the altar on behalf of the people. Even later, the church would learn more about the interpretive role. It would be another aspect of the diaconate that would expand.

While the word "servant" is what the church latched on to and it enabled many deacons to be ordained, further decades of living the ordination vows and charges would bring a new dimension to this overutilized word. It is noteworthy to consider here that the word was used and emphasized primarily by people of privilege. However, it was a start, a way into calling the church to be in touch with the diaconal ministry to which everyone is called, and the diaconal responsibilities and ministry to which the whole church is called.

Nevertheless progress occurred bit by bit.

By 1979, the first year of official use of the new prayer book, the National Centre for the Diaconate had moved to Boston. As the orientation of the church leaned more into a new vision of deacons, there were some who wished to honor the legacy of deaconesses. Thus one of the projects supported by the Centre was that of the Deaconess History Project. The ministry of a previous wave of the diaconate was being preserved as the church was living into another. But in addition to reports on that important project, newsletters from the Centre included foundational resources for deacons and deacons-to-be. These resources included new books, scholarly papers, the sharing of diocesan processes, news of conferences or regional gatherings, and snippets of special ministries in which deacons were involved. Some of those early ministries included: service and advocacy for the elderly, hospice work, prison ministry, and suicide prevention.

The work of the Centre insured that news of deacons was shared widely. Deacons in Hawaii were able to learn about deacons in New Jersey. Deacons in Central Florida could pave the way with their stories for those who were being trained in Rhode Island. In fact, the work of the Centre is testimony to what networks can accomplish, the ways in which they contribute to a movement, and the importance of uniting around things that are not always considered institutional priorities. They worked alongside the institution. There is no question about that. During the years of the church-wide studies, they worked to help with mailings, follow-up questionnaires, collating materials, and publicizing results. In true diaconal fashion, they walked alongside, working in the periphery, always there, urging the church into the next step and the next step. We are reminded in the first issue of DIAKONEO[1] sent from the new office in Boston that while the initial study on the diaconate (known as "The Church, The Diaconate, The Future") was commissioned by the House of Bishops and overseen by the Council for the Development of Ministry (at the Episcopal Church Center), it was actually funded by the Centre with funds carried forward from the Central House of Deaconesses and help from the Episcopal Church Foundation.

We thus see the beginning of the trend, the reality, of little church-wide help for the development of the diaconate, the heavy reliance on a network for making progress, and evidence that a vocational association was becoming the only place keeping records of deacons on a church-wide basis. To this day, the Association for Episcopal Deacons has the most complete record of deacons in the church.

Thankfully the Centre's work would also help many people hold "total ministry" and "servant ministry" in positive tension and balance. The Centre represented a community of deacon leaders who were prepared to do whatever they could to bring definition and clarity for the renewed vision of an ancient Order.

If it were appropriate to write in capital letters to emphasize how important this is, I would plead with my publisher to do so. But in lieu of that, it might be helpful to take a brief digression in order to explore more of the context of the BCP 1979 and the centrality of baptism.

The Total Ministry of the Church

"Digression" might be a misnomer here because having an understanding of the total ministry of the church is so foundational to what has emerged as our baptismal ecclesiology. I believe that understanding something of the impact of the revised prayer book in the life of the church is critical to understanding the fulsome relationships between the diaconate and the ministry of the people of God.

In a series of videos produced for an online course at Bloy House (the Episcopal Theological School at Claremont in California, and released late in 2011), those interviewed touch on the theology behind the revised rite of baptism as expressed in the BCP 1979. In one of the videos, Louis Weil explains to the listener that revising the baptismal rite was, in part, an attempt to correct the notion (what he calls "erroneous theology") of baptism as personal salvation. This is a theology that led the church to perform private baptisms and to ensure that infants were baptized so if they died, they would gain entrance to heaven. He explains that this is a theology that evolved and was practiced for centuries.

What was important to those developing the new rite for the 1979 BCP was to return to the understanding held by the early church—that baptism is an initiation rite. It is incorporation into a "faith-full community" as Weil describes it. It is as significant in the life of the community as it is to the individual being baptized.[2]

In these days many of our members are able to recognize this. And yet, one wonders if our church has fully explored what it means to be the "baptizing community." I borrow this phrase from Theodore Eastman, former bishop of the Episcopal Diocese of Maryland (1986–1994). Eastman wrote a book by that same name, published in 1992. His point was to examine what it would "mean for a congregation to explore a comprehensive attitude toward Holy Baptism as the keystone sacrament."[3]

Eastman acknowledged that the name of the book could be controversial because of our belief that it is God who baptizes, who bestows forgiveness and restores to new life, with the community simply being God's agent. But he also argued that "the church lags and wanders in its mission in direct proportion to the distance that baptism is allowed to stray from the center of ecclesial life. The Matthean formula for mission clearly places baptism at the heart of the matter, for the church is seen as the community that evangelizes, baptizes and teaches (Matthew 28:19). That vision, that priority, needs to be recaptured today."[4]

At the time Eastman was writing, the idea of the catechumenate was being explored in many dioceses and was the subject of wonderful and comprehensive books produced by our church—and others. The church began to take preparation for baptism much more seriously. Godparents were prepared more thoroughly. In the case of adult baptisms, the seasons of preparation similar to those of the ancient church were followed, with baptism often occurring at the Great Vigil of Easter, followed by a season of reflection.

Some of that continues. In fact even for those who were baptized as infants, some of our current Christian formation programs center on the Baptismal Covenant. But questions that remain for me are, "How is the community itself prepared? In what ways does it assess its role as it receives, nurtures, blesses, and continues to equip and walk with its members?" How, as Eastman asked, has the church "been reordered to reflect educational and missionary demands that the reformation of Christian initiation requires?"[5] And, I would add, if baptism is full initiation, what are the implications for ordination?

Louis Weil spoke to this, at least in a limited way, in his video about baptismal ecclesiology. Reminding the listener that baptism is the most important event in the life of a Christian (rather than ordination), we begin to understand that ordination becomes much less about "rank" and much more about "order." Weil comments, "If you put initiation in its proper place, everything shapes itself around that focus." He shares an image from one of his colleagues who explained baptism like the floor and walls of a room. "Lots of things happen in that room, but they are shaped by the framework, the context established by the floor and the walls." Weil believes he is still living into his baptism. I like to think of this as "living the covenant."

Returning to further implications for ordination if baptism is the primary initiation into the community of the faithful, Weil also mentions in the video that as he worked with the framers of the current version of our Book of Common Prayer:

> One of the major contributions of the '79 Book (one of the first stages, in a way) was to address the problem of clericalism. And in many ways the '79 Book is a step in the right direction of putting the clergy in their/our place. . . . I am not denigrating

ordination at all. But it does need to be kept in its place. . . . We suffer from the idea that ultimately it is the ordained person who calls the shots. . . .

An authentically collegial approach to the life of the church means a willingness to accept (and maybe one of the great gifts of a pastoral leader is to discern the gifts of others in the community) and to encourage development and expression of those gifts by laity—if I had been called to be a parish priest, I hope I could have embodied that—where I would do the ministry I was called to do in sacramental leadership . . . but to have working with me lay leaders . . . and deacons . . . who would have special gifts they would exercise also for the benefit of the common life of the church.[6]

This is what leaders in liturgical reform along with Church Center staff and administrative bodies meant when they talked about the total ministry of the church. As early as 1976, the General Convention held in Minneapolis had passed a resolution calling for "the Board of Theological Education and the Program Committee on Lay Ministries of the Executive Council, in full consultation with the Ministry Council, to be authorized to create a Study Committee on Total Ministry with special attention to the ministry of the laity."[7]

It also asked that the study include:

- an analysis of the concept of the total Christian ministry of laity and clergy in their mutually supportive and interdependent roles,
- an inventory of the resources available for the education and training of adult laypersons,
- consideration of the possibility for certification of laity for specialized training and skills, and further, for the recognition of their accomplishment in ministry.[8]

In a news release from the Episcopal News Service August 28, 1980, dealing primarily with staff changes in the office for the Council for the Development of Ministry, staff reiterated that "The entire Council . . . is serious about marshalling the Church's resources for total ministry."

Just a month later a three-day conference was held in Cedar Falls, Iowa, largely driven by provincial representatives to the Council for the Development of Ministry, to explore total ministry development. Thirty-two dioceses were represented. One of the presenters, the Rev. Daniel Eckman of Maryland, the bishop's assistant for lay ministry development, "told of that diocese's development of a total ministry support system which incorporates identification of gifts for ministry, training, theological preparation and spiritual formation."[9]

It is interesting to note here that Maryland was also among one of the eight participating dioceses in the early church-wide study of the diaconate. Clearly new deacons there were being formed in the context of total ministry and baptismal ecclesiology.

The early 1980s continued to see conferences, studies, and miscellaneous gatherings relating to the total ministry of the church. In the same year of second conference on the diaconate at Notre Dame (1981), the bishops of Province VIII held their own continuing education conference on total ministry. They explored, with the help of pioneer ministry developers, what it would mean for both clergy and laity to share in ministry. Conference leaders included: Jean Haldane, a lay professional from Seattle; Barry Menuez, a Church Center staff member for the Council on the Development of Ministry; Daniel Eckman Jr., a priest and ministry developer from the Diocese of Maryland; and Phina Borgeson, a deacon and ministry developer in the Diocese of Nevada. Interestingly, one of the conclusions they shared was that "lay ministry best takes place where ordained ministers have a clear idea of their role and function and where a congregation is clear about its mission."[10] That conclusion is reminiscent of what people were saying about the diaconate. The roles needed to be clearly understood, and the servant ministry of the church needed to be defined more clearly. There was a pattern, a need, for definition, and yet often that definition came by comparing things to congregational models and leadership that were pre-1979 Prayer Book.

Perhaps for this reason another of the conclusions of the bishops of Province VIII was that "Total Ministry helps to overcome the threat felt by some clergy when faced with concepts of lay leadership."[11] I'd like to think that total ministry, the *total ministry of the church,* was a way for presbyters to consider that we are all in this together—this ministry business. This is the antithesis of the understanding of total ministry as simply a survival mechanism for small congregations.

Because the official church-wide study on the diaconate extended through 1985, it's important to mention two more events that occurred during those years specifically addressing the total ministry of the church.

In January 1983 the Mutual Ministries Office of the Episcopal Church Center organized the third total ministry conference. The Episcopal News Service release opened by saying, "They came from throughout the country. There was a business professor from North Dakota. A New York City psychotherapist and a San Francisco business consultant were there. A wardrobe color analyst from Wyoming was among the 96 registered participants. The meeting was the Total Ministry Network of the Episcopal Church held January 14–16."[12]

The bishop of the Diocese of Nevada, Wesley Frensdorff, was the keynote speaker. We recall that Frensdorff was mentioned as in attendance at the conferences on the diaconate at Notre Dame, and as one who, early on, supported the renewal of the Order. The news release further tells us:

> The pervading theme for the weekend was that total ministry is not another program, but a *process*. It is not simply another group of those who happen to be interested in lay ministry, but a dynamic that must pervade and penetrate all aspects of the Church's work.
>
> "I disagree with those who say the ministry of the laity is in the world," said Frensdorff. "What that says to me is that the Church is the prerogative of the clergy. I believe it has to be both. . . . We want a view of the Church that is all sheep and all shepherd, all at the same time. . . . Ministry is moving from padre to cadre. It is a re-directing of the hired hands. . . . The biblical concept of *laos* means 'the people of God.' We need to develop a laity without laymen. The concept of a lay person is someone who doesn't know anything. Total ministry is not getting more people involved. It is finding a way for the Church to be truly alive, self-supporting, and indigenous in whatever context it is placed. That is my hope."[13]

My hope is that the reader will examine the paragraphs above one more time. The renewal of the diaconate, the redesign of the baptismal rite, and the emerging baptismal ecclesiology that underscores both, are important to consider together. This is the context in which the renewal of an Order was taking place. Clergy were not just threatened by having deacons—they were sometimes perplexed and at sea about more significant lay involvement, not only in the church, but what that meant about ministry in daily life. In fairness, not all clergy were threatened. Some were excited and ready for the challenge. We've already read of Bishop Folwell's commitment in the Diocese of Central Florida. Because he was committed not only to the diaconate, but to strengthening everyone's ministries, the Institute for Christian Studies had been established. People were being affirmed and equipped.

I suspect that because of this overwhelming renewal, one that included all the people of the church, it was easier for Commissions on Ministry and others to ask about the deacon's role in relationship to the priest or to the laity. Those were the traditional categories of thinking and acting. But seldom were questions asked about the best ways to be in relationship with others who had distinctive ministries and how to be partners with them. They were not asked of aspiring deacons, nor were they asked of most priests who would be working with deacons—other than when it was time to define roles and responsibilities in the form of a letter of agreement or job description. That would be a start, but the qualities and context necessary to building good partnerships, indeed living out mutual ministry, were not so much the issues of discussion, and the burden of creating them was often on the aspiring deacon.

In 1985, the year that the six-year church-wide study on deacons was completed, there was another conference on total ministry. In February of that year 125 Episcopalians gathered to "further the process of making Episcopalians aware of the ministry of all church members."[14] The Episcopal News Service reports that it included people who were just beginning to study the concept of total ministry, as well as those who had been advocating it for years.

The keynote speaker was Verna Dozier. The news release referred to Dozier as "one of the best known and most eloquent of the advocates," and challenged the gathering by "asserting that 'all of us have been called, in Jesus' own words, to do greater things than he did,' and then asking 'why have we been so slow to be about it?'" She suggested three blocks to that. The first was the "failure to see the full biblical story and its implications; the second, "the mistaken correlation between membership in the Church and membership in the Kingdom of God." The third was the "insistence on earning one's salvation."[15]

For those who are not familiar with Dozier, I count her among the modern-day prophets. Born in 1917, she grew up in Washington, DC. She spent her life as an educator, first teaching in public schools in the Washington area, and later as an administrator for the Washington Board of Education. Her obituary in the Episcopal News Service (adapted by Dr. Fredrica Harris Thompsett, retired Mary Wolfe Professor of Historical Theology at Episcopal Divinity School) stated, "Dozier may have been the first African-American to head a department in the area's newly integrated school system."[16]

Dozier was also a biblical scholar. She was devoted to careful study and teaching and was known for her teaching—in her congregation, in diocesan circles, in ecumenical settings.

It is tempting to provide a more extensive biography here because of the amazing life and witness Verna Dozier provided, not only in the Episcopal Church, but far and wide. But most importantly, she was devoted to equipping saints for ministry. She was tireless in her teaching and writing about the ministry of the laity, urging people "not just to worship Jesus, but to follow him." She was often referred to as a teacher of teachers, and her sermons and teachings were somewhat radical for her time. Of herself, she said, "I probably am one of the most radical voices in this church today, but people respond to me with great affection and love because I look like Aunt Jemima."[17]

To have had Dozier speak at the total ministry conference would only strengthen the resolve of many to live more deeply into what was emerging as a clear baptismal ecclesiology. And for those deacons in dioceses where the total ministry of the church was accepted as just that, it was not unusual for those ordained or soon-to-be-ordained deacons to talk about, wonder about, and work at ways in which their role was to be developers of ministry in others.

Pushed by the new baptismal rite and strengthened Eucharistic communities, the total ministry of the church—with a renewed diaconate as part of that—moved us toward reformation. With liturgical reform and new ways of thinking theologically, there would be few areas of the church that would be untouched, whether they had to do with education, scholarship, music, or canons and church governance, I believe we were witnessing a movement.

CHAPTER 4

Shaped by Living—The Fifth Wave as a Decade of Definition

In addition to the conferences, papers, and conversations that chronicle different aspects of the movement, deacons and deacons-to-be continued to live in the midst of it all, and the Centre for the Diaconate continued to chart the many ways in which this was happening.

A cursory review of the Centre's newsletters from 1979 to 1985, the years of the church-wide study, reveal at least three areas where deacons were active: direct service; educating each other and their congregations about the Order; and developing resources and educating the church. We owe the Centre gratitude for keeping track of much of it.

The examples of direct service were as varied as the individuals engaged in them. Some deacons were paid staff in nonprofit agencies and found ways to invite their congregations to participate with them in that work. Others were able to strengthen what were called "parish outreach" ministries by organizing, recruiting, and equipping more parishioners to serve in congregation-based feeding and clothing programs. No matter what the involvement, commissions on ministry, bishops, and others were still looking for people involved in some sort of "outreach" ministries. The implication was that outreach ministry was servant ministry. The 1980s remained most characterized, in terms of getting through the ordination process, as the decade of the "what-is-your-diaconal-ministry syndrome."

But almost without exception, whether in parish or diocesan-based ministry, it was up to deacons to educate others about the diaconate as they went along. As one of the first deacons ordained in my diocese (post 1979 BCP), I can attest to the constant need to define and teach. On our bad days we would say, "I'm so tired of telling people about this over and over." On our good days we would say, "This educating business simply comes with the territory." Years later we would say the same things, but with greater appreciation that, as time went on, it was deacons defining who deacons were, and others coming to understand clearly enough to help us proactively, whether in educating congregations, discerning vocation in the local community, or in helping assess the opportunities for diaconal ministry outside the church's walls.

The importance of deacons educating and resourcing each other can be seen, in part, by the development of provincial networks. (In The Episcopal Church, provinces are defined, by and large, by geography). By 1981 there is evidence of either newly formed or already-active networks in:

- Province I (northeastern U.S.)
- Province II (made up primarily of the Dioceses in New York and New Jersey, along with Haiti and the Virgin Islands and the Convocation of Episcopal Churches in Europe)
- Province IV (southeastern U.S.)
- Province VIII (far western U.S.).[1]

By 1983 we read of the first Province VII conference (bordered by Kansas and Missouri to the north, Arkansas and Western Louisiana on the east, Texas to the south, and New Mexico to the west). With that gathering, more than half of the provinces had brought deacons together.

Even though not all provinces had deacon networks, as more and more dioceses instituted formation programs and more ordinations occurred, diocesan gatherings of deacons became much more common. The Diocese of Kansas was one of the first to begin newsletters for deacons in its own diocese. The diocesan communities of deacons, in the early stages of the renewed diaconate, were often quite close, with people leaning on each other as trailblazers and encouraging each other in the formation and ordination process.

Again the Centre would often document the content and outcomes of these gatherings, newly established formation programs, and the numbers of deacons that each diocese was ordaining.

Concurrently, as some deacons were engaged in direct service and local education, others continued speaking, writing, advocating for the Order, and educating the larger church, even as they engaged in ministry in their local congregations and dioceses. None were more important in those early years of living the "new" prayer book than Ormonde Plater and Phina Borgeson. Newsletter after newsletter included reports of their work around the church. Plater refers in his own book to Bishop Wesley Frensdorff's contributions to the board of the Centre for the Diaconate. He was a forward-thinking board president, a longtime advocate for the diaconate, and outspoken proponent for the total ministry of the church. But it was also significant when, in 1983, Plater became the first deacon to serve as president of the board of the Centre.

He not only led the board, he was a contributing member of Associated Parishes for Liturgy and Mission (APLM), thus bringing a deacon's perspective to this very important organization as well as maintaining a helpful link from their work with liturgical reform to the larger community of deacons as represented by the Centre. Associated Parishes had advocated early on for the restored diaconate and was an Association that would remain friends with the deacons' Association, in its various forms, for decades.

In fact, encouraged by APLM, Plater and others associated with the Centre worked on a "set of guidelines for the diaconate in the Episcopal Church: the need for deacons (a theological and practical rationale), their selection, training and use."[2]

As a resident of the host diocese (Louisiana) of General Convention in 1982, Plater was responsible for seeing that deacons were a part of every Eucharist. The spring issue of the Centre's newsletter in 1982 reminded readers, "You are needed to function liturgically in services and remind the Church of the distinctive diaconate by your presence at the altar and near the Presiding Bishop."[3] To this day, deacons play a very visible and active part in General Conventions, including preparing the Prayers of the People for the Eucharist daily.

Plater and Borgeson both served as General Convention deputies in 1985, the year that the final report of the six-year study was completed and included in Convention materials. This was no small thing, as it was the first year that deacons could serve as deputies. (Two other deacons served as deputies that year in addition to those who served as alternates.) Plater reported three things that were of importance to deacons.

The first was the addition of Deacon David Pendleton Oakerhater to the Calendar of Saints. (Readers will remember Oakerhater as a missionary deacon to the Cheyenne people. His commemoration is on the liturgical calendar for September 1.)

The second item of importance was the stated intent of the Bishops' Committee on Theology to write a position paper on the diaconate. It was to include input from deacons and a discussion of direct ordination (ordination directly to the priesthood, without passing through a "transitional diaconate").

Finally Plater reported on the new canon for lay Eucharistic ministers, of special interest to deacons because the intent was for deacons to oversee this ministry. Plater's commentary points to the all-important grounding in baptismal ministry and commitment to the total ministry of the church. After reminding his readers that a new liturgy would need to be written since Communion under Special Circumstances in the BCP 1979 did not mention laypeople serving, he shared:

> This proposal was opposed by several prominent priests and other friends of the diaconate, who thought it would harm the order, but I find it hard to object to a ministry in which deacons enable lay persons. The only problem with this and other exclusively liturgical canons is their implication that lay persons serve chiefly by assisting the priest or deacon. As someone else has remarked, John Westerhoff I believe, it's a funny church that licenses people to hold a cup, but lets anyone teach the faith.[4]

This was also the Convention where Bishop Edmond Browning was elected presiding bishop, which was good news for deacons. His diocese, Hawaii, had been one that was involved in the study of "model dioceses," which were instituting deacon formation programs. This combined with his message that there would be "no outcasts" in our church was encouraging to all who were committed to those living on the margins—of either church or society.

In the meantime Phina Borgeson was preparing for a winter meeting of Sindicators, an informal "think tank" that met for some twenty-five years around issues of renewal and ministry development. Borgeson, especially in her role as ministry development staff in the Diocese of Nevada, was a key player in organizing these meetings. The February 1986 gathering was organized around a discussion about the relationship between the renewal of the diaconate and the diaconal work of congregations. In preparation for the meeting, Borgeson was putting together a dozen or so "vignettes of deacons who have worked with laity in outreach."

While I have shared only portions of the report here, it is still available in its entirety from the Association for Episcopal Deacons. It captures both timeless questions and timeless definitions.

Present at that meeting were then-bishop of Alaska, George Harris, and a young priest from Oklahoma by the name of Jim Kelsey. Both would go on to serve as bishop-representatives on the board of the North American Association for the Diaconate. All orders of ministry were represented at the meeting, and Borgeson's assembled deacon vignettes were part of the discussion, along with vignettes from laypeople who felt that their ministries were not encouraged by the church. The overall theme, once again, was "Laos and the Diaconate," and key questions were presented and discussions centered around several topics related to that theme:

- the primacy of baptism over ordination
- the deacon as icon of Christ's servanthood

- the role of the deacon in empowering the ministry of the *laos*
- intentional ministry beyond the "walls" of the gathered church
- structures and models for shared leadership
- shared servant leadership

We read in the discussion about the primacy of baptism over ordination:

> There was a refreshing and stimulating discussion of the diaconate, starting not from the comparison of the deacon with that of the priest, but rather by asking how the office of deacon in the church might support the ministry of all the baptized. The focus of the dialogue was on the primacy of baptism over ordination. All ministry is Christ's. All members of the *laos*, whether ordained or not, are called to share in the life and mission of the church. Ordination provides "offices." Persons are "ordered" to the church that it may minister in the world.
>
> We miss the mark when we think and act as if the challenge in revitalizing the diaconate is to get the priest to share his or her ministry. The role of the deacon, as indeed for the priest and bishop, can only be identified in direct relationship to the ministry of the *laos* as a whole.
>
> Clearly this orientation assumes a view of the church which is not hierarchical, but is characterized by shared servant leadership more accurately symbolized by a circle than a pyramid. Deacon Phina Borgeson offered the image of the amoeba: the nucleus (Christ) is ever-present and always the cohesive focal point, but the basic shape and structure of the gathered church must be flexible and adaptable to fit the given place and time in which the Body of Christ is called to serve. Leadership must be shared, based in teams of equal partners in ministry.
>
> Holding this view in our sociocultural environment is certainly swimming against the current of the popular world view. Indeed, there is an implicit danger in the revitalizing of the diaconate that some could accept it as a strengthening of the hierarchical structure of the church. Still, the rebirth of the diaconate as a distinct and separate office in the church seems worth the risk. When good teaching and modeling is used, the presence of the deacon in any congregation offers tremendous opportunity for affirming not only the basic vocation of all Christians to servanthood, but also the basic character of all Christian leadership as being that of shared servanthood. [5]

In the summary around the deacon as icon of Christ's servanthood, the report tells us:

> An icon is a window, or perhaps more accurately a prism, through which the divine light shines on creation. An icon is not an end in itself, but exists only to point beyond itself to the divine. So the deacon, as an icon of Christ's servanthood, is not an end in himself or herself. The existence of the diaconate in the church is not to honor those in that office, nor is it to bestow upon a certain group the responsibility of doing the ministry of *diakonia* for the rest of us. The presence of the deacon, in the liturgy, and in the life of the church, is to shed light upon the *diakonia* of Christ, the ministry of servanthood to which all members of the *laos* are called. . . .
>
> It is possible for devotion to an icon to become blasphemous. An iconostasis can be erected which seems to block one's access to God. This being true, is it possible that the revitalizing of the diaconate tempts some to fall into these sorts of traps? This seems to echo the discussion above concerning clericalism. If the deacon is seen to establish a hierarchy through which one must go to "get to God," we have problems. If, on the other hand, the deacon is seen as a true icon, as a window through which God is perceived and which draws us through to a broader vision of the ministry of all baptized, these dangers disappear.[6]

In these days, it's interesting to consider what it means to be an icon. This is a word that was used so frequently for years that I fear it lost some of its deep meaning—along with the fact that we now have "icons" on our computers. But perhaps we can consider an image that invites us into the intersection between spirituality and service. Often people think of the foot washing as such an image. Not only does Jesus perform an act of service in washing the feet of his disciples, he invites them into a way of life in which caring for each other, and for others outside their community— even Gentiles—is the norm. In a way, he confers a new authority, one that is humble but confident, collaborative but clear. Love each other. Remind each other. Make this your way of life. Yet lest we be tempted to sentimentalize this ritual, it is important to remember that on the night Jesus washed the feet of his friends, he also washed the feet of his betrayer. The intersection is not always an easy one to navigate.

In discussing the role of the deacon in empowering the *laos*, and in considering the importance of ministry beyond the walls of the gathered church, the participants (remember that all the orders of ministry were represented) agreed that there is a difference between training people for ministry where they live and work and training them for "church-sponsored" outreach, pointing toward the need for deacons to be ministry developers as well as ministry "affirmers." Phina Borgeson shared that it had been important to her to visit people in their workplaces in order to "understand better the issues, tensions and opportunities for carrying out a ministering and prophetic role."[7]

Sadly, in our own congregations, we seldom take time to be proactive in our presence with those who would benefit with tools for ministry in daily life. Our discernment committees are reserved primarily for discerning church vocation, rather than how we might approach a job change, or an issue around a child with special needs. We reserve much of our attention to what we call "pastoral care," rather than equipping the saints. What the participants in this discussion were talking about was not only the intersection between spirituality and service projects but service in everyday life.

One participant suggested:

> The better job the church does at supporting persons in their daily ministries out in the world, the easier it will be to motivate persons to pitch in and assist in the in-house ministries needed to maintain the fabric of the institutional life of the church. He suggested that there are two kinds of offerings: sacrificial offerings and offerings of the heart. A sacrificial offering is done out of obligation and leads to burnout. An offering of the heart is one that is in line with your gifts. The giving validates one's meaning, and thus it is given in love, and in giving love is received back. . . . If a Christian's life work is an offering of the heart, the church can help a person to identify this fact. In light of this, it could be expected that a person might also gratefully and energetically offer time, talent, and treasure, for the maintenance of the institutional life of the church.[8]

Finally in the discussion about structures and models for shared leadership, those present concluded that this challenge was rooted in many centuries of a hierarchical church. They affirmed that they were more supportive of a New Testament model of the church, one that was more "circular" in nature, and went on to conclude that changing mindsets rather than structures might be a first step toward shared leadership.

A small group then produced a list of characteristics of this kind of leadership in the church. Shared servant leadership is:

- always consultative
- opens up the system
- results in few unpleasant surprises and/or rude awakenings
- takes more time
- meets all "genuine" needs through expressing gifts collegially
- considers the context in which we minister and live out our life as church (especially in this information age)
- builds ownership of decisions
- uses and integrates the gifts of the whole community
- has to begin somewhere (must be modeled by those who have the vision)
- is spiritually grounded
- is under the discipline of (accountable to) the community
- is rooted in and inspires trust
- allows the possibility of calling any baptized person to any office, and involves discernment and election by the community (or representative body)[9]

The work of the group encouraged a shift from thinking about servant ministry in an individual sense to servant leadership in a community of equals.

Meanwhile, the deacon community church-wide was becoming stronger. In January 1986, just a month before the Sindicators' gathering, the National Centre for the Diaconate had become the North American Association for the Diaconate. Efforts were underway in the Anglican Church in Canada to renew the diaconate, members of the Associated Parishes for Liturgy and Mission were working across the same borders, and it was hoped that the more international approach would strengthen efforts in both countries.

Dioceses newer to recruiting and ordaining were, with the help of the Association, learning from those who had committed, early on, to the renewal of the Order. By the mid-1980s, for example, the Diocese of Central Florida had ordained sixty-four deacons. In the September 1985 issue of their newsletter, they reported, "Ten years ago the Diocese of Central Florida made history when it ordained 15 people to the permanent diaconate and took the lead in the revival of this ancient ministry of service. In the years that have followed, 64 deacons—53 trained at Central Florida's Institute for Christian Studies—have served in a wide spectrum of ministry: in nursing homes and hospitals; in prisons and half-way houses; in schools and colleges; in poverty shelters and medical services;

in counseling . . . in chaplaincies in civic and service organizations, in the hospice movement."[10]

Indeed, through direct service, educating, teaching, and advocating, the diaconate was becoming stronger as deacons lived the charges from the church as articulated in the BCP 1979, and learned more deeply the meaning of their vows in the community of all God's people.

By 1987 the North American Association for the Diaconate (NAAD) had decided to hold a conference every two years to ensure the community (of deacons) had a way to gather in a church-wide context. In June of that year the conference was held in Kansas City, with the newly elected presiding bishop (Ed Browning) in attendance. Deacons gathered there were encouraged by his presence, which clearly added to the visibility and the credibility of the group.

By that time, it was my sixth year "in the process." Once again my bishop sent me off to a conference and, once again, I heard from people who had clarity of vision about deacons and their place in the total ministry of the church. I was among those tremendously encouraged to hear from a presiding bishop who had a history of supporting deacons in his home diocese of Hawaii and was comfortable in their midst. He was also comfortable with the give-and-take in the meeting and, while giving deacons a challenge, was challenged himself. This was evident in the report from the Association, a portion of which follows here.

> Speaking at the conference banquet, Bishop Edmond Lee Browning made a pledge to encourage the diaconate in the Episcopal Church. But he also challenged deacons and called them to several tasks: To articulate with as much clarity as possible, to the whole church, a definition of diaconal ministry; To model, with intentionality, diaconal ministry in the church and in the world; To "join me" in making this church as inclusive as possible; To regular re-examination of the spiritual foundations of your ministry through study, prayer, theological reflection and worship.
>
> Bishop Browning referred to his own commitment to the diaconate, both "transitional and distinctive." The next morning, in a question and answer session, the primate faced heavy criticism from both deacons and lay person of the continued use of the transitional diaconate.[11]

Despite his encouragement, he was not off the hook! In that morning conversation there was a great deal of back-and-forth. Clearly Bishop Browning was still in favor of the transitional diaconate, but he was also listening carefully as people articulated the fact that transitional deacons were not trained to be deacons in the same way deacons were. Six months does not a deacon make! Bishop Browning reminded people that he was at the meeting to listen as well as to talk, and was gracious to all, encouraging the Association to continue its role as an agent in educating the church. He was especially appreciative of the suggestion that if, at the very least, the church was not going to do away with the transitional diaconate, it should extend it from six months to two years or more, for the purpose of training the individual in diaconal ministry.

I have pondered this over the twenty-five years I've been ordained as a deacon and the eight years previous to that in my holding pattern process. As I reflect on Louis Weil's suggestion that people still read the BCP 1979 through the lens of the 1928 BCP, I see a context for this tremendous reluctance by bishops and priests to give up the transitional diaconate. Not always, but often. The ordination service for a deacon in the BCP 1928 does mention those in need—but primarily within the confines of the parish.

However, the BCP 1979 helps us understand that the call to serve is extended at baptism. Each of us then looks at that call through a primary lens. For example, as a deacon who worked as a canon to the ordinary on diocesan staff for many years, I know that part of that job is to be present in very real ways to the office of the bishop, which includes guarding the unity of the church. I always had that in my sights. But that was not my primary lens. From my primarily diaconal perspective, I brought other things into the position: marginalized congregations; people excited about baptismal ministry—ministry in daily life; the needs of the communities in which our congregations resided. But the part I had in guarding the unity of the church didn't make me a bishop.

Likewise, bishops are called to diaconal ministry. Many of them are actively engaged in some kind of direct service or advocacy. But that is not their primary lens. It is a call that was extended at baptism, which they continue to answer. But that does not make them deacons.

While it's important not to get lost in this one issue, it was representative of things that deacons, and the church, were dealing with at the time. I share just one other thing about this particular discussion.

Winnie Crapson was one of the loveliest people I've ever met in the church. She was a resident in the Diocese of Kansas and a firm supporter of the renewal of the diaconate. She herself felt no call to ordination, but she obviously felt called to promote the diaconate. Winnie served on the board of the Association for many years, stayed in touch after she was no longer a board member, and continued to advocate throughout her lifetime. She died in 2010, still, by the way, advocating for direct ordination.

Winnie said to the presiding bishop, "As many people know, I don't even want to be a deacon. I think your comment about the rediscovery of baptism is the key to this. Because it's a very sad thing to realize that someone who is going to be ordained a priest, that the church has not made them aware of what they promised in baptism in terms of servanthood."

Bishop Browning responded, "I guess I think about my own ministry today. If I didn't have my ministry in the context of servanthood, I'd get out of this business real quick-like. Whether you're a bishop, whether you're a priest, whether you're a deacon, or whether you're lay. It's what baptism calls us to do."[12]

Precisely. To both. But the primary lens is different from person to person. And if one is called to be a deacon, it has not only to do with servanthood, but with all the other vows and charges in the ordination service. To this day, I believe the transitional diaconate is rooted in an identity that has more to do with ordination than with baptism. I do not believe that the source of confusion about any of this lies with deacons or with laypeople. But I suspect that if we were to do our homework around the priesthood and the total ministry of the church, it might make a difference. I suspect as well that for many young priests, who have known and worked with deacons, there is simply a clear distinction that does not require any sort of six-month incubation period, as if passing through it would strengthen a call to serve.

The conference was about much more than the transitional diaconate, however, and that discussion was just one part of a much larger program. Deacons talked about formation programs and deployment, liturgy and service, and there was a "deacons' fair" at which people shared the various ministries in which they were involved.

Deacon Phina Borgeson was the keynote speaker. Her speech reflects many of the ways in which the diaconate was being defined. While I share some of her words here, I believe her speech was such an articulate "recap" of how the diaconate was evolving during the 1980s that I have included it in its entirety in the appendix.

Borgeson brought a photo to share with the assembly about which she commented:

> I had this photo blown up because it illustrates so well where I feel we are with the renewal of the diaconate in the church. When you first look at it, it appears to be just another picture of just another invitation to communion. If you're into playing ecclesiastical who's who, you may recognize the presider as Stewart Zabriskie, the new bishop of Nevada. If you are from the Diocese of Nevada or receive our newspaper . . . you will

know that the photo was taken at Stewart's ordination liturgy in September.

What does this have to do with deacons? If you look closely, you will see four hands in the picture—the other pair of hands, holding the chalice, belong to Deacon Virginia Ferguson. Virginia, our diocesan treasurer, was one of two deacons serving at table and attending the new bishop.

Deacons *are* in the picture. Though sometimes faceless, though often unnamed (the original caption of the photo would've left observers believing that Stewart has what all bishops covet—an extra pair of hands), we are present in the church—serving with other ordained leaders at the community table and reminding all the faithful, by gesture and example, as much as by word, that the gifts of God are for them—the gifts of God for the people of God in service to the world.

Borgeson goes on to share observations about some of the changes that had been made since she was ordained in 1974, including the fact that the church had succeeded in changing canons so that deacons could vote, serve as members on commissions and committees, and be General Convention deputies:

> I frankly must say that I applaud the changes. To me, being a part of the decision-making processes of the church is basic to adult membership in the church—and I wonder how ordination can take that away. . . . I recall one General Convention . . . when the bishops were questioning how deacons could be in the House of Deputies when deacons are really the Bishop's People. I suggested to another deacon . . . that we get our respective bishops to propose returning to the ancient custom that deacons may represent bishops in their absence; then our bishops could both head to the men's room and ask that we be seated . . . but what I want to celebrate is that we *are* trying a *variety* of solutions and deacons are in the picture as the church takes council.[13]

She went on to talk about titles, collars, and resisting the clericalization of the Order. And then she shifted to what she called a less tangible change.

> When I first became a deacon it seemed as though most attempts to define and describe the office were done negatively, and with

reference to the offices of presbyter and bishop. You know the sort of thing. "What can a priest do that you can't? Is the parish priest or the bishop in charge of the deacon?" etc. More and more the arguments have shifted so that we speak of the diaconate positively, and with the entire body of Christ . . . as the reference point. We have come to see that the relationship we must understand and articulate is the relationship of deacons to the ministry to which all Christians share by virtue of their baptism: the ministry of Christ.

While at some level I knew this shift was going on in my own thinking, it was really brought home to me at the 1986 Sindicators meeting when my colleague, Jim Kelsey, [then a priest] pointed out how refreshing the shift was. We need to be sensitive to those who have still not made this shift—but we also need to forge ahead and build from our new perspective.[14]

Borgeson's words hold as much meaning now as they did nearly thirty years ago. They apply to all orders, not just to the diaconate, and to a kind of leadership that I believe we're still struggling in the church to define—one more collaborative, more affirming, one that worries less about the maintenance of the institution and more about God's mission, Christ's ministry, and where the *laos*, the whole people of God, come into a more mutual set of relationships that equip all the saints, sending them forth in confidence to meet the needs of the world.

Living in the Fifth Wave— Wading into a Sixth

From Definition to Interpretation

The last few years of the 1980s brought markers of further definition. One of the most important was the introduction of ecumenical dialogue around the diaconate. The dialogue was sponsored by the Faith and Order Commission of the National Council of Churches and was a part of the ongoing discussion around *Baptism, Eucharist and Ministry,* a document produced by the World Council of Churches. During those years of the discussion on the diaconate, relationships were made, friendships were built, and other denominations were interested in how we were handling the renewal of the Order.

Ecumenists tell us that most of their work is about building relationships. The same was true in discussions about the diaconate. At a time when defining this expression of ministry was a very new thing, those relationships were very important. The reminiscences of my friend and colleague Madelyn Busse give us a glimpse into that time and the idea that the diaconate itself is an ecumenical movement. Madelyn was a lay professional at the time she joined the dialogue group. Looking back, she remembers:

> I was introduced to the group in December of 1988. Brother Jeff Gros [a De La Salle Christian Brother and well-known ecumenist who died in 2013] was responsible for convening a large ecumenical conference in Dallas. I was new on the staff in Chicago and with the creation of a new church, a five-year study of ministry had been mandated by the constituting convention of the ELCA. The mandate was to consider a Lutheran adaptation of the three-fold office of ministry, which would help deal with issues that had been unresolved in the merger.

At the ecumenical conference there was a wide range of churches. Jeff was trying to get a handle on how the word "diaconate" was being used. I remember three different people representing the United Methodist Church (UMC). They all had different passions, but were all committed to the diaconate in some form. There were people from the United Church in Canada, from deaconess communities, Presbyterians, and other denominations where the diaconate was more of a congregational phenomenon, with deacons serving in congregations as property and finance managers.

I often call this my "roots" experience. It was an experience of hearing language for the call I'd always understood myself to have, even though we had no diaconal ministers in our church.

There were a lot of conversations about the meaning of *"diakonia"* and what it meant for the church. That included various denominational perspectives and sometimes broke down more into discussion about polity, rather than about vision. But the heart of it was pervasive and influential for me. I remember leaving that conference, lying awake, and getting up the next morning feeling sure that this was something for which I was supposed to advocate.

Jeff convened at least one other meeting, maybe two at Alma Matthews House in Greenwich Village (a United Methodist facility providing hospitality to nonprofit groups). During those meetings the group began to sort itself out. Those who remained were representatives from the ELCA, the UMC, and TEC. We brought a feeling of value for and to each other and gave each other courage and strength to pursue the development of the diaconate in our own denominations.

These colleagues became extremely important contacts and, at one point during our ministry study, some of them came to present their thoughts on the diaconate and how it was evolving in their respective denominations. All this had a deep influence on our denomination's proposal to have diaconal ministers in our newly merged church. While we had a strong and rich tradition of communities of deaconesses, it was the only expression of the diaconate at that time, and we felt it might be appropriate to broaden that expression. Eventually in its report to the ELCA, the Task Force for the Study of Ministry recommended not only having diaconal ministers, but ordaining them. The end result, however, was to adopt diaconal ministry as a "lay ministry" with consecration as the entry rite.

While our ecumenical group never produced a product, it was an important think tank—a partnership. We affirmed a common theology, reinforced each other, and addressed common issues. We were all facing the questions about whether having deacons or diaconal ministers would add to a clerical hierarchy, whether it would diminish the ministry of the baptized, or whether it would tread on the territory of other ordained people. Having each other gave us the impetus to continue.

As we continued to meet, even after expressions of the diaconate were instituted in our respective denominations, we learned from each other about formation programs, deployment, and continuing education.[1]

Madelyn was consecrated as a diaconal minister in the ELCA in 1997.

Working groups would meet together well into the 1990s. As leaders and denominational staff in their respective churches, the group not only shared their thoughts, they also provided considerable support and affirmation. Members of both the Evangelical Lutheran Church in America and the United Methodist Church brought helpful resources to the first gatherings of Episcopal deacon formation directors. While the group no longer exists, deacons, diaconal ministers, and deaconesses continue to share resources on an informal basis. As denominations in full communion with each other—the ELCA with both our church and the UMC; and with our full communion relationship with the ELCA and our current agreement for interim Eucharistic sharing with the UMC—it is my hope that further sharing about the diaconate, and between those engaged in diaconal ministry, will move us all forward in unity and in God's mission.

By 1988, there were over 1,000 deacons in The Episcopal Church. Education and advocacy were making their mark. Deacon formation programs were becoming part of more and more dioceses, and there were nearly 500 deacons in training throughout the church.[2]

The year 1988 was also the year for General Convention, held in Detroit, Michigan. Now nearly ten years into the restoration of the diaconate, the Council for the Development of Ministry (CDM) was proposing canonical changes that would be more reflective of the diaconate as a full and equal order.

To the extent possible, processes for becoming a deacon or priest were separated. References to deacons as "nonstipendiary" were removed, and deacons were enabled to be part of the Church Pension Fund if they were paid by the church. It was clear that the canon guiding the ordination process for deacons could no longer be used for those aspiring to the priesthood. While the means of studying for each was quite different in reality; the canonically required areas of competency remained the same for both.

What became known for many years as "Canon 9" (an abbreviated name for Canon 9 of the Title III ministry canons) was instituted to allow local training and formation for individuals who would serve as priests or deacons only in their local congregations. The intent of the canon was to enable small and geographically or otherwise isolated congregations that did not have access to the sacraments or other kinds of clergy leadership to train people locally to serve in that capacity.

Previous canons had actually never prohibited that. However, proponents of the canon felt it would ease the way for congregations exploring alternatives to the unsustainable model of a full-time, seminary-trained presbyter for every parish.

While compatible with a theology of ministry rooted in baptism, in some dioceses, the canon served more to create a clergy class system, and came to narrow the definition of the total ministry of the church. As a longtime proponent of a theology of ministry rooted in baptism, it is disconcerting to look back on the mixed results this canon produced. Rather than providing a way to affirm new and exciting forms of congregational development, the term "total ministry" came to mean "team ministry in otherwise unsustainable congregations." Rather than understanding the total ministry of the church as a theology of ministry rooted in baptism, "total ministry" became associated with a particular method of training and configuring teams. Rather than providing affirmation and encouragement, the canon was simply viewed in some situations as "ok-to-use-if-you-can't-afford-a-priest." To this day, many such creative congregational ministry configurations have received little acknowledgement. However, now that fewer and fewer congregations can sustain a traditional model, changes in education, building use, and other aspects of parish life are being reexamined. Perhaps economics will drive the status quo toward living more deeply into a theology of ministry rooted in baptism. As it relates to the diaconate, Canon 9 was not particularly necessary. Deacons had always been trained locally (and still are) and, as time went on, we often observed that where the canon was being used to train local presbyters serving with teams, deacons were not often part of those teams. (A caution: This was not true in every case, but it was in many. In dioceses where the canon was used thoughtfully for the development of congregational ministry teams including all orders of ministry, the canon enabled effective education for all members of the local team.)

Finally, 1988 also brought the Lambeth Conference (a gathering of bishops from throughout the Anglican Communion, held every ten years).

While there were no resolutions on the diaconate that came from the 1988 Lambeth gathering, it was still a topic of discussion, observing that the deacon's role is "to focus on or be a sign of the ministry of the servanthood in the church and in the world" and "to remind the whole church that the essence of ministry is service."[3]

It is notable that The Episcopal Church is still one of the few provinces in the Anglican Communion where the diaconate is well developed. Interestingly it is also one of the few provinces in the Communion that has a Baptismal Covenant. One wonders, then, do these things contribute to our differences or provide an opportunity for building on a new foundation? It is my belief that no matter what the context of our differences, whether Communion-wide, across denominations or faiths, geographical boundaries or other contexts, *diakonia* unites. Joining with others in service is often common ground, easily identified. Working together for justice, albeit often with differing methods and challenges, unites us even more deeply—even when the gains come one step at a time.

In looking back, it is clear that this period or "wave" of definition would continue well into the next decade. However, it is with a speech at the 1989 biennial meeting of the North American Association for the Diaconate where we clearly see the beginning of a shift into the sixth wave—one of interpretation.

Remembering that the Association name had come from the intention of including deacons and their friends in both the United States and Canada, that year the keynote address was given by Deacon Maylanne Whitall (now Maylanne Maybee) from Toronto. In her remarks, Maybee spoke to the theme of the conference, "Citizens of the World—Servants of Christ."

She reminded the participants:

> As deacons, we are on a journey. The theme of this conference, "Citizens of the World—Servants of Christ," is a signpost of where we are on that journey. For many good reasons, as individuals and as an organization, we have been concerned with our identity and status, with internal questions of canons, of the difference between deacons and priests, of title and dress, with the transitional diaconate and *per saltum* (direct) ordination.
>
> But our journey does have a goal, reflected in our theme and workshop topics. We are not primarily members of an institution. We are also members of the Body of Christ, members of a society, citizens of the world, creatures of the planet earth. And as such, we go with a clear vision."

Maybee went on to reflect on the goal as building the realm of God on earth by using the account of the wedding at Cana in John's Gospel. She observed:

> For where we fit in, the details of this story are interesting. It's a short drama, but there are lots of actors, and where do the servants fit in? Mary is the one who notices the need ("They have no wine"), and she is the first to speak to the servants ("Whatever he tells you to do, do it"). Jesus gives a practical, short-term order ("Draw the water from the jars"), and the servants obey. The governor of the feast is delighted, but not curious—the servants are the ones who know the source of the wine. The bridegroom is the one who gets the credit ("But you have kept the best wine until now"). The disciples observe and believe. And the guests get to celebrate.
>
> What does this tell us about being a servant? It tells us we may get our orders from unexpected places . . . not always the obvious ones. It was not the governor of the feast who gave the orders in this instance, but Mary, who was part of the community and saw the need. It's not necessarily the bishop or the rector of the parish who are going to be the ones who give us our orders. It tells us that by listening to others, we become receptive to what Jesus asks of us. It tells us that we may not always have the full picture of what we do; we may not always understand or see the consequences of our action. It also tells us that we might not necessarily get credit for what we do; and that as servants, we might not even get noticed by those who benefit by what we do.
>
> But servants, by their attentiveness, responsiveness, by their faith and obedience, are the ones who enable transformation to happen. They know their business, and that knowledge is the source of their influence and their power. . . .
>
> The leadership of servants comes from making sure that people's highest priority needs are being served. We must always ask ourselves if those we serve, no matter how destitute or seemingly self-sufficient they seem, grow as persons, whether they are more likely themselves to become servants.
>
> Above all, servants know the goal, the vision, and command trust both by their competence and spirit. . . . They're in touch with reality, they can see and hear things that others don't. . . .
>
> Our job as servants is to make the people of God a more serving people, to make the organized church a more serving

church. As deacons, we are like trustees, whose influence is from knowing and asking questions—hard questions, searching questions, ones that can't be answered superficially. We take our orders not primarily from the institution, but from the human context where there is need, and brokenness, and suffering. . . .

So we have to ask ourselves, "What *is* our context? What *are* the prophetic voices we listen to?"[4]

She went on to suggest that being attentive to our context means listening, really listening, displacing ourselves—moving beyond our primary experience into the contexts of those we serve, and to make ourselves inconspicuous—"to leave room for God to act, to avoid creating dependency, to recognize our self-interest, our need as well as those we serve, to be healed."

While this author is very cautious in using the term "servant," Deacon Maybee's remarks are significant in demonstrating an understanding of servanthood that is more Christ-like and less informed by dominant culture, more about serving God and less about thinking we understand what it means to be a servant with a human master. It is for that reason I share more of her thoughts here and have included the full text of her speech in the appendix.

In a privileged culture, we look through privileged lenses. Unless we have been domestic servants, or have close relationships with those who have been treated as servants or slaves by those who are part of dominant culture, I question how valuable it is to talk about being a servant or a servant leader. The concepts are not completely irrelevant, but I believe we must engage them with great care.

Most importantly, for some of us, Maybee addressed the authority of deacons in relationship to the whole church:

If we're going to be agents of transformation, we have to look at what's holding people down. If we're going to make the church a servant church, we have to look at a different emphasis . . . and that which is specifically and emphatically ours as deacons, is the realization that the real crisis is the existence and nature of human beings. Through involvement with the poor, with people who are oppressed, with those whom our society and culture are marginalizing, we come to understand God and Jesus the poor servant. We do not flee the world as a mystic community . . . As servants of transformation, we take the incarnation seriously, we recognize that here and now has priority, we acknowledge creation as good.[5]

Maybee also addressed some of the skills necessary to be agents of transformation. She talked about the need to be "critically aware of our context . . . to be skilled in human relations—in communication, in listening, in diagnosing need not apart from, but together with others, not as experts, but in dialogue with those whom we are concerned about, not as rescuing angels, but as partners."

She challenged participants by saying:

> As agents of transformation we need to be knowledgeable about institutions and organizations. We need to understand how they work; we need to realize that these can be vehicles of oppression or transformation. But if we don't know how they work, we can't help to make the difference.
>
> As agents of transformation, we need to learn how to do social analysis, to observe systems and structures of the economic, social, political and religious aspects of our society. We need to be astute politicians. This is a complex and difficult task, but an absolutely vital one if our actions are to be part of a liberating and transformative process, and not merely aspirin solutions which reinforce existing structures.
>
> I want to give you an illustration—one you may have heard of before, but it bears repeating. It has to do with a woman who is standing on the bank of a river, and sees someone drowning. She takes off her jacket, and she jumps in and she saves the person. A few minutes later, someone else is drowning, and she does the same thing. A crowd starts to gather. And this happens a few more times. But when the fourth person that she sees comes along, she puts her jacket back on, and goes away! Those who were standing by in admiration and fascination said, "Where are you going? You can't leave these people to drown!" And she said, "I'm going up the river to see who's throwing them in."[6]

Here we begin to see the fullness of the charge for deacons to interpret to the church the needs, concerns, and hopes of the world. What Maybee described is the deep need for deacons to understand various contexts and to understand them well enough to interpret between them. This was no small thing and, I believe, she was giving voice to what many deacons had been feeling, sensing, even living, but had been limited in articulating because of the church's emphasis on servant ministry as outreach ministry. For some it was encouraging, affirming, and helpful in returning to their local contexts, equipped to articulate this role more fully.

The words in the ordination service are not just part of a ritual. The bishop says on behalf of the gathered people of God, "You are to interpret to the Church the needs, concerns and hopes of the world." In other words, you are to be a living reminder, interpreter, reading the signs, moving us to take the strength of our gathered community of faith to those who wait for us. You will remind us we are called to be God's healing presence in the midst of life's wounds. When we see you at the altar, just as we see the breaking of the bread, the sharing of the wine—we will see the basin and the towel, and our charge to take them out and use them.

Indeed Maybee was speaking about the authority of deacons, not only to offer solace, but to offer renewal—for God's people and for the world. She was saying plainly that charity and justice are both important, but to achieve justice, it takes an understanding of context. It takes the ability to equip others to read the signs, to bring them to the community and to mobilize. It takes the willingness to ask hard questions, including questions about what is getting in the church's way of moving more boldly into places of need, of learning more deeply, not only about others' needs, but about others' gifts. She was talking about deacons as those who not only interpret, but who equip the saints for diaconal ministry, and who affirm and strengthen those engaged in it.

It may be helpful, once again, to remember two things. First is the rhythm of the waves. An emphasis on direct service found in the fifth wave of "defining" would continue in many places. But the sixth wave—the meaning and owning of the interpretive role of deacons—that role was clearly emerging.

Secondly it is important in considering how praying shapes believing, to remember the words of Louis Weil—that it could take as many as fifty years to live into the implications of the Book of Common Prayer. Indeed deacons would continue to live into these vows and charges, grounding more deeply as time passed, in both the meaning of service and the role of interpreter. Just as importantly, the church would be living more deeply into the Baptismal Covenant.

In addition, new scholarship, pointing the way toward an expanded definition of the Greek word *diakonia*, would contribute to the evolving understanding of the diaconate. In 1990 a major work was published by John Collins entitled *DIAKONIA: Re-interpreting the Ancient Sources*. Even though his work was the subject of debate, Plater chose to incorporate his ideas into both editions of *Many Servants*. This was particularly significant because Collins's work moved away from translating *diakonia* and Greek words with the *diakon* prefix as mere servanthood or waiting tables. With Plater's book as the definitive volume on the contemporary diaconate in the Episcopal Church, many began to see the shift away from the mere "table waiter" or "servant" understanding of the Order.

Collins suggests there were other ways in which references to deacons and *diakon-* words were used. The terms were used in three ways: first, in the sense of being a "messenger" or a go-between; second, in the sense of "agency" or serving as a someone who facilitates operations, organizes, gets things done; and third, in the sense of "attendance," or as someone who cares for the needs of others and sees to their comfort.

He also tells us that when "early Christians wrote of a 'deacon' of the church, they meant an agent in sacred affairs, who worked closely with the bishop, spoke for him, acted for him, and attended him. "Even when the context of the agency was care of the needy, they perceived the activity as ministry to the Lord and not as ministry or service to the poor and the widows."[7]

While we cannot discount the fact that tradition has pointed toward a direct service aspect of diaconal ministry, clearly in emerging scholarship, the words of the Book of Common Prayer (to interpret to the church), and lived experience, deacons are called to much more.

Between the new books published (Plater and Collins), the changes in canons, the growth in the number of dioceses involved in restoring the diaconate, and the steadfast gathering of practical tips and stories provided by the North American Association for the Diaconate in its newsletters, the definition and vision of the diaconate became clearer and clearer.

With the release of these new books, along with a video entitled "Signs of Service," significant resources had become available for the church, resources which addressed the reality, vision, and experience of contemporary deacons.[8] At the same time, more intentional activity was beginning in Canada. After an agreement at the 1989 Synod of the Anglican Church in Canada to examine the restoration of the diaconate, a task force had begun in Ontario. By 1991 the Ontario Province had approved guidelines for its seven dioceses. The strategy there was one of creating a "community for deacons" right from the start. In the States, diocesan communities were evolving, some stronger, some not. The North American Association for the Diaconate, following on the heels of the Centre for the Diaconate, was providing the opportunity for church-wide community. However, what the province of Ontario was intending to do is relevant today and perhaps something to be reclaimed more intentionally. In a report offered on behalf of the task force in Ontario, The Rev. Donald Thompson wrote:

> At least until the diaconate is fully received and integrated into the life of the Anglican Church of Canada, it needs to have a vocational base in a diaconal community structured very much

along the lines of a religious order, to be known as the "community for deacons."

The purpose of the community is not to regulate the exercise of the ministry of deacons . . . but rather to receive, affirm, nurture, and promote the vocations of those whose practice of the faith has stirred others to see in them an enabling presence of servant ministry.[9]

The report suggested four primary purposes for gathering the community. The first would simply be to develop a model and standard of prayer, Scripture study, sacramental life, and reflection. The suggestion was made that a "deacon for deacons" serve as a convener and that a chaplain be provided, both to serve along with the bishop to guide the community. The second purpose would be to simply provide a place where people could share something about their journeys, and where affirmation, blessing, and ongoing discernment could take place. The third—especially consistent with the remarks from Maylanne Maybee to the North American Association—would be to examine different styles of servant ministry and the education and resources necessary to carry them out. This would include working for justice and speaking prophetically as well as appropriate pastoral care in seeking to be the church outside its boundaries. Fourth would be the sharing of liturgical practices, among other "programmatic aspects of the ministry of deacons."[10]

How the diaconate has evolved in the Anglican Church of Canada is slightly different than in The Episcopal Church, but the idea of this community is remarkable and helpful. Likewise had it not been for the community known as the Central House for Deaconesses and their willingness to share their resources with an emerging community of deacons, the Centre for the Diaconate would not have been able to do the things it did—at least not as quickly. Had it not been for the Centre, with both its ups and downs, it is questionable how effective the North American Association for the Diaconate would have evolved. Had it not been for deacons and their friends, who shared a vision and united with each other, educational efforts, canons, best practices, and moral support would have been much slower in coming. In fact, wherever there are strong deacon communities, one is likely to find a strong diocese.

Association newsletters, as always, included stories from deacons, teaching on "how-tos" in liturgy, in direct service and in mobilizing others, and news of dioceses and ordinations. What we also began to see were ordination sermons. Clearly this was a way for preachers to educate congregations about deacons, but it was also a way to interpret diaconal ministry itself. Not only were bishops preaching at deacon ordinations, but deacons were preaching at deacon ordinations. And while initially the emphasis, in many places, was on the role of the deacon who was being ordained, slowly but surely we began to see more emphasis on the role of deacon as icon and animator in relationship to the community, pointing the way for all God's people to engage in diaconal ministry, defining more clearly the relationship with the congregation.

By 1995, the church-wide community of deacons represented at the biennial conference of the North American Association for the Diaconate was clear enough in their understanding that they took a very important step. The membership of the Association passed a resolution "calling for a facilitated conference of program directors and other involved persons for the purpose of creating general guidelines for deacon formation programs, evaluating the usefulness of General Ordination Examinations for deacons, compiling benchmarks for measurement, and considering how the canons of the church might be changed to apply better to the diaconate."[11]

While in retrospect the outcomes seem somewhat more prescriptive than might be helpful (i.e., numbers of contact hours, which would point to a more traditional "school" mode of study), this was a serious and successful attempt to provide guidance for dioceses that, after fifteen years, were either just entering the deacon formation business, or were revisiting their own programs. Several years later the guidelines would be amended to include an outline of a competency-based program, and allowances for dioceses in which deacons were trained with ministry teams. However, there were several outcomes that were helpful and pointed toward how to speak to the church effectively around issues of deacon formation.

I had been elected to the board of the Association at the biennial conference in Des Moines in 1995. By that time I had been ordained for six years and was serving on diocesan staff as the director of the Institute for Christian Studies. Within the next year I would become the canon to the ordinary with further responsibilities for ministry development, deployment, and discernment—both with individuals and congregations.

At one of my first board meetings, I was asked by Br. Justus Van Houten, then president of the Association, to facilitate the first gathering of formation directors. We held that first gathering January 31–February 2, 1997, in New Orleans. I was committed to a new process I'd learned about called Open Space Technology,[12] a process where space is made, literally, for the topics important to every participant. It is one that requires people to take responsibility for facilitating their own conversations around issues that concern them most, and it is one that is particularly compatible with making room for the Spirit.

Using the Open Space format, participants formed groups around the theme question: "Given the data which indicates there is little uniformity in deacon formation programs, and taking into consideration the experiences of our own dioceses, what are the challenges, opportunities, and possibilities in working toward standards which establish uniformity, but allow for flexibility in those programs?"[13]

"Uniformity" was a word that brought its own assumptions. Since that time, we've realized the deep value we all place on context and flexibility but, at the time, we needed a ground of commonality. It was at least a question that launched appropriate and helpful discussion, and was part of what led to the development of a vision statement to be used as a guide for the formation of deacons. It read:

> A deacon is a baptized person called and empowered by God and the Christian community to be an icon illuminating Christ as a model of servanthood for all people.
>
> The role of the deacon in liturgy mirrors the role of a deacon in the church and world.
>
> The personal gifts the church looks for in a deacon include spiritual maturity, compassion, and flexibility. Under the authority of the bishop and the church the deacon serves as an evangelist and catalyst with others.
>
> The deacon fulfills this calling through action and example as servant leader, witness, intercessor, facilitator, visionary, nurturer and interpreter among diverse people. The deacon is messenger and proclaimer of Christ's presence among us.[14]

Establishing this common ground as a base for developing formation programs was helpful. It was reflective of lived experience. Now after sixteen years of living with the 1979 BCP, the definition was strengthened and the practical experience that was reflected at the gathering of formation directors would serve to interpret the Order to the larger church. One of the important things that emerged from those early meetings was the stated need for more spiritual formation. While not stated as an area of competency required in the canons, it was clear that the diaconate had a lively and distinctive spirituality that should be developed and strengthened. Over time the results of these meetings were published, and the Association for Episcopal Deacons (AED and formerly NAAD) continues to facilitate annual meetings of formation directors and archdeacons.

This was not the only important thing that happened as a result of the meeting in 1995. At the board meeting following that conference, we learned that the bishop who had been elected to the board would not be able to serve. As a result, Bishop George Harris, who had by then retired from the active episcopate (Alaska), agreed to assume the four-year term.

George Harris, first of all, was a personal mentor and friend. What he brought to the NAAD Board was the reminder that all ministry is Christ's ministry and that we go about it as the people of God. No one has a corner on the market. We all exercise priestly ministry, diaconal ministry, episcopal ministry in daily life. Harris had served in the Philippines and was a full believer in developing indigenous leadership. He was a staunch proponent of the total ministry of the church and leaned heavily on the work of Roland Allen. (Allen was a British missionary who served in both China and East Africa in the first half of the twentieth century.)

Harris was also a colleague and friend of many of those involved in liturgical reform and committed to a theology of ministry rooted in baptism. One of his friends and mentors was the late Boone Porter, one of the architects of the BCP 1979 as well as an advocate for the church in small communities.[15] Harris's manner was quiet but convicted. His presence was encouraging to deacons. His commitment to the people of God, and the gifts each brought for ministry, was unwavering.

As we began conversing immediately after our biennial conference in San Francisco about the conference to be held in 1999, Harris pushed us to consider something new, suggesting that we (NAAD) work with Associated Parishes to cosponsor a National Conference on Baptismal Ministry.

The first idea for a National Conference on Baptismal Ministry came from Bishop Tom Ray (Northern Michigan, who had been a keynoter at the NAAD conference in 1995) at a meeting of the Associated Parishes Council. In March 1997 an initial planning meeting of Associated Parishes was held to determine possible sources of support and interest. Porter and Harris then worked to select a tentative site and date, which proved to be St. Olaf College, Northfield, Minnesota, from June 9–13, 1999.[16]

I had also heard about this potential gathering as a member of the Living Stones Diocesan Partnership (a group of dioceses covenanted around the total ministry of the church, local formation, and new configurations of ministry).

At the first planning meeting for "Living the Covenant," as it became known, "we talked about our hopes, our concerns, and our passions for ministry. It was a dialogue between all the ministers of the church. Two laypersons, three presbyters, two bishops, and one deacon later, we had the basic design. The first day would be given to discussion about what we mean by ministry, that is, ministry rooted in baptism, understood broadly and inclusively. The second day would have as its theme how the church organizes its communal life. That is, how does the church order its life, discern gifts for ministry, and call persons to fill those positions in accordance with their gifts. Finally, the third day would be given to how the church 'forms' people to move into ministry and orders, particularly through worship, spiritual development, education and training."[17]

Planning for the consultation was both challenging and gratifying. Sitting with well-known pioneers in liturgical reform and ministry development was a privilege. Being one of only two women and the only deacon sometimes made it a challenge. It was also a lesson in how difficult it can sometimes be to live the visions we dream.

During the two years of planning, our target was to reach 250 registrations. By the time the consultation rolled around, we had 450 registrations representing all orders and most interest groups in the church. In fact, I believe that this was a watershed event. Now twenty years into living with the BCP 1979, this event was a glimpse into the richness of baptismal ecclesiology.

In addition to the keynote each day, the consultation offered at least forty workshops with room for people to organize additional conversations daily. About a dozen of those workshops were designated as "of special interest to deacons." Among others, the offerings included: "Issues Related to the Revision of the Ministry Canons" by Deacon Ormonde Plater; "The Baptismal Covenant and Diakonia," by Br. Justus Van Houten; "Ministry and Social Change," by Deacon Maylanne Maybee; "Ordered Ministries in a Disordered World," led by a layperson, priest, deacon, and bishop; "Lambeth Perspectives on the Diaconate," led by Bishops James Jelinek and Russ Jacobus; "The Care and Feeding of Deacons," led by Deacons Denise Leo and Bill Jones.

There were others. But the richness of the consultation was in the many perspectives that were represented: liturgy, music, ministry development, orders, mission development, Christian formation, theological reflection, and many others. The gathering included active lay leaders, seminary deans, Christian educators, specialists in liturgy, professors, and members of congregations from both urban and rural communities.

Sadly Boone Porter was not among the participants. He died just four days before the consultation began, but his life and witness were celebrated and his influence felt all during the gathering.

In one of the keynote addresses, Professor Timothy Sedgwick captured the essence of baptismal ministry as a movement, saying:

> As with all renewals or reformations, this vision of the Church
> seeks and claims to draw us back to Christian faith, in this case
> to draw us back from a clericalized, institutionalized church
> seeking its own self-preservation. So we seek a fuller under-
> standing of Baptism as initiation into a community of faith.
> We see worship as communal and not something done for the

people by a priest. The Eucharist is in this sense the work of the people, as a thank offering, as table fellowship, and as a reenacting of Christ's full offering of his life to God. What is celebrated in worship is the life lived in Christ. Ministry is then not something the ordained do for others or that which is done for the sake of the Church. Ministry is the life of faith lived out in the world. And the concerns for ministry development are focused on what is needed to make this understanding a reality—what needs to be changed in governance and canons, in liturgy and worship, in opportunities for service, in education and formation, in the role of the ordained, and in spirituality, so that the connections are made and life in relationship with God is deepened. The list goes on, especially as we address the specific challenges of particular communities of all sizes, in all locations, and with all different kinds of people.[18]

There is a very important lesson here. A movement does not focus on one small area, even though it may have a primary, or even secondary, goal. It takes into account as many perspectives and stakeholders as possible. It makes room for both liberal and conservative, activists equipped for immediate action, and educators who are in it for the long haul.

We sometimes lose sight of the length and breadth, the necessary diversity and grassroots buy-in, that are needed to make meaningful change. I have watched goal after goal remain unmet as the round of "priorities" or funding changes from General Convention to General Convention. Three years is often not long enough for new and important visions to take hold. While the intentions are laudable, the three-year cycle of governance and limitless resolutions often serve to shift the focus from one thing to another. Attention and financial resources are often prematurely diverted. This doesn't mean that all goals and priorities are unmet. It is simply to say that networks of stakeholders are closer to what is needed, the more perspectives integrated into a movement, the stronger the movement, and important things take time—sometimes a maddening length of time, but not always. Taking stock of the health of a movement, a goal, a structure, an organization, is always helpful. With "Living the Covenant," we had a twenty-year benchmark. It was testimony to deacons and others that we remained squarely grounded in the Baptismal Covenant, and in relationship with the total ministry of the church. It gave others similar ways to reflect on their organizations and endeavors in equipping the saints and moving forward in mission and ministry.

Deacons on the ground made up one-third of the participants at the "Living the Covenant" consultation. They made their presence known in significant ways in the midst of that gathering of educators, liturgists, and others. While not every deacon came away with the same lessons and questions, most came away with a sense of affirmation and a place of depth and richness in the total ministry of the whole people of God.

The need for definition was winding down. In formation programs, in letters of agreement, in interaction with other ministers, deacons themselves had a good sense of who they were, even if they still needed to be engaged in helping others understand. This confidence, this lived experience, the assistance of national and North American platforms, would serve as further undergirding for the emerging interpretive role.

CHAPTER

The Sixth Wave—Interpretation and Prophetic Voice

Late in 1999 a question emerged that further convinced me of the emerging interpretive role deacons could serve and were serving. I had been elected as president of the deacons' Association during the "Living the Covenant" consultation. In that role I was called upon to write and speak to communities of deacons and others in the church.

Not long after the consultation, I received an e-mail from Deacon Dutton Morehouse. Morehouse served for several years as the editor of *Diakoneo*, the Association newsletter. After our watershed gathering, he wrote, "We have seen far more than a beginning of the restoration of the historic diaconate; we have seen the beginning and development of various concepts of total ministry; many thinkers are beginning to come to grips with the fact that we are going to have to come up with new ways of 'being church' if we are to continue to grow and capture the minds of 21st century people." And then he added, "If deacons are truly the bridge between the church and the world, are we also the bridge between a church that is somewhat stuck in the old ways of doing things and a world that has journeyed light years away from the mind-set of Thomas Cranmer's time?"[1]

That question served as the centerpiece of much reflection in my own vocational life over the next years. I reflected in dialogue with others and in writing on possible answers and possible ways to think about moving forward. The thoughts I shared, first at a gathering of deacons in the five dioceses of Michigan, and later in various venues, went like this:

> So if deacons are truly the bridge between the church and the world, are we also the bridge between a church that is somewhat stuck in the old ways of doing things and a world that has journeyed light years away from the mind-set of Thomas Cranmer's time?

I think we are. I even think we're asked to be a bridge between a church that is stuck, and a church that is moving forward; a church that is anxious about her survival, and a church into which the Spirit's breath is blowing vibrant new life.

Nineteen years ago (when we first started using the BCP 1979), not unlike churches in Nevada, in Alaska, in Northern Michigan, who were fighting for survival, we were fighting for an order to be renewed. We frequently concentrated on the question, "What is your diaconal ministry?" We thought about the diaconate primarily as ministry in the soup kitchen or the clinic or the homeless shelter or the prison. We defined ourselves over and over again as servants. Indeed, that is a part of who we are, the ones on the margins, and the ones who seek to serve. But for all of those things we do, and all of those things we invite others to do, that is not our only definition. We do not promise, when we stand before the assembly, only to visit shut-ins or to cook meals or to sit with those addicted to drugs.

We promise to interpret to the church the needs, concerns, and hopes of the world. We ask the church to enter life's wounds. We ask God's people to join with us as we look to be the church outside its walls. And as Deacon Ormonde Plater has said, "We stir up the dust of a musty old church. We break down the hegemony between two monochrome parties called lay and clerical. Our role is not only to make holy trouble. We are ordained to be leaders in a *laos* of great vitality and variety." Ormonde goes on to say, "This is why I don't like the word 'servant' as a definition of a deacon. In our culture it suggests an inferiority that is unscriptural and untraditional."[2]

Think about it. Can you even count the number of times when someone has seen a deacon cleaning up after a meeting, or offering to be helpful in some other way and has said, "After all, that's a deacon's work!" That is very nearly always said with a smile. But I sometimes wonder if that's not really what they and we let ourselves think. When we talk about the servant nature of Christ, or the servant nature of Christ's church, we are not talking about a mere cleanup detail. We're not talking about bowing or scraping or about setting some above and some below. We are not talking about doing these things only on behalf of others.

Jesus told Peter, as he knelt to wash his feet, "Peter, I know you don't understand. But unless I do this, you have no part in me." I think we often forget about the authority of the basin and the towel. Jesus gave them to us as new symbols of power, of love, of mutuality. And that is what we seek to claim as deacons. That is what we seek to hold before the people of God as we invite them to exercise their own *diakonia*, to kneel before friends and strangers *and* betrayers in daily life, and to claim the power of the basin and the towel.

Early in the days of total ministry talk, and sometimes even recently, I have heard clergy describe how theirs is to give the power away, to give the ministry away. Theirs, they say, is to get out of the way and let ministry happen. But the deacon in me always wants to say, "It is not our power to give away. It is not up to anyone to hand it out or to get out of the way." It is, I believe, about being present in a new way. It is being willing to change our own styles of leadership, recognizing that whatever power is there comes from God and is meant to be shared. It is about being willing to recognize and honor the gifts in each person.

Honoring those gifts means looking for, expecting to find, and celebrating our discoveries in the stranger, in those on the margins we would ask to be our companions. And it means honoring the gifts, interpreting the hopes to a vital and vibrant and diverse people of God. That is what the community asks us to do on its behalf. That is the part of us that is interpretive and prophetic. And at this point in the church's history I think we are called, not only to invite others into ministry beyond the church's walls, but to ask the church to look at her very structure and to create, as Gordon Cosby has suggested, "a structure which does not isolate the poor while serving them, but recognizes that the poor are true leaders and works alongside them in their struggle for a just world. A structure that provides the opportunity for the privileged and deprived, rich and poor to be together." And then he adds, "A structure which serves the poor is one thing; a structure which serves the poor while evoking their gifts and leadership and nourishing genuine friendships is quite different."[3]

I do believe that ours is to offer the gift of a new kind of leadership; one that walks alongside, that is inclusive, that encourages mutuality and interchange between all of God's people, one that affirms the gifts of the stranger, and is excited every time the church's doors open wider and her people venture farther.[4] Indeed I believe that we are called to be the bridge between a church that is somewhat stuck in the old ways of

doing things and a world that has journeyed light years away
from the mind-set of Thomas Cranmer's time.

It makes me anxious sometimes when I begin feeling like
a prophet in my own country. When I begin feeling like the
diaconate is becoming institutionalized, just as we have institutionalized other orders. When we invest so much time into how
it is deacons are trained or deployed or evaluated or supervised,
I feel like we're taking steps backwards. I'm sometimes tempted
to ask, "Who is it that supervises bishops? Or priests? Who is
it that supervises the saints in the pew who are about ministry
every day of their lives? Sometimes I know we're tempted to
ensure that the order is here to stay, rather than taking advantage of the fact that we are an order renewed, and that we have
the opportunity to chart the course into new forms of leadership. Is it possible that mutual accountability can replace supervision? Is it possible that covenants between congregational
leadership can replace employer and employee paradigms?

Is it possible that we can, in our interpretive and prophetic
voices, ask the church to cut through everything that keeps it
from returning to the waters of Baptism, emerging clean, with
countless others, ordained to share in Christ's ministry?"[5]

The message was meant to be strong in encouraging deacons in their
roles as leaders in a *laos* of great vitality and variety. It was no longer about
dragging the church into acknowledging the diaconate, but about claiming
who we were, who we'd become, and acknowledging a clear identity. That
didn't mean there hadn't been challenging times in educating the church
and building credibility. Nor did it mean that there wouldn't still be uphill
battles. But it did mean that our working at and living our definition were
real. Perhaps it was no longer so much about struggle as it was about living
into that identity. We were an Order restored.

The church-wide community of deacons continued to share their stories, primarily through the newsletter that NAAD published four to five
times a year. We were beginning to see more deacon archdeacons, a greater
variety of assignments, and deacons as members of committees and commissions, not only in a diocesan context, but in a church-wide context.

A listserv for deacons had also been established by Ormonde Plater in
1999, and deacons flocked to it and the opportunity to share with each other.
The list continues to this day and has over five hundred members. It is a
place to share questions about ministry assignments, offer new resources,
ask about best practices, and simply to be in touch with the larger deacon

community. Like any listserv, there are times of complaining, or disagreement, or domination by one person or another, but unlike many listservs, those times are exceptions. The beauty of the medium is that it includes not only deacons in leadership in diocesan and church-wide contexts, but deacons on the ground, and many more of them. Topics range from capital punishment, to feeding programs, from asking support for overseas ministries, to sharing good resources—whether in liturgy, community organizing, preaching, or a wealth of other concerns to deacons.

Entry into the new millennium brought another deep loss as well as a great gift. In May of 2000, Bishop George Harris died. From his steady but gentle prodding to take part in "Living the Covenant," to his own careful listening to the hopes and dreams of the larger deacon community, he had served as a good mentor and friend to the diaconate. His understanding of the total ministry of the church, his involvement with organizations and associations committed to baptismal ministry, were such gifts.

In the wake of his passing, a newly elected bishop was chosen to serve on the board of the Association. Bishop James Kelsey of Northern Michigan shared many of the same values. His nonhierarchical and collaborative style, along with the fact that he was an active bishop in the church, pushed the Association in new ways. In addition, he was a member of the Standing Commission on Ministry Development. At the time, deacons in many places were talking about the need for canonical change. Through very hard work over the next three years, Kelsey took the written suggestions from a committee of the Association straight to the Standing Commission. Most of the suggestions were incorporated into new canons at General Convention of 2003 with little change. In many ways these were landmark changes, as we'll see in upcoming pages, but the journey of writing, negotiating, testing, and rewriting required a significant period of commitment.

This was also testimony that the period of definition and lived experience produced strong results. The church-wide community of deacons, at least as represented by the Association, was clear in its interpretation of what was important to deacons in selection, formation, and deployment. While it sounds like deacons were only interpreting themselves to the church, deacons were interpreting what was needed in an infrastructure that would enable them to further engage the *diakonia* of all believers.

However, with the new millennium, we were not only interpreting our needs to the church, we were very publically walking with the church as she read the signs of the times.

For example, in the Diocese of Louisiana, there were several deacons—and many others—involved in prison ministry, especially at the Louisiana State Penitentiary, known as Angola. It is a prison that houses death-row inmates, and a place in which conditions are questioned from time to time. It has been written up in the media and has been the subject of movies and documentaries. It is a prison that has received the attention of faithful Episcopalians, led by faithful deacons and priests. They have held vigil with those on death row. They have been present at executions. They have dealt with families. The ministry of deacons at Angola was the subject of several articles in the Association newsletter. But in 2001, the community of deacons in the Diocese of Louisiana took their work a step farther.

In June of that year, they issued a statement. They shared it far and wide, both within their diocese and outside of it. In fact, Ormonde Plater posted it on the listserv (mentioned earlier and known as "anglodeacons") with these words: "The Community of Deacons of the Diocese of Louisiana issued the following statement this morning, following the execution of Timothy McVeigh. We invite deacons in other dioceses to adopt and publish it also." The statement follows here:

From Death to Life
A Statement on Capital Punishment

While we acknowledge that Christians of good conscience hold a variety of opinions about capital punishment, and while we recognize the depth and difficulty of this subject, the Community of Deacons of the Diocese of Louisiana speaks out now on the issue because of its importance and timeliness.

We believe that capital punishment should be abolished for the following reasons:

- It is unnecessary for public safety and civil order.
- It has unsubstantiated and dubious value as a deterrent.
- It is less effective than life imprisonment, which addresses the legitimate need of society to punish the worst kinds of criminal behavior.
- It is applied in an inconsistent, unfair, and discriminatory manner.
- It involves the possibility of execution of innocent persons.
- It perpetuates violence and destruction.
- It deprives the criminal of the opportunity for reform, rehabilitation, and restitution.
- It deprives survivors of the opportunity for forgiveness.
- It is at odds with the teaching and example of Jesus Christ to fight evil with good and to forgive injury.

While abolition of the death penalty is not a simple solution for the complex problems of crime and violence, it can and should be part of an overall approach that supports human life and dignity, spiritual healing, and restoration. We invite all Christians and others of good will to join us in calling for abolition of capital punishment.

Community of Deacons
Diocese of Louisiana
11 June 2001

What followed, in the community of deacons online, was a reasoned discussion. Not every deacon held the same opinion, but it is one of the conversations that modeled the way the church can get along when it disagrees. More importantly this was a clear sign of what the church charges deacons to do: to interpret the needs, concerns, and hopes of the world to the church. As important as their work inside the prison, so was this statement that invited others to consider alternatives.

Here I hearken back to the remarks made by Maylanne Maybee:

As agents of transformation we need to be knowledgeable about institutions and organizations. We need to understand how they work; we need to realize that these can be vehicles of oppression or transformation. But if we don't know how they work, we can't help to make the difference.

As agents of transformation, we need to learn how to do social analysis, to observe systems and structures of the economic, social, political and religious aspects of our society. We need to be astute politicians. This is a complex and difficult task, but an absolutely vital one if our actions are to be part of a liberating and transformative process, and not merely aspirin solutions which reinforce existing structures.[6]

As of this writing, there are thirty-two states that still have the death penalty.[7] The issue has come to the fore once again because of botched executions by lethal injection. The point here is not to debate capital punishment, but to illustrate, once again, that deacons are involved in both direct service—with serving God as the core motivation—and in serving as interpreters about issues we face as a community. The deacons in the Diocese of Louisiana took a stand, but they also invited others into conversation. They were familiar with the institutions that are a part of what it takes to kill someone legally. They had walked with victims of crime, and with those walking the long walk toward execution.

A few months after the deacons in Louisiana had issued their statement, Ormonde Plater wrote for an Association newsletter:

> But what happens when deacons and others bring Christ
> to those outside? Are they in the world then apart from the
> church? I don't think so. When we bring the body of Christ, we
> are the church and we bring the church. The people in Loui-
> siana who, led by a deacon, bring Christ to prisoners in Angola
> have not only brought church, they have established church in
> that grim prison, a community of inmates formed by baptism
> and eucharist. And the ministry team at Angola is our main
> farm club for deacons!
>
> Just as we bring church into world, we bring world into
> church. There is something otherworldly about eucharist, but
> there is also something worldly. The role of deacons is to bring
> the world, with all its joy and pain, into the otherworld of the
> gathered assembly. We do this when we proclaim the good
> news to the faithful poor, when we stir them up to pray for
> those in need, when we gather bread and wine and set them on
> the table, when we feed the hungry and thirsty, when we tell
> them to go—go into the world, but not into a world bereft of
> church. That's a role we the church consider central, this role of
> deacon, and thus we ordain certain members to the role.[8]

There are many more examples in addition to prison ministry. There
are countless stories about deacons in the pages of Association newsletters and diocesan newspapers. Whether the issue was literacy, immigration, health care, elderly services, racism, economic inequality, or one of
countless others, we were seeing deacons serving in an interpretive role in
more and more ways. More and more they were serving as those with a
finger on the pulse of their own communities, as well as in the nation and
the world. As they interpreted, they also invited the people of God into
those places. In many cases they were instrumental in identifying people
in parishes who were already engaged in social ministry and advocacy,
and worked to strengthen their support.

The "how-tos" that we read about included projects like establishing
commissions on mental health, working ecumenically in small communities when dealing with social issues, and educating people on labor unions
and the importance of fair wages.

On a church-wide basis, the deacons' Association continued to work
on major canonical revisions. Board members sought feedback from colleagues in their dioceses and regions. The anglodeacons listserv was used

for information-sharing and for gathering feedback. Thanks to Deacon Joyce Hardy, who was serving on the Standing Commission on Ministry Development, along with Bishop Jim Kelsey, significant canonical changes were shepherded through General Convention 2003. It was a landmark convention, with the approval of the first openly gay bishop in the Episcopal Church. Thankfully, with the skill and persistence of our friends on the Standing Commission, we ended up with canonical changes that more clearly defined the needs and realities of deacons. The changes were comprehensive, and not without some controversy after their passage.

In broad brush, these were some of the most significant changes:

- The selection process included nomination by the local community. Previously the canons had required the clergy in the local congregation to assist with the nomination, and the vestry to endorse it. In the new process, nomination could be made only after a discernment process locally. This made it clear that whether the local community had first identified a good candidate for ordination, or whether the individual had first initiated exploration of the call, the local community would be involved. In the nomination letter the congregation was to indicate how they would be involved and supportive during the applicant's ordination process. This was significant and helped move the church away from ordaining clergy that had "self-selected," or who were nominated only by clergy, and kept the community of faith engaged all during the process.
- After the nomination was provided to the bishop in the diocese, the bishop and the commission on ministry, or a committee of the commission, would interview the applicant. The diocesan group would report with a recommendation to the bishop about whether to move forward with postulancy.
- There was no time limit on postulancy. Previously a six-month time period was required, but this was no longer the case. It was during this time that the relevant background checks and medical and psychological examinations would be performed, rather than prior to the first interview with the commission on ministry.
- At any time after these checks and examinations were completed, the applicant would be interviewed again in order to determine candidacy. Again, the congregation needed to endorse the applicant for this stage, and an interview by the commission on ministry would take place. Once the commission made a recommendation, and if the bishop concurred, the applicant could be made a candidate. The major change here was that candidacy was required in order for the applicant to pursue study and preparation for ordination. Previously, candidacy often was not

granted until after the applicant had begun a period of preparation. Unfortunately, if it wasn't granted after preparation had begun, the applicant would have spent time and money unnecessarily on a program of study.

- The program of study changed significantly. Rather than providing the same subject areas for both deacons and priests, the new canons provided for education more relevant to deacons. The new areas included:
  O Academic studies including the Holy Scriptures, theology, and the tradition of the church. (This meant that several areas of academic study included in previous canons were subsumed by this one.)
  O *Diakonia* and the diaconate—here was an important change. The church acknowledged that knowing about the history and tradition of the order, and its scriptural foundations were all important.
  O Human awareness and understanding—the importance of building relationships was acknowledged, especially relationships between people who differ.
  O Spiritual development and discipline—this was an area that had been articulated, again and again, at gatherings of formation directors and archdeacons. Finally it was acknowledged in these important canonical areas.
  O Practical training and experience—many dioceses were requiring Clinical Pastoral Education. In some situations that was not the most helpful model. This opened up the possibility of alternatives, and for mentored practice and fieldwork, both in congregations and in agencies in the larger community.

- Another important change was that the canons articulated the importance of formation in community. "Wherever possible," they stated, "formation shall take place in community, including other persons in preparation for the Diaconate, or others preparing for ministry." This change enlarged possibilities. One would hope that people in the congregation or diocesan region are preparing for ministry all the time. This would build collaborative and helpful relationships.

- Another remarkable change was that a whole new canon was added on the life and work of deacons. Again, this was an attempt to distinguish the diaconate as a distinctive order for which people prepared differently. Primary features included the following:
  O A statement that deacons serve directly under the bishop, and in the absence of a bishop, the Ecclesiastical Authority of the diocese.
  O The provision for deacons in the diocese to create a community of deacons that would meet from time to time. In addition, it was suggested that the bishop might appoint one or more deacons to serve as archdeacons, to serve in advising on formation, deployment,

supervision, and support of deacons and deacons-to-be. (It might be useful to hearken back to the Canadian proposal for a community of deacons mentioned earlier in Chapter Five).

O The provision for the bishop to establish a Council on Deacons to study and promote the diaconate.

O The suggestion that deacons could be appointed to serve in a variety of capacities. That is, rather than being limited to serving in one congregation, they might be appointed to serve more than one, or they might be appointed to "other communities of faith or non-parochial ministries." With the advent of this suggestion, we began to see more deacons in diocesan advocacy roles, as people building relationships between congregations around social ministry, etc.

O There were also provisions for letters of agreement, reports to the bishop, and the reiteration that deacons could serve in the governance of the church. In addition, there was a provision for mentoring during the first two years after ordination, as well as continuing education for all deacons.[9]

While the canons were greatly changed and improved, it is interesting that the life and work of deacons, in those canons, is more about relationships and the life and work of priests is set forth more as a job description. Regrettably, one of the changes that was not made was the one that had been suggested for years—that of direct ordination. Therefore, people who are preparing for the priesthood still need to say they feel called to the diaconate, even though they have not had appropriate training to be deacons.

As for the deacon canons, it had taken twenty-four years to accomplish the kind of canonical change that was reflective of both the vision articulated in the BCP 1979, as well as the lived articulation by a real community of deacons. Again we are reminded of Louis Weil's words of wisdom about how long it might take to live into the implications of the prayer book. And yet, through prayer, through living the vows and charges in the ordination service, in collaborative relationships with others, both inside the church and out, the vision was becoming a reality. (Note: The canons have been modified since these major changes, particularly in regard to postulancy and candidacy.)

Another important event occurred in late 2003. Deacon Edwin (Ted) Hallenbeck retired as executive director of the North American Association for the Diaconate. Ted had first become a member of the board in 1987, became president of the board in 1991, and soon became director. For nearly a decade Ted had served as the face and voice of the Association. He had built on the early work of others, expanding the membership list, serving as shepherd of Association finances, expanding the publishing arm of the organization, creating publicity, and generally overseeing the important work of the group. He was presented with the George Clinton Harris award in 2003 for his contributions. Part of the citation read, "As servant to the servants of God, you have served. . . ."

Indeed Hallenbeck was servant to the servants of God. His contributions were many, including bringing NAAD into an association of associations called DIAKONEO—World Federation, and its regional association DOTAC (Diakoneo of the Americas and the Caribbean). He nudged the board consistently, moving them to understand, more and more, that the diaconate is a worldwide ecumenical movement. Overseeing the Association booth at General Convention, speaking with deputies, bishops, and others, along with building this important infrastructure, made it possible for important efforts that would help us "wade" into a seventh wave—one of integration. I was chosen to succeed Hallenbeck as executive director of NAAD, and began work in January of 2004. As we began wading into a new wave, there were countless times that I gave thanks for a sound infrastructure as we took steps into new areas.

Of course, attention would now be turned to how best implement the canons. In fact, they would serve as the primary topic of conversation, study, and program development when formation directors and archdeacons gathered annually. The group had worked hard to produce guidelines under the previous canons. While it wasn't necessary to start from scratch, there were so many changes, it would take time to implement them in each diocese's context.

It's important to pause here for some additional commentary on these gatherings. They themselves point to the importance of deacon community. Not all of the participants at annual gatherings of formation directors and archdeacons were deacons, but most were. This was a good representation of deacons in leadership around the church, certainly in the United States, but Canadian deacons also attended as they continued to build their programs. At any given time, close to sixty dioceses were represented, with some of the representation changing from year to year. There are few dioceses that haven't been a part of this gathering, so there is a fairly steady opportunity to spread new ideas, best practices, challenges, and creative new programs. The gathering is extremely collegial. People come planning to share. They come planning to take something away. And they are always reminded to thank their bishops and others for making it possible for them to attend. The Open Space Technology that is used continues to make room for conversations of most import to the participants.

It is important to remember that Open Space often has a theme question based on the issues facing the group. It is not simply a free-for-all. I believe it is safe to say that few people leave one of the gatherings without feeling that they both contributed to the work of others, as well as that they are taking important new things back to their dioceses.

Thus, at the first meeting after General Convention, in the spring of 2004, the group set to work on integrating the new canons into already existing formation and continuing education programs, expanding content areas, and looking at new pedagogical styles, including online teaching and learning.

In the meantime, however, a phrase was emerging in the church-wide community of deacons. It was being used both by individuals and was the topic of conversation in groups. That phrase was "prophetic voice." Deacons had grown through the waves of transition and definition and were now examining, much more deeply, the interpretive role with which the church had charged them.

The term had been used in a variety of circles—in diocesan groups, private conversations, and at the formation director and archdeacon meeting in New Orleans in 2005. I distinctly remember one of the participants saying that year that she wanted to talk about prophetic voice in an Open Space group. She was concerned about the church's relevance in today's world, and felt that the charge to deacons to interpret led directly to the need, on occasion, for a prophetic voice.

Almost all of the participants at that gathering took part in that conversation. As a direct result, plans were made for a presentation on prophetic voice at the gathering in 2006. Roderick (Rod) Dugliss, the dean of the School for Deacons in California, calls himself a passionate advocate of the deacon's role as prophet in bringing about the kingdom of God.

During that gathering he offered several thoughts for reflection. Among them were:

- reflections on the prophets themselves
- the meaning of a diaconal hermeneutic, that is: prophet formed; gospel based; baptismally realized; systemic, critical, and analytical, heartbroken, and real
- aspects of formation including: a scriptural foundation; understanding the principalities and powers; understanding and living with the marginalized; interpreting to the church the needs, concerns, and hopes of the world, among other things

In addition, the Vocational Development and Lifelong Learning task force of NAAD recommended offering an online course on "the prophetic voice of the deacon." NAAD had entered into an agreement with the Church Divinity School of the Pacific (the first seminary willing to offer online courses for deacons) in which NAAD members could receive significant tuition discounts for continuing education courses online. As a result, the first online course on prophetic voice was offered in the fall of 2006. It has been offered annually since that time and has always been subscribed.

It has been a joy to be the facilitator of that online learning experience. In consultation with others, I've presented a set of skills, far from exhaustive, but at least enough to build on as deacons develop their identity as interpreter.

The first has to do with grounding or regrounding in the prophetic tradition. Attention is given here to considering that the prophets acted out of their love for God and for God's people. As they became aware of God's call to them to speak to the people, they were sometimes reluctant, sometimes afraid, sometimes more effective than others. They complained. They fretted. But they were asked to articulate God's vision. So the church has asked deacons to interpret to the body of Christ. What are the needs and concerns and hopes of the world?

This is perhaps the most challenging task with which we have been charged. It is not so much about being a thorn in the church's side, or about making trouble (though we are often involved in both), it is, as Walter Brueggemann reflects in *Prophetic Imagination*,[10] about being both critical and analytical, as well as people who energize with hope.

Other skills that are discussed are: the importance of knowing how to facilitate dialogue; understanding what it means to advocate, and how to do it; how models of service learning (especially in schools and universities) can enrich our mission experiences. Another way of saying this is that we simply must do theological reflection on our mission experiences, and ask questions about what we've been learning, what the causes are of the problems we see, and how we can act beyond direct service. We also discuss what professional interpreters do. Rather than just translating words from one language to another, they interpret deeper meanings, the cultural values they carry, the similarities and differences that can make or break conversation or build relationships. Finally we consider asset-based-community-development, a method in which we face challenges by discerning the assets and gifts we have to bring to them.

While the course didn't begin until 2006, I had tried out its design in a presentation in late 2005. It was a rich experience, and a poignant one. I share it as an example of a deacon community doing the work of reflection on their interpretive role and a prophetic word to the church.

In November of that year, I had the privilege of spending a weekend with the deacons in the Diocese of Mississippi. It was the first time they had been together since Hurricane Katrina struck the Gulf Coast that August. We were to work during the weekend on the meaning of the interpretive role and prophetic voice of the deacon! Amid stories about what they had witnessed, the work in which they were currently engaged, gratitude for the camaraderie with deacon colleagues, laughter and exhaustion, they reflected on the meaning of their own interpretive and prophetic roles. We discussed prophetic criticizing and prophetic energizing. We rested in St. Augustine's wisdom that "hope has two beautiful daughters, anger and courage; anger at the way things are and courage to make things other than they are." Before we ended our time together, I asked them what they would say to the church. This is some of what they replied:

- There seems to be no place for the poor in the rebuilding plans for the Coast. It is our hope that others will join with us in making that happen and that the poor will be engaged in the conversation.
- Thirty percent of children lived in poverty before the storm; there is the potential for even greater poverty now—or for things to be better as we rebuild.
- Christ spent as much time with those in power as those who had no power. If we expect to effect change, we must dwell with and have compassion for the powerful, in order to bring them to a place of willingness to share that power.
- It may be that our nation no longer represents hope and generosity, but rather bullying and self-interest.
- If everyone who works a job in Mississippi were employed at the average wage rate of Mississippi, the state would still have the lowest per capita income in the nation. People survive by sharing. And yet Mississippi has one of the highest rates of proportional giving to the church.
- We have an opportunity to share a different vision of how things should be, to redefine both our church and our communities.
- We may be about transforming our theology—moving beyond understanding the storm as "an act of God" to understanding it as an unfortunate disaster in which God is present.
- We hope that the deacon community and those in our congregations who speak with similar voices will support those on the Coast in speaking with authority. The church must sit in places of power and decision-making.

Diaconal leadership asks hard questions, speaks from a position of strength, and energizes with hope.[11]

As the months went on, we would learn more and more about the ways in which deacons were part of the Hurricane Katrina recovery effort. In the spring of 2006, the annual gathering of formation directors and archdeacons would take place at the camp and conference center in the Diocese of

Mississippi. In his welcome to the group, Bishop Duncan M. Gray III told us how almost every major area in their organized response to the hurricane was coordinated by a deacon. He had not set out to appoint deacons to these areas, but realized early on that the people most in touch with the needs and potential responses were all deacons.

I recently asked Bishop Gray if he would reflect on that experience, once again. He also provided additional thoughts that he had shared, only recently, with the deacons of the diocese as he prepares to enter retirement. It is with gratitude that I share his words here.

> It was an idea that had been kicked around for a number of years. Could we design a combined Lutheran and Episcopal social service ministry that would start small, learn its way through the distinctly different ecclesiastical cultures, and tap into the unique charism from each church. The vision and energy around such an idea came from the diaconal community in the Diocese of Mississippi and became a reality in February 2005.
>
> Thus, it was to the Lutheran Episcopal Services of Mississippi (LESM) that I looked to coordinate our church's response to the devastation wrought by Hurricane Katrina in August 2005. The executive director of LESM was the Rev. Deacon Carol Stewart (now Spencer). The chair of the LESM board was the Rev. Deacon Frank Spencer. Deacons were scattered across the Gulf Coast where Katrina had done her greatest damage. Each were to contribute in their own unique and life-giving ways, but in the center of that community of deacons was the Rev. Deacon Nick Roberts who would play a major role in the coordinated response by LESM across the coastal region.
>
> Deacon Stewart became the overall coordinator of the early efforts of relief and recovery, shuttling back and forth from Jackson to the Gulf Coast. Deacon Spencer found the necessary logistical and structural support from an organization still in its early infancy and ill-equipped to handle such a dramatic challenge. Deacon Roberts contributed in a variety of organizational ways at the very beginning, eventually becoming the site director at Camp Coast Care, the epicenter of our Episcopal Church's response.
>
> These deacons were not chosen for these leadership positions because they were deacons. Rather, they were chosen because they were already doing the servant ministry work that this critical moment in our history required.

I am enormously proud of the work they did in those very difficult months and years. It was one of this church's finest hours.

As I approach my own retirement and begin to reflect on my tenure as bishop many things have become clearer than they had been before. One bit of clarity relates to the relationship between bishops and deacons. Supposing as I had that the deacons were in this unique relationship in order to receive guidance, direction, and accountability, it became abundantly clear that there was another, terribly important, if unintentional, reason for this unique relationship between deacons and their bishop.

The bishop, by virtue of his/her vocation, is called to be the pastor to the institution. This means the spiritual health and vibrancy, not of individuals, but of an institutional structure that serves this spiritual health of individuals is the bishop's primary concern.

In the midst of this deep (and appropriate) focus on institutional realities comes the deacon, tugging on the bishop's sleeve, stirring the pot, shaking up the institution, forcing the bishop's attention back to the world and saying, "Remember your baptismal calling." It is so easy to forget why a bishop does what a bishop does. Deacons are God's gift to bishops, not the other way around. They are there to remind him/her of their foundational calling. They become the instrument through which God saves a bishop's soul.[12]

Wading More Deeply into the Seventh Wave—Up to Our Waists Integrating All We've Learned

Unexpected consequences. If we hearken back to the study on the diaconate requested by the House of Bishops in 1977, I suspect few could have foreseen the clear description that we read in Bishop Gray's words. Indeed they were written some thirty-seven years later, but I believe they point to a maturity in the Order of Deacons, and a deep grounding in the words and actions articulated in the BCP 1979.

For example, it's taken a while for the liturgical role of the deacon to seep into our consciousness. Sometimes, very little emphasis has been placed on that role for fear that we would end up with primarily liturgical deacons. At others, a great emphasis has been placed on liturgy, often in more Anglo-Catholic congregations and dioceses. Doing things right can sometimes become an obsession. And yet, no matter what the liturgical style of a diocese or congregation, deacons have grown into a space that dictates attention to thoughtful liturgical practice, but that mirrors their place in the church and the world.

One way to think about this is to consider what it means to stand at the side. Whether at the altar with a priest or bishop, whether in daily life with parishioners or members of the larger community, we walk alongside. While the ordination vows and charges suggest that deacons assist the priests and bishop in public worship, I wonder if we might consider a deeper understanding than one of simply being a helper. Perhaps we can consider the deacon as one who "attends," who anticipates, who companions. As one who has stood to the side for some twenty-five years, I know that there is a difference between standing at the side, and being pushed to the side. I have come to look on that position in several ways:

- as one who stands in that radical equality of Christ, but attends and anticipates as a good companion. What might this person need? Are things placed as they would find comfortable? Is everything in order? Can I be a spiritual presence as we break bread together?
- as one who expands the images at the altar, who with the sacrificial feast and the bread and the wine, brings the symbols of the basin and the towel. Just as we consider the supper at which Jesus washed feet and broke bread, can the people see themselves as they break bread in daily life, mop up, or offer hospitality?
- as one who exists in the periphery of the vision of the presider—who serves, not only as companion, but as a living reminder of those who remain on the margins.

I once talked with a clearness committee (several individuals helping me consider where I was vocationally as a deacon and what might be tweaked in my vocational and personal life), about what it meant for me to stand at the side. The bishop and the priest both could relate to what I said about existing in the periphery. One of them remarked that sometimes it was helpful to know that someone was right there in their peripheral vision. It was encouraging. The other remarked that other times having something constantly in the periphery was irritating. They both agreed. Perhaps that's the cost of asking questions about the church, but it is my hope that those seeming challenges are always tempered with what it means to be a good companion, standing alongside.

It is important here to speak to the mutuality within the relationship of bishop and deacon. If, as Bishop Gray suggests, deacons are always shaking up the institution, deacons also need to hear, and are enriched by hearing, about the importance of the unity of the church. I say this from a little different perspective than most deacons because there is a bishop in my living room. And yet, having worked as diocesan staff, I understand how important that unity can be, even if we need to challenge the church on occasion. My challenges needed to be thought through, tempered (not tamed), and offered with solutions in mind. I am lucky to have had several good relationships working with bishops and priests as full partners and colleagues. How I wish that more congregations could truly experience how rich we are when the total ministry of the church, and the different perspectives we bring, is in balance.

Indeed deacons need to be reminded about unity and bishops need to be reminded about institutional pitfalls. On our ornery days, the bishop and the deacon in my house can say things like, "Guarding the unity of the church can seem dangerously close to selling out." To which the response might be, "And prophetic voice can seem dangerously close to shrill accusation and judgment!"

But on our good days, the richness of episcopal and diaconal identity give us both a glimpse of the best of what the church can be. This image is what Bishop Gray offers, and I believe it comes both from the maturity of deacons as well as openness by bishops and others to embrace what the church has asked us to do. This, perhaps, is one of several signs of maturity and integration that we begin to see in the seventh wave of the diaconate in the Episcopal Church.

By the middle of the first decade of the new millennium, several things were occurring that would have an effect, directly or indirectly, on the church-wide community of deacons. First, the primates had established a task force on education in the Anglican Communion called the TEAC—Theological Education for the Anglican Communion. The Episcopal Church had been invited to share expertise on the diaconate. At nearly the same time, the North American Association for the Diaconate received the first of two large grants for vocational development and lifelong learning.

In addition a church-wide task force on theological education was established to examine the state of theological education. This task force came to be known as Proclaiming Education for All (PEALL), and included the perspectives of theological and Christian formation educators, as well as ministry developers.

Other significant initiatives included: a report on The Diaconate and Called to Common Mission (the agreement between our church and the Evangelical Lutheran Church in America); new models of ministry for deacons that moved beyond the traditional parish-only assignments; and, finally, recognition by church-wide offices that deacons could be helpful in many social ministry efforts facilitated on a church-wide basis.

More about each of those initiatives and situations follows here.

Theological Education for the Anglican Communion (TEAC)

While the work had begun on a design for this task force after the primates met in 2001, the first face-to-face meeting was not held until June of 2004 outside Johannesburg, South Africa. In a time of questions about the future of the Anglican Communion (after the Episcopal Church's General Convention in 2003 in which the first openly gay bishop was approved), the importance of theological education was something about which the primates agreed. By and large, they were all supportive of this initiative to offer guidelines for theological education throughout the Communion. That did not by any means suggest a process of standardization, or of expected conformity, but would simply provide guidelines, and a way to build a ground of commonality.

Five target groups were identified, which included: one on training programs for bishops; one for priests; one for vocational deacons, cate-chists, and licensed lay readers; one on other lay vocations; and one on the Anglican Way.

It may be important to note that I was the only resident from the United States who was a member, and the only deacon from the entire Communion who was part of the group. I simply want to be clear about my point of view. While there was a member of TEAC who was part of the American Convocation of Churches in Europe, he had lived abroad for over thirty years. In addition, there was a priest who was an employee at Trinity Church, Wall Street, in New York, but he was actually a resident of Canada, and is now one of the bishops in Haiti. It was a challenge, with emotions running high about our General Convention decision. It was a challenge, as well, because most places in the Communion do not have a well-developed diaconate.

Between November of 2003 and January of 2006, the five target groups worked online and at two face-to-face gatherings. During the first phase of our work, we established common understandings of various minis-tries. We later began work on the content and format of theological edu-cation most beneficial to each. Each subgroup worked with a grid which, with only minor variations between groups, included a competency-based approach to the same basic areas of concern. The grids address four time periods for evaluating competencies, including: the discernment and selec-tion process; the point of licensing, commissioning, or ordination; three years after that point; and finally what must be demonstrated in order to teach in one of the competency areas.

The competency areas suggested during each of those periods included vocation and discernment; clarity about the nature of ministry; spirituality and faith; personality and character (self-knowledge, strengths, limitations, self-care); relationships (ability to relate to many kinds of people, sexual boundaries, conflict); leadership and collaboration (leadership style and local expectations, supervision, etc.); awareness of context (social, political, economic contexts); biblical and theological competence; practical compe-tence; mission and evangelism; the Anglican Way; and spouse and family.

After submitting thoughts and expectations from around the Communion, the grids were refined many times, including during our time in South Africa. We also identified potential resources and possible ways to make those resources available. For anyone who has designed educational programs, the content in these grids is not surprising.

Note that the grids are not so different than what our own Episcopal Church canons recommend. The question is whether we are willing to take a look at a tool like this with others around the Communion. Assuming that we are, there are three levels of consideration to keep in mind.

The first set of considerations has to do with circumstances *globally* with which we need to be familiar, including the fact that there are places where people are ordained, including bishops, who have no formal education. (This should not be interpreted as being without any education, but that education could be strengthened with additional guidelines and resources.) There are places where the church is growing so fast that there is not time to wait for people to go through multiyear residential training programs. Even those who do must depend on local leaders who do not have theological education of any kind.

There are places where resources are so limited that theological education, or education of any kind, is a challenge most of us cannot fathom. There are no texts in languages the people can understand, if they can read at all. There is no Internet. There is no food. There is no peace. And if you are a woman, there is no chance.

Finally, we have learned that our best help is not to give people our old books—or sometimes even our new books—but to encourage scholarship through financial and other types of assistance in order that the contextual theology so important to us is also a possibility for others; or to make concerns about theological education part of our companion diocese relationships; or to consider long-term exchanges or relationships dealing in local formation as well as seminary and theological school education. Our best help might be to take a hard look at where we are in our own part of the world, not just in our own context, but with consideration for how we are a part of the rest of the Communion and the world. For example, what are we learning about the scholarship taking place in other parts of the world and about the kind of contextual study that is occurring in Africa, in Asia, and in Latin America?

This leads to the second level of consideration—the importance of the work of the Anglican Way subgroup. It was my feeling that this was the one upon which everything hinged. If we were to talk about theological education in the Anglican Communion, it was important to have a common understanding of the Anglican Communion. To this day, I'm not sure there is. I've often said that the Windsor Report does a good job of addressing the meaning of "Communion," but that I'm more concerned about whether we have a common understanding of the meaning of "Anglican." It was clear at each of our meetings that "Anglican" means different things to different people. For some of us it has to do with a common beginning, based on common prayer and Scripture as interpreted through the God-given lenses of tradition and reason. For others it means "sola scriptura." For others it is a word that is avoided whenever possible, because of the long history of British imperialism and colonialism. What do we mean by "Anglican"?

Finally, the third level of considerations. These are much larger issues. When I think about the relationship between our own church and the work of TEAC, I have wondered:

- What relationship does our theological education (on all levels) have to do with the Communion? Are we truly knowledgeable about any contextual theology outside our own? And what does the average Episcopalian know about the Communion?
- Because I believe that issues of sexuality are merely the "tip of the iceberg" in the Communion and in other contexts, what is the rest of the iceberg? For instance, what about disparities in wealth and resources? Again, what about our understanding (or lack of it) of contextual theology outside our own? What about access to theological education? Who decides? What about the place of women in the church around the Communion? What about the fact that violence and poverty are dramatic and undeniable concerns around the world, including here at home? In Kenya, domestic violence, particularly violence against women, is incorporated in every part of the curriculum in one theological school. How are we really educating about globalization, about racism, about sexism? I'm not sure, but I think if we were educating well, we would not have seen those searing pictures from New Orleans in August of 2005—pictures of people desperate for help to survive—receiving little or no response.
- Is our privilege blinding? Does it blind us to the lessons of other ways of life?
- Are we educating for mission? And what does that mean?
- We've somehow claimed a baptismal theology and ecclesiology without processing the full implications of that. Not everyone in the world has a Baptismal Covenant comparable to ours. Is that another entry point for discussions around the Communion?[1]

I have included this extensive report for two reasons. First, the Anglican Communion looked to The Episcopal Church because of our well-developed diaconate. I believe that was a sign that the Order had matured recognizably.

Second, Anglican Communion issues are not resolved. Things may be quiet for now. Dioceses abroad have split from the Communion, as they have here. But there are issues that remain—the issues under the tip of the iceberg. While mine is not to speak about the overall place of the diaconate in the Anglican Communion, I do believe that Episcopal deacons have a responsibility for looking at our life and work in the Communion through a diaconal lens. It is my hope that this report might push us to incorporate more about the meaning of "Anglican" into our deacon education programs.

I admit that I have never believed that I am an Anglican. I have always been an Episcopalian. Born, perhaps, from an Anglican tradition, I believe that we have clearly gone our own way in the Episcopal Church, really from our beginning. I am happy to be part of the Anglican Communion, but it is important to be clear about what we mean by "Anglican" with its leftover overtones of imperialism and colonialism. (The same could be said about the word "American.") Nevertheless, should there be a Lambeth Conference in 2018, it is my hope that bishops will attend with the knowledge that, at home if not in person, there is a deacon or deacons in their peripheral vision, urging them to consider the place of *diakonia* in their deliberations.

The Constable Fund Grant for a Partnership Project between the Office for Ministry Development and the North American Association for the Diaconate

In 2005, the North American Association for the Diaconate partnered with the Office for Ministry Development (OMD) in New York in applying for a grant. The grant proposal was entitled "Filling a Gap—Vocational Development and Lifelong Learning for Deacons."

There was a gap because funding appeals for theological education were usually aimed at seminaries, or for those aspiring to the priesthood. Seldom was there extra help for deacon formation programs.

While individual dioceses determine their own formation programs, the church-wide deacon community had learned how helpful it could be to strengthen those programs through hearing from colleagues. With the canonical changes, we had an opportunity to consider how best to structure lifelong learning (the term we preferred over "continuing education"). The North American Association had never considered itself a credentialing body, nor had it subscribed to the notion of creating a single national standardized program for deacon formation. However, we had learned the advantages of annual peer review, of sharing things that worked, and of working collaboratively to make good things even better.

In fact, it might be said that, in recent times, the diaconate has really been the first consistent example of what we call local ministry formation. While many of us considered the existence of a variety of deacon formation programs helpful, we also recognized the need for producing experiences and resources that would benefit all deacons. The church simply had not, and has not, contributed to deacon formation and education in comparable ways as it has in its support of seminary education, recruitment, and lifelong support for priests, or the very expensive "College for Bishops."

While the Association had been the primary church-wide community for deacons, as a vocational and professional organization it had no full-time staff. With its limited financial resources, only so much could be done, and yet it had served as the primary player in bringing forth best practices and making space for the educational concerns of deacons.

The partnership between the OMD and NAAD received a grant for $75,000, with the suggestion by the grant makers that after the first phase of the proposal, additional money could be requested.

The funds covered the cost of planning, executing, and debriefing three regional conferences held in 2006. The purpose, following on the heels of canonical changes mandating continuing education, was to encourage and reward innovative ways of thinking about lifelong learning. The conference content was built around the Baptismal Covenant and the deacon ordination service. Methods of skill development, creating learning goals, and defining the competencies needed to meet those goals were also part of the program. In addition, there was time for reflection on how these things would be applicable to members of our congregations as they carry out diaconal ministry in daily life.

Our goal in funding the regional conferences was to provide a quality experience to thirty-five deacons in each region for a nominal fee. We reached thirty-five or more in every region, with a waiting list in case of cancellations. Excluding several deacon facilitators, 113 deacons attended. Conference venues were: the Duncan Gray Center in Canton, Mississippi; Savior Pastoral Center outside Kansas City, Kansas; and the University Guest House in Salt Lake City, Utah.

The participants of these conferences were not the "usual suspects." As we had hoped, making lifelong learning accessible, financially and geographically, drew many deacons together who would not otherwise have had such an opportunity. In fact, this was the first time that some deacons had met with any deacons from outside their own diocese.

We learned several helpful things from those in attendance. Among them:

- There was a deep hunger for continuing education where "process" is the "content." Of course, deacons are anxious to continue learning about practices in their own specialized areas of ministry. However, the interpretive and prophetic roles, especially evident in the ordination charge to "interpret to the Church the needs, concerns, and hopes of the world," require skill in particular processes that were not often covered in formation and lifelong learning programs.
- At the time, there were many dioceses that did not have a plan for continuing education. There were (and still are) many dioceses where deacons receive no financial support for continuing education.
- Deacons do understand that they are developers of diaconal ministry in others.
- Large "national" conferences are one way to draw deacons together, but time and expense make attendance prohibitive for most deacons. Regional gatherings are much more practical.

At the end of each conference, we asked participants to complete a questionnaire. We asked about skills deacons were using in ministry and what they were seeking to improve. We asked what areas they would like to reflect on with other deacons, and what areas they might like to teach other deacons about. We also asked about whether anyone felt they were being called in to a new area of ministry and what new skills and ideas they would need to prepare for it.

Finally, we asked about preferred methods of learning, what the continuing education requirements and processes were in respective dioceses, and whether there was a process in place for developing lifelong learning plans.

Not only did the participants of these regional conferences benefit, but the planners and facilitators had good insights to take back to the larger deacon community, to the Office for Ministry Development, and to the Episcopal Church's task force called PEALL (Proclaiming Education for All).

After the three regional conferences were held and debriefed, the NAAD Advisory Committee on Vocational Development and Lifelong Learning prepared the "themed agenda" for the gathering of formation directors and archdeacons in 2008. As always, there was also time available for Open Space groups. In fact, "continuing education" was a topic the group had suggested while meeting the previous year, and some of the participants had also been in attendance at the regional gatherings.

Using a World Café format (where participants change tables with each new question in a series of questions, like changing tables with each "course" on the menu), we asked the following questions:

- How can lifelong learning be built into our processes from the time of discernment and call?
- How can lifelong learning be helpful to us as developers of diaconal ministry (not only in our congregations, but elsewhere)?
- Where can we connect lifelong learning with larger systems in our dioceses?

We had deliberately chosen the term "lifelong learning" over "continuing education" because "continuing education" is so often associated with a requirement or a number of contact hours.

The group was energized. Not only were there exciting new ideas and models taking shape, people were enthusiastic about the idea of connecting with larger systems and other colleagues within their dioceses.

In 2008, OMD and NAAD once again applied for a Constable Grant. The focus this time around would be to further bridge the data collected from the regional conferences in 2006 to action. It was our hope that this would help us develop locally adaptable frameworks for lifelong learning, identify best practices in deacon formation programs, and examine possibilities for new partnerships, for example, with seminaries, between diocesan programs, and with other educators.

We hoped that in doing these things, we might see the development of new resources or practices, including competency-based strategies, alternatives in Clinical Pastoral Education, new ways of developing mentored practice, and new online studies.

The grant enabled NAAD, in consultation with OMD, to hold a consultation of twelve people who had rich experience with developing deacon formation programs. They included nine deacons, two laypersons, and one priest from across the country.[2]

In a report on the consultation for the Association newsletter, Dutton Morehouse wrote:

> The participants at the consultation began their discussion by considering one overarching question: "Why is deacon formation a gift to the church?" As the three days progressed, this became the central theme, with parallel consideration of an additional question: "What are the principles common to the most effective formation programs?"

Participants concluded that, "Deacon formation can be considered a gift to the church because local formation programs, based on the five canonical areas of competency, have proven to be a successful, practical, and holistic model of formation for all the baptized and their ministries in the world. Specifically, diaconal formation models servant leadership; is counter-cultural; empowers deacons and others to live into the Baptismal Covenant more fully; is inexpensive, proven, local, and adaptable; provides a way of being and growing more fully into Christ; models sacrificial giving (Deacons do not have the luxury of tuition assistance or devoting three uninterrupted years to a residential education program.); provides a model for lifelong learning; proclaims justice and mercy as ministries; and models local and national and international collaboration.

Participants concluded that key principles common to the most effective formation programs were: flexibility; a focus on outcomes and what people have learned; integration of content, experience, knowledge and spirituality; competency focused; collaborative".[3]

Based on the work at the consultation, a program was prepared for the spring of 2009 to test some of our conclusions at the annual formation director and archdeacon gathering. Asking the group to look at the first draft of the "Principles of Deacon Formation Programs That Work," we created ten scenarios in which those principles could be followed. Examples of those scenarios:

- Create a social ministry – focused field education experience for a deacon in formation who lives in a small town (200 people) and an Episcopal congregation with an average Sunday attendance of 15.
- A deacon in formation needs to have a field experience outside her own congregation. The nearest Episcopal church is eighty difficult miles away.
- As archdeacon for deacons, you have just concluded a meeting with your bishop who has moved "continuing education" to the top of his priority list. There is no practice or culture of ongoing learning in the diocese, particularly among deacons. You have been charged with motivating and organizing the deacon community to get serious about continuing education. How are you going to do that?
- So many people think deacons need CPE (Clinical Pastoral Education), but it's predominantly hospital-based. Many of our deacons will have

little interaction in hospitals or medical settings. Also, they have full-time jobs and can't take ten weeks off to work in the local hospital. What are we to do?

- We have students take online courses from one of our seminaries. They each do this work on their own. How can we integrate their work into the diocesan formation program?

By the end of that annual gathering of formation directors and arch-deacons, we had a completed set of principles that we began sharing throughout the church. Some sixty participants, representing fifty-two dioceses in the United States and three dioceses in Canada, contributed to refining the principles we now share on a regular basis.

Principles Common to Quality Deacon Formation Programs

The programs are:

- **Competency based**: Expectations are clearly stated so that outcomes can be recognized and achieved in a variety of learning experiences and opportunities. This affords the possibility of different learning plans for different individuals.
- **Holistic**: By engaging in all five competencies,[4] holistic Christian formation occurs for the individual (personal, psychological, relational, spiritual, and academic) as a person in and of the world, empowered to live out the baptismal and diaconal vows. The sacred and secular, church and world are involved and integrated.
- **Integrative**: The content is not learned in a vacuum, but includes attention to experience, content, reflection, ministry and life context, knowledge, and spirituality.
- **Collaborative**: Collaboration means that what affects me, affects you and we work alongside one another. Cooperation and coordination are also important, especially in our processes with the Commission on Ministry and others, including agencies, congregations, and individuals. Partnership with other organizations is encouraged and developed. Collaboration means that we decide on things together, that we are both prepared to give things up as well as benefit from mutual gifts.
- **Flexible and innovative**: The program allows adjustments for life experiences, level of education, life circumstances, and learning styles. The program is oriented toward a changing church which honors the past but allows for current trends and future possibilities. Various

alternatives exist for fulfilling requirements, i.e., CPE alternatives. Being innovative is acceptable and necessary.

- **Focused on adult learning**: The program focuses on outcomes. The learners gain new knowledge and skills that empower them to apply that knowledge and those skills to relevant situations. When we place the focus on learning, we are able to learn from our mistakes as well as our successes. In order to focus on learning, supervision, mentoring, and coaching are important. Adult learning is experiential, inductive, collaborative, appreciative, and reflective. Current prevailing adult learning principles are applied; different learning styles recognized; and new technological opportunities employed (i.e., online courses).

- **Oriented toward lifelong learning**: The program authenticates that learning is ongoing and provides the learner with the foundation and resources for lifelong learning. The learner understands the program is simply one stage along the lifelong learning spectrum and is able to set learning goals and prepare learning plans beyond the prescribed program.

- **Clear in their focus on leadership development**: The program provides opportunities to engage in a broad spectrum of leadership possibilities in the church and community, locally, nationally, and globally.

- **Clear in their focus on theological reflection with praxis (doing ministry) within a peer group**: The program teaches a variety of methods for theological reflection and the program provides opportunity to theologically reflect with peers on the ministries in which the learner is engaged.

- **Community based**: Learning occurs in community and out in the community. Growth in human awareness and understanding of self and others and the ability to relate to and appreciate "the other" are important aspects of formation.

- **Relevant to diaconal identity and the Baptismal Covenant**: The program focuses on the understanding of the diaconate as outlined in the Book of Common Prayer (deacon ordination, catechism). It integrates an understanding of the diaconate that includes both the Baptismal Covenant and the ordination vows and charges. Deacons realize themselves as a part of the *laos* and are developers of diaconal ministry in others.

- **Relevant to Christian mission (needs and concerns of the world today)**: Ministry focuses on situations and needs in the world and current social issues are engaged. Practical training and experience in the church and world occur.

- **Contextual**: The program takes learner and diocesan context into consideration. This includes geographical, economic, social, ethnic, and racial identities. The program helps the learner to grasp the drama of the story of salvation and how the learner fits into that story so that the learner acts in congruence with the drama of salvation.

- **Clear in providing assessment opportunities that are always done in the context of learning**. The assessment process is a learning and empowering process.
- **Clear about the place of discernment**. Discernment is foundational and integral to formation. The learner realizes that discernment is lifelong as well as critical prior to beginning formation. Christian discernment begins at baptism and ends at death.
- **Clear in their focus on the place of spirituality**. Spiritual practices are incorporated and the integration of those practices is an essential part of formation.

While I've provided a great deal of information about these education initiatives, they are testimony to the ways in which deacons were integrating much of what had been learned over the three decades since the BCP came into use. They were also testimony to the fact that we needed financial assistance to move these endeavors along. Indeed the church-wide deacon community owes its gratitude to the Office for Ministry Development for its help. Now that the OMD has been eliminated, there is little opportunity for systematic help from the larger Episcopal Church. Indeed we are truly grateful to those years between 2005 and 2008 when so much was accomplished. In years that overlapped with these educational events, there would be one more initiative in which deacons both influenced the larger church and were influenced by it in the area of theological education.

Proclaiming Education for All (PEALL)

PEALL was an initiative that resulted from combining two General Convention resolutions on Christian Formation and Theological Education. It too was funded by a Constable grant in cooperation with the church center's Office of Ministry Development and the Ministries with Young People Cluster.

Donn Morgan, Ph.D, and dean of Church Divinity School of the Pacific, served as chair of a sometimes unruly group. I remember, in one of his reports to the Executive Council of the church, that he described our first meeting using the metaphor of oil and water.

It was hard work bringing people from many different perspectives into a common mind. Membership of the task force included Christian educators whose primary focus was children; others young adults; others represented ages in between. It also included seminary deans, professors, diocesan ministry developers, and educators whose primary focus was in a congregation. I was also a member, asked to bring the perspective of deacons and their educational needs, though I could never entirely separate that from my deep commitment to ministry development.

The vision of the group was for all people in our churches to have access to quality education, whether lay or ordained, and from cradle to grave. In a brochure members of the group created for the 2006 General Convention, PEALL described itself as: a strategic planning team, charged with thinking about the future of theological education and Christian formation in the Episcopal Church; a network, creating opportunities for connections between people involved in educating, across the church; an advocacy group raising awareness of the importance of education for the Church; and a collaborative enterprise, bringing together diverse perspectives in order to create a model for Christian education working toward a common vision of Christian discipleship.

Over a four-year period, the group generated significant reports. One subgroup wrote a history of theological education in the Episcopal Church from the 1950s on; another was responsible for outlining and finding support for a Charter for Lifelong Learning. Of major significance to deacons was the offer to conduct a survey about deacon education and formation. This was important for several reasons:

- PEALL represented so many perspectives and groups. Here was an opportunity to increase awareness about the diaconate in general, but also about educational strengths and vulnerabilities specifically.
- There had never been another church-sponsored survey after the one conducted in 1978. Thirty years later, the same researcher would work with NAAD to create a questionnaire about formation that was related directly to the vows and charges in the deacon ordination service.
- Results of the survey could be shared with the many groups represented at PEALL. Members of NAAD, bishops, and commissions on ministry would also receive copies of the results.

The study was titled "Deacons and Their Ministries in the Church as Reported by Deacons in 2008 and 1978." As the first comprehensive study in thirty years, we were blessed that the same researcher who conducted the studies from 1978 to 1985 was available to do this research in 2008.

Adair Lummis, PhD, Faculty Associate at the Institute for Religion Research at Hartford Seminary, brought historical insight, openness, and clarity to the project. The North American Association for the Diaconate brought the insight that comes with the view of the big picture, primarily as a result of regional meetings, national conferences, and a dedication to vocational development and lifelong learning.

The content areas of the survey included:

- a recap of the 1978–85 research;
- research on the diaconate in 2008 (Two surveys were a part of the overall study: one an e-mail survey to directors of diocesan formation programs; the other a web survey for deacons.);
- personal characteristics of deacons past and present (This included questions about employment, education, and age.);
- formation of deacons. (This was an overall summary of the characteristics of diocesan programs and their effectiveness.);
- assessment of educational areas taught—with deacons evaluating how well they felt they had been prepared to fulfill ordination vows and charges. (This included questions about how well content was integrated with experience, relationships with instructors, and quality of content in general.);
- the overall value of the education received and areas participants thought should have been included;
- deployment and types of ministries in which deacons were involved;
- liturgical duties;
- complementary roles, including diaconal ministry development with people in the congregation;
- continuing education. (This included whether an orientation toward lifelong learning was incorporated into the formation program from the very beginning. It also included areas where deacons were looking for more education.);
- the financing of diaconal ministries. (There is little in the way of help with education, whether pre- or postordination, and the existence of deacon discretionary funds had improved, but was still somewhat spotty.);
- deacons' membership in wider church associations (NAAD, Church Pension Group, Church Deployment registration);
- and diocesan involvement, including what deacons would like to recommend to Commissions on Ministry.

There were important learnings from the study. Some conclusions from the study follow here. However, the complete report, with all its nuances and insights, provides additional valuable information.[5]

One of Dr. Lummis's special notes reported that "rather dramatically and in accord with the 1978–1985 vision of developing formation for a 'new style' deacon, diaconal formation has improved greatly in providing 'factual and conceptual background' in: world issues affecting the Church, particularly international problems of poverty and hunger; and contemporary issues in the United States, particularly issues of race, class, and gender. However, more education in these areas was desired by a number of deacons."[6]

It was also clear from the study that living into the words and meaning of the BCP 1979 brought new understandings. As I wrote in the summary report, "With a focus more on baptismal identity, new collaborations and partnerships in carrying out the mission and ministry of the church are encouraged. That is one of the reasons that the North American Association for the Diaconate encourages the use of the Baptismal Covenant and the Ordination vows and charges to assess our ministries and learning plans each year. We would, in fact, advocate that our annual parish meetings include a major report booklet on how each person in the congregation has done in fulfilling their baptismal promises each year, rather than only the business and accomplishments of committees and commissions."[7]

We were also not surprised to learn from the study that the ordination charge for which deacons felt least prepared was the one to "interpret to the Church the needs, concerns, and hopes of the world." We'd heard, in various meetings and conversations over the years, a plea for more skill development and more process orientation in the interpretive role.

Finally, we also had a document, sponsored by a church-wide body that would help others see that the diaconate was real and growing. There had been a four-fold increase in the number of deacons since 1978. And dioceses that were not ordaining deacons were (and are) the exception, rather than the rule. In fact, this study was as much a commentary on the church as on the diaconate.

The Diaconate and Called to Common Mission

At the General Convention in 2000, The Episcopal Church approved a concordat of agreement with the Evangelical Lutheran Church in America. The document, entitled "Called to Common Mission" (CCM), outlined important areas of agreement in our common life, including our understanding of ministry and ministers. In section 9 of CCM, we read:

> Important expectations of each church for a shared ordained ministry will be realized at the beginning of our new relation: an immediate recognition by The Episcopal Church of presently existing ordained ministers within the Evangelical Lutheran

Church in America and a commitment by the Evangelical Lutheran Church in America to receive and adapt an episcopate that will be shared. Both churches acknowledge that the diaconate, including its place within the threefold ministerial office and its relationship with all other ministries, is in need of continuing exploration, renewal, and reform, which they pledge themselves to undertake in consultation with one another. The ordination of deacons, deaconesses, or diaconal ministers by the Evangelical Lutheran Church in America is not required by this Concordat.[8]

I had the opportunity to vote on the agreement at General Convention, and did so, in the affirmative. I also had the opportunity to attend the liturgical celebration of the agreement at the National Cathedral in Washington in January of 2001. However, I was still somewhat troubled (as were other deacons) by the idea that nothing more definitive or committal had been said about the diaconate.

This, perhaps, is a good example of how bishops and deacons look through different lenses. The bishop of my own diocese, C. Christopher Epting, had been the chair of the writing team from The Episcopal Church (working with a team from the ELCA, chaired by the Rev. Martin Marty) that created this concordat of agreement.

Clearly, in the interest of unity and partnership, this was the best that could be done around the issue of the diaconate. However, many of us felt there was enough clarity that expressions of the diaconate (though they were slightly different between denominations) might have served as another entry point for common mission. One of the issues was that while deacons in the Episcopal Church are ordained, diaconal ministers in the ELCA are consecrated. They, along with deaconesses, are part of a lay roster (a list of those authorized to serve in the ELCA).

Nevertheless, "Called to Common Mission" came into being, and at the 2001 conference of NAAD, Bishop Epting was in attendance. By then he had been appointed as the presiding bishop's deputy for ecumenical and interfaith relations and was working in New York. The associate executive director of the ELCA Division for Ministry was also in attendance. They both assured participants that further study would be done and, by August of 2001, both of their offices partnered with the Office for Ministry Development to begin that study. At that time a conference call was held between representatives of those aforementioned offices, as well as an ELCA diaconal minister, an ELCA deaconess, and an Episcopal deacon.

The group agreed that a writing team should be identified to create a document on our respective understandings and recommendations.

They also agreed that there were several areas that should be included in the resource including: history; canons and policies; call process and bishop assignments; mission and vision; liturgical roles and situations of exchange; examples of practice; and identification of areas for continued work, renewal, and reform. Overall the discussion had, as its initial focus, the exchange of deacons, diaconal ministers, and deaconesses between the denominations.

By March of 2002, the group had their first meeting in New York. An excerpt from the report titled "The Diaconate and Called to Common Mission" tells us:

> While the discussion about the areas that had been delineated . . . was fruitful, a question that seemed to give both focus and energy to the meeting was, "Are we being called to something much more radical than a concept of exchange?" This arose in part because some of the team was aware of ongoing discussion about the diaconate on a worldwide ecumenical level. In addition some were aware of what had come to be known as "The Hanover Report—The Diaconate as Ecumenical Opportunity"[9] and the positive recommendations it offered.
>
> In sum, the conversations led to exciting and creative thinking about the mission of the church, the possibilities of joint social ministry and friendship with those on the margins of society, formation and continuing education opportunities, and a desire to offer diaconal leadership . . . to the Lutheran Episcopal Coordinating Committee.[10]

Over the next three years, a painstaking review of all the areas initially mentioned were addressed by a writing team and reviewed by a working committee made up of representatives from both churches. The writing team included Madelyn Busse, a diaconal minister in the ELCA, and myself from TEC, in close consultation with ELCA Deaconess Nora Frost.

This fifty-plus-page document demonstrated just how much we had in common in our understanding, even though our particular expressions of the diaconate were different. Our histories were somewhat intertwined, our consecration and ordination liturgies were very similar, our roles in the church were more alike than different, and we'd already been cooperating with each other before CCM had been ratified by our respective churches. Much of that cooperation was a direct result of the National Diaconal Dialogue Group sponsored by the National Council of Churches. Other efforts resulted from membership in DIAKONIA—World Federation and its regional affiliate, and additional efforts resulted from the NAAD Board's intentional liaisons with diaconal ministers and deaconesses.

In Philadelphia, some Episcopal candidates for the diaconate were attending the Lutheran Theological Seminary there. Likewise, the annual formation event for Lutheran diaconal ministers in Gettysburg, Pennsylvania, included a presentation by an Episcopal deacon.

Several other examples of cooperation, including joint ventures in social ministry, were offered in the report, including overlapping leadership in prison ministry community agencies, health-related ministries, antiracism training, community organizing, and advocacy; a partnership with an Episcopal deacon, fluent in Spanish, provided Bible study for an English-speaking ELCA congregation seeking to reach out to the Latino community; and an Episcopal deacon who served as director of health ministries in a large ELCA congregation joined with an Episcopal church in offering diet classes, Habitat for Humanity projects, and other health programs and Bible studies.

The full report showed that while Called to Common Mission had asked for further study, the threads of understanding, both empirical and theological, were undeniable. Further affirmation for that came from work that was being done by the Lutheran World Federation. That work would play a significant part in a theological statement adopted by the North American Association for the Diaconate several years later. However, their work also influenced our report from 2005, in a section on "A Diaconal Call to Common Mission." Part of it is cited here.

> We acknowledge with gratitude the many kinds of diaconal work that the Church has carried out throughout the centuries and which necessarily continue in our own day. This work is now challenged to move toward more prophetic forms of diakonia. . . . Diakonia is central to what it means to be the church. . . . As a core component of the gospel, diakonia is not an option, but an essential part of discipleship. Diakonia reaches out to all persons, who are created in God's image. While diakonia begins as unconditional service to the neighbor in need, it leads inevitably to social change that restores, reforms, and transforms. . . .
>
> In order to be effective and credible agents of prophetic diakonia, all levels of the church regularly need to assess internal structures and governance models for the sake of transparency and accountability. Member churches and their diaconal ministries should structure diakonia so that it is effective, visible, credible.[11]

We hoped that the document "The Diaconate and Called to Common Mission" would at least be a start to that.

Finally, the report offered specific recommendations:

> In the spirit of being called to something much more radical than the concept of exchange, entering ever more deeply into the concept of common mission, this task group strongly recommends the identification and development of new resources and projects that will strengthen the presence of deacons, diaconal ministers, and deaconesses as "agents of the church in meeting needs, hopes and concerns within church and society." (CCM, paragraph 8, page 5)
>
> To that end we submit the following summary of recommendations to the Lutheran-Episcopal Coordinating Committee for their review and action:
>
> - That the Committee establish a process whereby it regularly asks how our full communion partnership is contributing to prophetic and practical *diakonia* and to equipping our various members to take up their call to serve . . . identifying areas of mutual concern (social services, disaster services, etc.) and how we might strengthen those efforts. This might include financial support for joint ministry, resources for establishing local partnerships, or training sponsored on a church-wide basis.
> - That the Lutheran Episcopal Coordinating Committee take steps to include an Episcopal deacon and an ELCA diaconal minister or deaconess in its membership, thus keeping *diakonia* before the church. . . .
> - That consideration be given to a diaconal ministry subcommittee to consider areas that could expand common mission, link common resources, and build shared mission through diaconal leadership (new patterns of stipendiary and nonstipendiary ministry, shared theological education, etc.).
> - That Episcopal deacons and ELCA diaconal ministers and deaconesses be allowed to serve in one another's liturgies according to the principles developed in the "Suggested Customary" or guidelines for liturgical exchange. (This customary is included in appendix 3.)
> - That the Lutheran Episcopal Coordinating Committee and others review the current customary for joint liturgies

between our denominations so they might more closely reflect some of these recommendations.

- That the concepts of exchange of deacons, diaconal ministers, and deaconesses be approved, allowing service under call in one another's parishes and agencies. This exchange would include flexibility related to consideration of stipends for Episcopal deacons and nonstipendiary service under call for ELCA diaconal ministers and deaconesses. (This was an attempt to acknowledge that while not all Episcopal deacons are nonstipendiary, and not all ELCA diaconal ministers and deaconesses are stipendiary, those are the norms in the respective denominations).
- That the Lutheran Episcopal Coordinating Committee look at what can be offered in future ecumenical dialogues regarding the diaconate.[12]

It is disappointing that ten years later we have seen little movement on these recommendations. At the Episcopal Church's General Convention in 2012, the charge for further study on the diaconate was sent, once again, to the Lutheran Episcopal Coordinating Committee.

While it would be easy to become discouraged about the place of the diaconate in our ecumenical partnerships, it is clear that there is a gap between the more formal "faith and order" perspectives, and the way we live together in our practical and personal relationships. Thus, the effort described here is offered to remind us that important foundational work was done, upon which further relationships can be defined and strengthened.

It is my hope that rather than waiting for bishops or others to encourage Episcopal-Lutheran partnerships in our dioceses, deacons will take the initiative to create mutual relationships that move us more adeptly and in more unity toward addressing the needs of the world in which we live. Clearly we know that oftentimes what we can do together is clearly more than what each of us can do alone.

Changing Assignments in Diocesan Contexts and New Relationships with Church-Wide Offices

By the time the ministry canons were revised in 2003, there were a number of deacons who were serving on the church-wide Standing Commission on Ministry Development. I had been appointed to the church's initiative called 20/20, which was a strategy group to consider how the church might double its average Sunday attendance by the year 2020. At the initial meeting, then-president of the House of Deputies, the Rev. George Werner commented to me that we had a tremendous diversity represented on the strategy group. I agreed, but pointed out that I was the only deacon of the over-sixty members of the program committees that were part of the initiative.

From that point on, while he remained president of the House of Deputies, George Werner was very conscientious about appointing deacons to church-wide committees and commissions. This was and remains an exception. While it is still discouraging that deacons remain on the bottom of the list when it comes to those appointments, I remain (as do other deacons) deeply grateful for his leadership and attention to all the ministers of the church.

When I married Christopher Epting in 2001, he was serving as the presiding bishop's deputy for ecumenical and interreligious relations. As a result, I moved to New York, and the Church Center really became the community in which I was grounded. While I visited and attended many congregations in Manhattan, I maintained my canonical residency in Iowa, and often served at the Eucharist at the Church Center.

I had worked with many of the staff who were employed there. As a former deployment officer and canon to the ordinary, I had worked with the Church Deployment Office, the Office for Ministry Development, the Jubilee Office, and others. It was a gift to know so many members of the Church Center community.

While I worked with some of them in New York, both as volunteer, and as a paid consultant, once I became executive director of NAAD, I was persistent in asking whether it would be helpful to some ministries if we involved the church-wide community of deacons.

One of the first people who wanted to engage with us was the Rev. Carmen Guerrero. She was serving as the director of the Jubilee Ministry Office in New York. Her office was a part of the larger Justice, Peace and Integrity of Creation initiative at the Center. She was charged with helping to identify and develop "Jubilee Centers" across the church. Such centers were located primarily in local congregations. The Jubilee effort was aimed not simply at local outreach programs, but at overcoming the injustice that lies at the heart of poverty and suffering.

Guerrero felt that because deacons both serve, and interpret, on behalf of those in need, that they would be "naturals" at being part of the Jubilee initiative. As a result, she invited deacons to be part of a cadre of Jubilee Center Site Visitors. The job of those individuals was to visit potential

Jubilee sites for which congregations follow an application process. They learned to perform assessments and made recommendations about whether the site would be approved. In other cases, they visited sites that were already designated as Jubilee Centers to see how the site was doing with core goals, and whether they were in need of additional resources.

The training took place over a long weekend in Los Angeles. Fifteen deacons were trained and certified. Guerrero also wrote letters to bishops in order for participants to receive continuing education credit for their efforts. As a result, the relationship between deacons and Jubilee Ministries was strengthened and mutually beneficial.

While this is one of the clearest examples of how deacons were becoming further integrated into the life of the larger church, smaller steps were being made in other offices. With the expanded effort to have a significant delegation at the United Nations Commission on the Status of Women, several deacons were able to attend that event over several years as a part of the Anglican Communion delegation.

By 2005—and beyond, we were also seeing changes in deacon assignments. Part of that was in response to the changes in ministry canons in 2003, encouraging bishops to appoint archdeacons for deacons. In 2005, there were fifty-eight archdeacons in the church, representing forty-six dioceses. By the end of my time as executive director in 2013, there were some seventy-six archdeacons representing sixty dioceses. Clearly this had become an important ministry.

Archdeacons were tending to diocesan communities of deacons. They were (and are) an important liaison with the bishop. They often collaborate with the bishop in deployment, pastoral care, gathering the community, and providing education about the diaconate to individuals and congregations.

In addition, we were beginning to see more deacons involved as formation directors or teachers in deacon education programs.

One of the ways we know how effective deacons can be is through the Stephen Recognition program that was started by the North American Association for the Diaconate. At each biennial (now triennial) gathering of the Association, deacons are nominated by their bishops to receive this recognition. From 2005–2010, we saw new assignments recognized and affirmed, some of which are highlighted here:

- regional leadership and ministry development in eight congregations
- fieldwork supervisor for deacons and facilitator of the Diocesan Peace and Justice Commission
- health ministry coordinator in five congregations
- leader in area-wide community organizing

- leader in mission and relationship with the Diocese of Haiti
- facilitator of Diocesan Strategy and commitment to Millennium Development Goals

In addition to these more regional and diocesan ministries, deacons were also recognized for ongoing work in prisons, hospitals, feeding programs; in affordable housing, benefits assistance, shelters, and all the while inviting congregational participation and skill development in these areas.

Thirty years after we had begun to use the BCP 1979, we were clearly continuing to grow into the implications of the visions, prayers, and theology articulated there.

Seven Waves and Room for More

Interpretation, Integration, Ebbing, Flowing, and Unexpected Consequences

Sometimes the waters swirl. Sometimes it's impossible to distinguish where one wave ends and another begins. I believe we are still living into the sixth wave (interpretation), even as the seventh continues to emerge (integration). In fact, we still have deacons in our midst who were trained with a picture of the third wave in mind, one more oriented toward pastoral and sacramental activities. And yet, they bring us the lessons of steadfast and faithful responses to what the church asked of them. They bring those lessons into the fast and furious shifts and changes of a world that becomes more global by the day. Let us give thanks for each perspective and for every steadfast deacon who has been faithful to the charges they were given by the church, whatever wave they were a part of. And let us give thanks that we are an Order that is dynamic. We change on purpose. It's not always clean. It's not always easy. But the needs, concerns, and hopes of the world change. Yet with all the shifting and changing, we now remain grounded in a vision articulated in the BCP 1979.

Are we all in the same place? No. Are all our formation programs the same? No. Does every diocese have a strong and well-developed community of deacons? No. Is every deacon a member of the Association for Episcopal Deacons, working for vocational development? No. But perhaps the way in which we are in touch with those differences, the way we attempt to integrate, the willingness to ground through diaconal lenses, perhaps those are gifts to the church. While it may take us fifty years of living into this prayer book to understand some of the implications it brings with it, I don't imagine that there will be a special sign that says we've arrived in 2029. Even then, I imagine we'll be living into new ways of being, maybe even a new prayer book, new vows, charges, and prayers that the body of Christ has embraced.

But despite the fact that we are far from monochrome, in this emerging seventh wave, there are characteristics that undergird who we have become and who we are becoming. It is my hope that as we continue to claim them, and the church claims them with us, that even more creative ways of "being church" will emerge. More creative and authentic ways of being a reconciling and justice-making force in the world will become realities. These characteristics are the undergirding for who deacons are, just as Scripture, tradition, and reason are the undergirding of who we are as Episcopalians. Just like the waves, they blend into each other from time to time, with one informing the other, or all serving as lenses to look at a single issue, but they are identifiable, and a deep part of diaconal identity in today's church.

There are unexpected consequences. They may be *logical* consequences of the vision of the diaconate articulated in the BCP 1979, but if we probe their depth, we may have gotten more than we bargained for. We may have received both a call to revisit the meaning of baptismal ecclesiology, as well as a push, an admonition to the church, to let go of her sacred cows. I don't imagine that these characteristics are exhaustive, but they are remarkable. Let us, then, explore them.

First and foremost, our identity is primarily **baptismal**. We believe that baptism is the first call to ministry and we know we step out of the glorious *laos*, the whole people of God, called to be living reminders of the *diakonia* to which we are all called. We are **adaptable**. From the earliest church described in the Book of Acts, to four recognizable types of deacons in our church over the course of two hundred years, we've been adaptable. We've learned from the different waves, and in ministry on the ground, we often have to be creative with few resources. We are **contextual**. We have always been trained and grounded locally. Understanding our own contexts allows us to develop and use appropriate tools and education with ourselves and others, whether geographically, culturally, or socially. It also gives us an appreciation and respect for the contexts of others, and enables us to stand more effectively in solidarity with them. If we know the neighbor next door is hungry, we often understand hunger far away. We have glimpsed the importance of a **strong deacon community**, whether in dioceses or church-wide. We know the importance of networking. For example, without it, we might still be waiting for canonical changes or appropriate continuing education. In the last thirty-five years, we've claimed our charge from the church to be **interpreters** in ways that have been unexpected but critical. We have moved steadily away from an understanding of servanthood that means "reaching down," to one that reaches out and under the issues we face in the world today.

All of these characteristics have implications for the diaconate; how we train for it, how we develop educational resources, and how we deploy deacons (both in location as well as ministry). They also have implications for the church. The reflections that follow are far from exhaustive. They are offered as an invitation to further expand on distinctive realities, to wonder, and to imagine new possibilities.

Baptismal Identity

On those days when diplomatic language is elusive, and I find myself surrounded by clergy "ranks," I simply want to ask, "What is it you don't get about the radical equality that comes with baptism?" Those are the days when I'm likely hearing about "the bishop's staff" (rather than diocesan staff) or "the bishop's vision" (rather than the vision of the diocese) or whether "the bishop will be supportive of such and such." Sometimes it's when deacons are complaining about how they can't get so-and-so to jump on a particular social issue, rather than listening for what the reluctance is, or whether other issues are more important to people in the congregation. Still other days, it's when hearing priests declare that they are "permission givers," or hearing that "so and so will not do that at my altar."

Often we know that members of the congregation expect clergy to do things that they could do themselves. If we hearken back to Louis Weil's sharing about the framing of the BCP 1979 and the attempt to address clericalism, perhaps we can recognize that it takes a long time for people to adjust to the radical equality that comes with baptism—whether lay or ordained.

That's what I try to remember on my good days. It takes time.

In his article entitled "Exodus from Privilege: Reflections on the Diaconate in Acts," Bishop Thomas Breidenthal opens with these words:

> The 1979 *Book of Common Prayer* brought the ministry of all the baptized front and center. If baptism is full incorporation into the body of Christ, then every baptized person is fully authorized to be a minister of Christ's reconciling work. Not surprisingly, this insight has led to a fresh examination of all kinds of authority, particularly that of the ordained. As we live into the ministry of all the baptized, what role, if any, should bishops, priests, and deacons play? The tensions packed into this question are nowhere more evident than in the church's ongoing reflection on the diaconate. The rise of the modern diaconate is inextricably bound up with the recovery of the ministry of all the baptized, and could be said to be its precursor.[1]

Breidenthal then describes the tension between the idea (held by some detractors) that the diaconate takes the servant ministry given to all and assigns it to the ordained, with the idea that the diaconate actually challenges how we think about ordained ministry. "Perhaps," he writes, "the recovery of the diaconate, far from demoting the laity, presages a flattening of our hierarchy, a redistribution of ministerial power that calls the very purpose of ordained ministry into question. It might be that the diaconate, far from resacralizing servant ministry, charts a path toward lay presidency of the eucharist or, still more radically, the elimination of orders altogether."[2]

Those are weighty questions—questions asked by many who take baptismal ecclesiology seriously. In fact, I believe it would be helpful for the church at large to consider these questions in a church-wide forum, to revisit the importance of baptism and Eucharist in how we live, rather than to focus its efforts on restructuring in governance and administration.

Be that as it may, the questions about our relationships with the whole people of God have been part of the diaconate since at least 1979. While the North American Association for the Diaconate (now known as the Association for Episcopal Deacons—AED) has always been a vocational association, its mission statement includes reference to the *diakonia* of all believers, which is the diaconal ministry to which we are all called.

In 2010 The North American Association for the Diaconate adopted the following theological statement. If we hearken back to the period of definition (fifth wave) in the 1980s, we can see the ways in which the community of deacons church-wide has become more confident and determined in its theological grounding. A small group from the board worked hard to adapt and contextualize the statement for the Episcopal Church. The Association produced a brochure soon after. It has now been distributed far and wide. It points toward the total ministry of the church and to diaconal leadership in the midst of the whole people of God. It is set in the context of baptism and Eucharist. The statement opens with an acknowledgement and reads as follows:

> The board of the North American Association for the Diaconate/ Association for Episcopal Deacons and the directors of diaconal formation church-wide are profoundly grateful to the Lutheran World Federation for their statement, *Prophetic Diakonia: For the Healing of the World*. This prayerful and profound work has both inspired us and served as the foundation for our statement on behalf of deacons and of all who engage in the *diakonia* of all believers, both in The Episcopal Church and the Anglican Church of Canada. We are especially grateful for

the permission of the Lutheran World Federation to adapt their words.

On Engaging the *Diakonia* of All Believers

Diakonia is central to fulfilling the church's mission as servant leaders. *Diakonia* is not optional in the gospel of Jesus Christ; rather it is an essential part of discipleship. *Diakonia* reaches out to all persons created in God's image. While *diakonia* begins in unconditional service to neighbor in need, it leads inevitably through advocacy and prophetic proclamation to bear witness in word and deed to God's presence in the midst of our lives.

We are shaped to serve others through worship, where we celebrate God's gift of grace in the Word, water, bread and wine, through which we glimpse the fulfillment of God's promise. In this broken world where sin and injustice abound, God in Christ through the power of the Holy Spirit shapes us as a gathered community. Thus, we become the voice, hands, and feet of Christ and agents of grace for the healing of the world.

All Christians are called through the Baptismal Covenant to live out *diakonia* through what they do and how they live their daily life in the world. This is the first and most fundamental expression of *diakonia*. Organized expressions of *diakonia* occur at the congregational level as well as through those who are set apart as ordained deacons. Deacons are to model and lead by inspiring, empowering, and engaging every baptized person in living out the *diakonia* of all believers in everyday life. Deacons do not—cannot—"do" *diakonia* on behalf of the baptized, but they help to lead all people, including the ordained, into the servant ministry of all believers, which is the essence of our Baptismal Covenant.

Because of the holistic mission of God, *diakonia* is deeply interrelated with *kerygma* (proclamation of the Word) and *koinonia* (sharing at the Table). *Diakonia* is witnessing through deeds. It is rooted in the sharing of the body and blood of Christ in the Eucharist. The mutual sharing inherent in the communion of the church bears witness in word and deed to the unjust power relations that often are present in some diaconal work, such as between "wealthy givers" and "poor recipients." In *diakonia* those serving and those served are both transformed; the purpose of *diakonia* is to make Christ's redemptive love known by word and example not to proselytize.

Diakonia is not the strong serving the weak, which can lead to paternalism by assuming that some churches are unable to engage in *diakonia* because of their lack of resources or expertise. As Episcopalians, we envision that *diakonia* is part of the calling of all churches, regardless of size and all Christians, regardless of wealth, because we believe that all of God's people, individually and as communities, are blessed with gifts to share.

We must challenge all theological interpretations that do not take seriously the suffering in the world, a world afflicted with poverty, violence, and injustice. We must also challenge all theological interpretations that do not take seriously the systems, structures, and powers that foster, or even benefit from, poverty, violence, and injustice. As Episcopalians, we are shaped by both an incarnational theology and a theology of the cross. In the incarnation, God's identification with all of humanity compels us to identify with all of our sisters and brothers. Christ's suffering on the cross compels us to identify especially with those of our sisters and brothers who suffer today, moving beyond politeness and pretense, breaking the silence and risking speaking truth to power, even when this threatens the established order and results in hardship or persecution. This is the heart of the prophetic diaconal calling.[3]

What if we were to take this statement, and hold it with the list of characteristics that was produced by the group at Sindicators so long ago: **Shared servant leadership** is always consultative; opens up the system; results in few unpleasant surprises and/or rude awakenings; takes more time; meets all "genuine" needs through expressing gifts collegially; considers the context in which we minister and live out our life as church (especially in this information age); builds ownership of decisions; uses and integrates the gifts of the whole community; has to begin somewhere (must be modeled by those who have the vision); is spiritually grounded; is under the discipline of (is accountable to) the community; is rooted in and inspires trust; allows the possibility of calling any baptized person to any office; and involves discernment and election by the community (or representative body).

This, in combination with regularly revisiting the Baptismal Covenant and the ordination service, gives us a good picture of the ways in which deacons see their identity as primarily baptismal. And the implications and questions for the church?

If the diaconate, as articulated in the BCP 1979, was to draw the attention of the church to Christ's servant nature, and her own in his stead, how does the church understand her servant nature today, specifically as she seeks and employs resources?

How do we honor, develop, and affirm the total ministry of the church today? Is the one priest/one parish model still the best way to reach out in ministry and mission? Are there possibilities for partnerships that involve more people in the leadership of congregations—in liturgy, in administration, in mission? (Once again, the terms "total ministry" and "total ministry teams" may hold value for how to start, but the possibilities are endless.)

Why do we so often see discernment, formation, and deployment policies for deacons changing when a new bishop comes to town? While our ministry is adaptable and contextual, the diaconate does not need reinterpretation by every bishop. How clear are the members of our commissions on ministry in holding to the meaning of the diaconate, and what place does constructive and proactive experience with the diaconate have in elections of a new bishop?

Some of us are still waiting for the "bishop's staff" to emerge as partners in a diocesan ministry rather than to serve as an enclave of episcopal hierarchy. And for those who like to think of themselves as partners, what does it say that they belong to the bishop—as if they were owned by one person instead of embraced by the body of Christ? The argument that priests and bishops should be able to choose their own staff feeds into a hierarchical model that seems far from authentic when we use words like "shared," or "mutual," or "collaborative."

How can our structures support our theology? Asking for money and moral support from working class and less privileged people for meetings abroad, or meetings that are held during the work week, or for extended periods, is not consistent with embracing the poor. Nor does it instill confidence that the institutional church is in touch with the needs, concerns, and hopes of the world.

If mission is so important, are we ready to do the hard work of building relationships with people who do not frequent our buildings? Are we prepared to see their gifts and the spark of the divine that resides in them— whether they venture inside our walls or not?

If we believe that everyone has gifts for ministry—and if we believe that engaging with Christ every day, no matter what we're doing at work, at school, at play involves our response to God's love—then with God, we can offer goodness, possibility, and healing transformation in the world. We take that into our identity as baptized people and we take that into our identity as deacons.

That means—we're in this together.

Just as we promise together in the Baptismal Covenant to seek and serve Christ in all persons, loving our neighbors as ourselves, deacons promise that "at all times in our lives and teaching we are to show Christ's people that in serving the helpless, they are serving Christ himself." We are charged with that responsibility by the church, the people of God, and by the bishop on their behalf and in their presence.

Just as we promise together in the Baptismal Covenant to strive for justice and peace among all people, and to respect the dignity of every human being, so deacons are charged by the church to "interpret to the Church the needs, concerns and hopes of the world."

We are in this together. If deacons are developers of diaconal ministry in others (presbyters, laypeople, bishops), we see that the skills that we need and the things that we learn to equip us in this special ministry are skills that others need. Sometimes others teach us about their skills as they engage in ministry and mission in daily life. Then it is up to us to take the lead in asking the church to affirm and bless those efforts. Likewise, we learn from bishops about the importance of oversight (one hopes with "undergirding" to counterbalance it), and from presbyters about sacramental living, reconciliation, how we keep the lore scripturally and traditionally, and how we keep the community strong.

When we talk about the importance of shared ministry, and about sharing in Christ's ministry, we need to be sure we have good relational skills, skills that we define in the canons as those having to do with human awareness and understanding. We need to take time to incorporate changes in how we educate deacons and others so that we understand things like how to learn the make-up of the communities around us—what their needs, challenges, and gifts are; what it takes to be good companions and partners with those who may not be regular inhabitants inside the walls of the church; about cultural differences and about economic differences—as well as about shared hopes and fears. Indeed it is our job as deacons to hold the vision, the possibilities of what does and can exist beyond our institutional enclosures, but we are all in this together.

If we return briefly to Bishop Breidenthal's article as he reflects on both the "exodus from privilege," and the diaconate, we can see hopeful possibilities for relationships, indeed partnerships, between bishops, deacons, laypeople, and priests. It is something well worth contemplating as we consider the place of the church in the world today.

In his article, Breidenthal writes:

> If there is no "higher" or "lower" among the three orders—if ordination is not stepping onto a ladder of ascent—then there

is no "higher" or "lower" when it comes to comparing the laity to the ordained. We are all disciples of Jesus who are called to follow him into the wilderness. Some of us are invited by the baptized to be deacons, priests, and bishops, in order to help the whole body stay the course when so many forces urge us to turn back. But there is no privilege here. Each order serves the whole body as it struggles toward exodus.[4]

If there is no privilege, we might consider rethinking the clergy super-majority at General Convention. While deputations look "equal," they are not representative of the whole people of God. With four clergy and four laypeople in each deputation, the laity are overwhelmingly underrepre-sented. And with a whole House full of bishops only, the hierarchy is very much alive. If there is no privilege, if there is trust and equality, might it be possible to build a new, unicameral structure, in which everyone is rep-resented (even deacons) and our work is done together? What are other possibilities?

I don't suspect that we'll see this type of radical change any time soon. I wonder, however, how we might practice this radical equality in our own contexts?

As for mission, what happens if we take baptismal identity outside the church's walls?

If there is one thing I love to imagine when we gather around the font for a baptism, it is the body of Christ welcoming the newly baptized with all the power and potential of the welcome God confers on Jesus as he rises from the Jordan. "This is my Son, my Beloved, with whom I am well pleased." (Matt. 3:17) How deeply we rejoice when our community of faithful people is enriched by another member.

In an essay on "Post-Baptismal Catechesis," Robert Brooks has written:

> The baptismal covenant talks about the lifestyle of prayer, com-munion with others in the Christian community and Eucha-ristic sharing, of repentance and returning again to the Lord, seeking and serving Christ in all people, striving for justice and peace, respecting the dignity of every human being. You see . . . seeking Christ presumes that there is a Christ to be found in all people. We aren't told, "Wait for the Christ to jump out of the other person, grab you, throw you down and pin you and say, here I am."
>
> The baptismal covenant calls upon us to commit *ourselves* to seek the Christ in that person, which is an *action*, and when we have found the Christ, knowing that the Christ is in all people,

to serve that person. That's why we can strive for justice and peace and respect the dignity of every human being, because the dignity does not depend on their credit rating, or where they live, or their job; it depends upon the fact that God has put within them eternal life. . . .

God has already done that and we're simply celebrating and praising that.[5]

If we take that seriously, perhaps we can see more readily that each person has gifts as well as needs. If we look for those gifts, while we seek to fill those needs, we stop seeing people as "needy" people. In our culture today, "needy" is a somewhat pejorative term. So is "whining." But if we take the strength of our baptismal promises away from the font, I believe we will look for the brightness of the gifts in everyone. Likewise, we will be able to hear under what might be called "whining" the plaintive longing of those who are hoping for help. May we never take away the hope of the poor.

When we look through a diaconal lens, I suspect that many of us can see that hope. That's often second nature to many of us. But we need tools and prayers, training and reflection in order to build effective relationships outside the church's walls. Simply talking about "mission" doesn't engage us in it. Engaging in God's mission includes the willingness to see with God's eyes.

I once heard a member of a commission on ministry ask a deacon postulant, "What's the difference between good works and ministry?" She was quiet for a minute, and then responded, "Jesus."

We engage in ministry and mission because we love God. We take all the power and possibility of the basin, the towel, the words of the prophets—especially Jesus, the prophet, and the love we share—beyond the walls of the church. While deacons stand at the intersection between spirituality and service, sending the people of God into the world to be the living gospel, we are, after all, in this together.

The Diaconate as Adaptable and Contextual

Simply looking at the waves of the diaconate in the Episcopal Church helps us see how deacons have adapted to changing times. It also helps us see that it has taken time for the Order to root deeply in the ordination vows and charges. From the first wave to the seventh, deacons have adjusted to the times and to what the church has asked. Has it all been smooth? No. Have we seen progress? Yes. Yet it has required intentionality. It has taken time. Most of all, it has taken a collective attitude and willingness to engage each other, and the church, in building a foundation to support that growth and change.

From the first gathering of deacon formation directors in 1997 to its gathering in 2014, we can see growth, development, and adaptability. While it took eighteen years to move beyond "each diocese for itself" in looking at formation, deployment, and other issues related to deacons, we now have almost as long with experience in collaborative initiatives that we share openly. Members of the church-wide deacon community have defined formation priorities, concerns in administration and building communities of deacons, and have offered new resources to the church. All the while, both individual deacons, and the community of deacons have adapted and contextualized new resources, new assignments, and new challenges. A cursory review of the topics of those annual gatherings shows us:

- From 1997 to 2001, guidelines for preordination education were created and finessed.
- In 2001, a job description was created for archdeacons. Having archdeacons who were deacons, assigned to work with the deacon community, was a new thing.
- From 2001 to 2006, revisions to the ministry canons were discussed, drafted, offered for General Convention approval, and then revised again.
- From 2005 to 2007, the idea of the "prophetic role of the deacon" was explored and discussed. In addition, the canonical revisions required a whole new round of discussion about how to adapt what had been created previously. In fact, we began to see that if we were to ground more deeply in our interpretive role, more tools and resources would be needed.
- From 2005 to 2009, attention was given to lifelong learning. Approximately two-thirds of our dioceses, along with several Canadian dioceses, were involved in exploring new options for education—online, learner-centered and driven. This was about more than simply reporting the number of continuing education units each year. Rather the community explored and implemented a series of methods to encourage lifelong learning.
- From 2008 on, alternatives to Clinical Pastoral Education were explored, methods of mentored practice (sometimes a combination of fieldwork and CPE) were shared, and best practices were brought for everyone's benefit.
- In 2010, the idea for a theological statement on "Engaging the *Diakonia* of All Believers" was conceived and the statement developed. The church's

resolution on domestic poverty from the 2009 General Convention was also discussed and an initiative to provide the deacon community with resources on the issue was implemented.

- From 2010 on, a young adult program was proposed, feedback received, and funding acquired for its implementation. By 2012, attention was given to social media—its use in both formation programs and practical ministry.
- In 2013, the community had asked for more resources and grounding in community organizing. This has come to be an important aspect of many deacon formation programs as we seek to interpret the world to the church and build relationships in our larger communities. Community organizing ranges from formal training programs like PICO (People Improving Communities through Organizing) to less formal and extremely accessible programs like ABCD (Asset Based Community Development).

It is important to acknowledge that sometimes the theme topics came out of new developments in diocesan communities of deacons. Sometimes it began with a need, sometimes with a new practice or program. Other times the topics came from deacons in leadership as they looked to improve and strengthen their programs. Still other times the staff and board of the Association for Episcopal Deacons provided themes to test based on a big picture of the diaconate—its trends, its strengths, and the feedback received from its members.

In many ways, adaptability in programs was not unlike the waves themselves. The early years were about definition, then years of transition into new canons with widespread implications. Later, like the wave of interpretation, came the request for new skills and resources, and finally, the integration that came with a young adult program, a domestic poverty initiative, a theological statement, and a review of the waves and the place of the diaconate in today's church. Through it all, deacons in the field, along with deacons in diocesan leadership in programming, deployment, pastoral care, and lifelong learning, have been willing to adapt.

We also see this clearly in deployment or "assignment." In *Many Servants*, Plater suggests that within the contemporary diaconate (what he terms the "fourth wave"), there have been "three stages, in a rough and overlapping sequence."[6] I have linked these stages with new waves, rather than defining them all as stages of a fourth wave. I have done so simply to emphasize the shifts, the growth and maturity, the reality of living more deeply into how we pray and live our vows and charges.

When I wrote to Plater in 2012 about my thinking that perhaps a "fifth wave" was emerging, he agreed and pushed me farther. "I agree," he wrote.

"There is evidence that bishops are using at least some deacons outside the traditional congregational structure, allied directly with the bishop (instead of parish priests), and assigned to specific community ministries, especially ministries connected to the church. That's all for the good, in my opinion. The trend tends to restore the earlier use of deacons as diocesan staff members or cabinet ministers with specific responsibilities for different areas. I think advocacy and community organizing are the most important areas, in our time at least, and we need to focus selection and formation on getting deacons with gifts in those areas."[7]

Thus adaptability is evident in how deacons have been deployed: The fourth wave (1970s and 1980s) was one of transition. Deacons adapted from being pastoral and sacramental assistants to caring for the poor outside the church. This came with an emphasis on deacons being in the world, and we often heard of priests having "in-house" ministry, and deacons having "out-house" ministry. This was far too dualistic, but a clear move to ensure that individuals understood themselves (and others understood them) to have a clearly diaconal or service ministry.

During the fifth wave (mid- to late 1980s to the mid- to late 1990s), the period of definition, deacons engaged with the congregation and encouraged and equipped the faithful for diaconal ministry in the world. We begin to see an expanded understanding of the deacon as developer of diaconal ministry in others and a deeper role in interpreting to the church the needs, concerns, and hopes of the world.

During the sixth wave (late 1980s to 2009 and beyond), the period of interpretation, we see deacons looking for more ways to speak to the church. I remember at the meeting of formation directors where people wanted to talk about "prophetic voice," that there was a concern about whether the church was relevant in the world. Deacons were more openly questioning whether church structures were contributing to mission (not unlike much of the rest of the church) and what our dwindling numbers meant. Plater says that during the decade leading up to the publishing of the revised edition of *Many Servants* in 2004, we were reinventing the ancient concept of deacons as bishop's agent, and in the process, finding the virtue of diaconal community. He suggests further that the dramatic changes in ministry canons in 2003 bear witness to that. Advocating and organizing became a primary role for deacons, whether in public policy, on behalf of the church, or in direct advocacy and action for individuals and groups who desperately needed the church's help. This continues around issues of gun violence, domestic poverty, immigration, and many other issues.

The seventh wave (from about 2005 to the present), one of integration, is one in which we see many of these things coming together: engaging the *diakonia* of all believers, equipping the saints, interpreting the world, and advocating—not only in congregations, but on behalf of the diocese. We see that deacons are confident in their identity, that there are more strong diocesan communities of deacons, and that bishops are actively involved in expanding their vision of assignments for deacons. There are archdeacons in about two-thirds of our dioceses who are helping to build community and articulate diaconal vision. I believe that the example that follows helps us see both an interpretive and integrative deacon assignment.

Elaine Clements is a deacon in the Diocese of Louisiana. I was drawn to ask that she share her experience because of a posting on the anglodeacons listserv. Elaine wrote about the importance of asset-based community development and contextual Bible study in developing congregational "outreach." These are both things that have been, or are regularly being, incorporated into deacon formation and education programs.

Elaine served as a social worker with children in Texas for many years, and later with a child advocacy organization in Washington, DC. After moving to Louisiana, she was ordained as a deacon in 2007. She began the formation program with Hurricane Katrina on August 29th in 2005 and shares that her diaconal learning was very much on-the-job training. She developed ministries on a pickup truck at sites where volunteers were gutting homes, and interned at St. Anna's in New Orleans, an historic church at the juncture of the Bywater, the Treme, and the French Quarter, where she developed a "murder ministry." The ministry involves calling attention to the victims of violence, and continues as an Episcopal city-wide prayer-based ministry.

In 2009, Elaine began working directly under the bishop, first with Episcopal Community Services of Louisiana, and now as a deacon on the staff whose primary assignments are as Diocesan Disaster Coordinator and as the resource person for congregations developing outreach ministry. She also serves on the board of the local Episcopal Service Corps program.

As disaster response coordinator, she has worked to respond to the underserved in disasters including hurricanes, floods, and the immigration crisis. This includes the crisis with children, often unaccompanied, crossing the border to come to the large Honduran community in New Orleans.

She also serves as a partner in Response and Long-Term Recovery for Episcopal Relief and Development's Domestic Disaster Program. In that capacity, she visits dioceses on their behalf. After a disaster, she helps determine need, capacity for response, and funding options.

I was also drawn to hear more from Elaine because she is living a new model of deployment—beyond a congregation-based ministry. In her role as a resource for developing outreach ministry in the diocese, she provides training and assistance to parishes for the purpose of identifying and expanding capacity for outreach ministry. This is where we see how new tools have been incorporated into deacon education, as well as the deacon taking those tools into local ministry development. In response to an inquiry from a colleague about how to raise awareness, in a congregation, of possibilities for community ministry engaging more effectively in the world, Elaine wrote:

> I don't know what the "capacity" of your congregation is in terms of gifts, time, abilities, and interests, but that's typically a pretty good place to start in designing outreach so that the process becomes a "bottom up" process rather than a "top down one." The bottom up process tends to make the congregation more invested in the outcome because they thought of it, designed it, and developed it. It is, thus, more sustainable and has broader based support. I see the deacon's role in that as one of coach—asking good questions, having information about community need (or knowledge of who to ask into the group to speak about need), and information about the program planning process.
>
> There are three critical questions to ask when planning:
> - What are we going to do?
> - Who is going to do it?
> - How will we know when we did it?
>
> This process takes some time. The last congregation with whom I worked took ten months to figure out what they wanted to do, but they have developed a program around which they have great enthusiasm, lots of volunteer capacity, and tons of support. They also developed a program that was sorely needed in their immediate neighborhood—certainly not where they started looking at the outset of the process. Too often I think we have an idea of what we want the congregation to do and what we think the need is. The program is sustained more readily when the congregation is engaged in the questions of "how can we dream together?" and "what do we see when we look with God's eyes?"
>
> There are some tools to use to get ready to have this conversation. One excellent one is contextual Bible study, which developed out of the liberation theology movement and is designed to get congregations to get to the issues of justice in the Bible in their study groups. It works beautifully. It does take some

time to do properly but can be done in a couple of hours. Community/neighborhood walks that result in a community map is another good tool. Invite folks to walk with you and look at the neighborhood through God's eyes. What do they see? Another good exercise to develop capacity for outreach (after some time with contextual Bible study, preaching justice from the pulpit, community walks, etc.) is using local newspapers to identify the justice issues they see emerging in the community. You can also do gifts/talents assessments—not necessarily formalized questionnaires—but rather a simple session of

- "What's your dream?"
- What are the gifts of your head (what do I know)?
- Your heart (what do I care about)?
- Your hands (what can I do or teach)?

Last but probably most important, you can do one-on-one conversations with individuals in the congregation who have enthusiasm around outreach. The purpose of the learning conversation is mainly to get to know folks, find out what they care about, and begin to assemble a "table of care" with other folks who care about the same things. It is not a conversation to get volunteers.[8]

What good advice. Deacon Clements's integration of experience and knowledge, both in her own life, and in discerning and developing ministry with others, is an excellent example of the maturity and integration of the many things we've learned about diaconal ministry and the diaconate.

When I talked with her about the waves of the diaconate, as I perceive them, especially in view of our interpretive role, and the many models of ministry we see, she reflected in this way:

I think the "new deacon," more than ever, has to be prepared to be a coach, empowering congregations and their work in the world. Relationship building is key to this process. People must be engaged to identify the gifts of their heads, their hands, and their hearts. Otherwise those things are simply talents—or skills. There is an action component implied. The call to biblical justice has to be clearly preached, translated, and supported by leadership, both clerical and lay. The deacon's role becomes one of inspiring, forging connections, building capacity through training, information-gathering, and asking critical questions.

It is pushing rather than pulling, organizing and facilitating rather than directing and planning.

The liturgical role of the deacon, acting as an icon for service ministry, is only effective in the context of relationship. Being at the altar or reading the Gospel are meaningless if no one understands what the deacon is acting as a window (icon) for. I'm simply a stranger at the altar doing liturgy and wearing my stole differently. I can't "proclaim" the gospel unless people understand how I am living out the Good News. Similarly, I can't effectively call people to the Prayers of the People or dismiss them to "love and serve the Lord" unless they understand my connection to the cares and concerns of the world.

To complicate things, it is abundantly clear to me that we need to be able, as deacons, to work with people outside of our congregations to engage them in the process of becoming coworkers with us in the larger community. No longer can we, as ministers of change in the world, decide what that change should look like, decide what programs are needed to effect that change, and then lead the work ourselves, recruiting volunteers along the way. Rather the process should be one of shared outcomes, shared ministry, shared transformation, and shared resources. Similarly, congregations can no longer build sustainable outreach by identifying community needs in a vacuum; rather they must build relationships in the community, begin to see the community with God's eyes, and then work within that community to develop ministry WITH, not ministry TO.

This is, undoubtedly, a much messier model than the more traditional ministry development model of identifying a need and developing a needs-based program model which then delivers services to "clients" in need. It takes a broad network of relationship-building and of people talking and meeting, often in facilitated conversations. It takes good coaching and training and lots of biblical perspective.

The skills that the deacon needs in their tool kit would include some of the following:

- coaching skills
- preaching skills
- leadership skills
- asset-based community development (community organizing skills)
- communication skills

- program planning skills with identified outcomes: what are we going to do, who is going to do it, and how will we know when we did it
- skills at teaching capacity building models such as: contextual Bible study[9]

Clearly we have come a long way from the initial struggle to define the diaconate, and the traditional canonical areas of required competency. We have adapted to a changing church and a changing world. We have learned what we need in order to be effective at what the church has asked us to do.

Are there implications for the church at large? I think so. When supporters of the diaconate smile and say that there should be at least one deacon in every congregation, perhaps we can see why this is a good idea. If there is no deacon, perhaps there should be a coordinator or facilitator of diaconal ministry to help the congregation have a sense of what it might mean to be a diaconal congregation. How do we create servant structures? How do we build relationships with our neighbors? What gifts or assets do we have to bring? How do we incorporate these things into Christian formation programs? Are we adaptable? Have we always done it this way?

We might also consider, with commissions on ministry, diocesan schools. and seminaries:

- How we are adapting for a changing church? Educationally? Theologically? For example, the idea of using contextual Bible study, or introducing contextual theology, might be helpful in how we understand ourselves, our communities, and the world in which we live.
- We are using social media to keep our parishioners informed of events, illnesses, programs. How can they use social media to strengthen ministry in daily life? Deacons who have studied online, but met with others locally, might have some insight. Deacons and others who have done fieldwork, or mentored practice, might be good at preparing for "mission" trips, and theological reflection on them.
- How are we adapting together? Do we understand each other's contexts geographically and culturally? Are we trying?

Some are doing well with congregational adaptability. In our church-wide offices, staff are adapting by tuning in to geographic and cultural needs. Professionals who work with youth and young adults know how important it is to be adaptable. Perhaps having an "adaptability assessment" would serve our communities well. Turning to deacons and others, who can walk alongside in that process of adapting, can only enrich our ministries more deeply and equip the saints more effectively.

The Importance of Diaconal Community

While the waves of the diaconate have ebbed and flowed in the contemporary Episcopal Church, the history of the Order is marked by the importance of communities of deacons. We've observed in earlier sections of this book that had it not been for the deaconess community, the many resources for study and action, for the contemporary diaconate, would not have been available.

Had it not been for its successor, the Centre for the Diaconate, some of the earliest resources, relevant to the vision of the diaconate articulated in the BCP 1979, would not have been available to dioceses working to implement this new vision. Deacons and their friends educated, cajoled, advocated, and gathered the small community of deacons that existed back then, along with would-be deacons and members of congregations and dioceses who were working for ways to move forward in preparing people for ordination.

With the North American Association for the Diaconate came a legacy of deacons leading their own vocational and professional association. The make-up of the board included more deacons than priests and laypeople, and only one bishop. While working together with other Orders was always important, deacons working for deacons, identifying new leadership and spreading the wealth, were equally important.

- A community of deacons and their friends did the groundwork for canonical changes.
- A community of deacons in leadership gathers every year to discuss formation, the very best formation and education possible—new pedagogies, new content, new processes, new challenges.
- A community of deacons created a theological statement on "Engaging the *Diakonia* of All Believers."
- When deacons gather every three years for the assembly of the Deacons' Association, they provide nurture, care, and affirmation for each other. They exchange ideas and best practices. They fuss about things that don't go well, and they challenge each other not to become domesticated. They share visions and chart the course for new possibilities.
- When deacons gather in a diocese, or on a deacons' council, they discuss the concerns of their community, not for the sake of the diaconate, but for the sake of the church. They discuss lifelong learning and new methods in ministry. They pray and enjoy each other. They identify issues that regions of the diocese are facing. In fact, in the Diocese of Chicago, the community of deacons receives a special charge at the end of each diocesan convention to work on a particular project or issue.

As we live in the ebbs and flows of the sixth and seventh waves (interpretation and integration), two examples of community initiatives and community involvement come to mind. It's important to note that the Association for Episcopal Deacons does not represent every deacon, nor does every deacon belong. However, as the only church-wide opportunity for collective action and reflection, and considering the significant contributions the Association has made over the years, I believe it is a good measure of the community, its experience, and its maturity.

In 2009 the General Convention of the Episcopal Church passed a resolution on domestic poverty. Titled "Establish a Community Development Initiative with Native People," the resolution was that "the Episcopal Church recognize the pressing challenges to those living in poverty and the working poor throughout this nation and call for new and innovative strategies to address issues related to nutrition, employment, childcare, education, healthcare, environment and housing, as well as equal protection under the law and cultural affirmations."[10]

The resolution further directed that:

- the church establish a community development initiative in Native People's communities (recognizing Native People live in some of the poorest counties in the United States)
- the initiative emerge from the visions and voices of the local Native People, and that asset-based community development models be used, advocacy issues be addressed at local, state, and national levels, and that the resources of the church be made available
- the Executive Council work with those affected and involved in evaluating the initiative
- the church's Advocacy Center sponsor asset-based community development training throughout The Episcopal Church and include people living in poverty, and the working poor who are members of our congregations

Underfunded, as usual, this was a commendable action by the church—particularly in looking to involve the voices of those most affected by poverty, and looking toward a solution that incorporated an asset-based approach.

Because many deacons are so close to those who are affected by poverty, as executive director of the Association for Episcopal Deacons, I took that resolution to the next gathering of deacon formation directors and archdeacons. Because the gathering includes so many deacons in leadership in their dioceses, it seemed a good way to test how the church-wide community of deacons could bring its own assets to the intent of the resolution.

At the meeting in March 2010, a large Open Space group discussed the question, "Given the Church's recent commitment to addressing domestic poverty, what are the opportunities, possibilities, and challenges for a deacon-led initiative to address domestic poverty?"

Some ideas were grand. Some ideas were small and measurable. Again the deacon community recognized the need for the gifts of many: visionaries, nurturers, activists, planners, sustainers. Pages of experience, ideas, methods and hopes were recorded. As a result, the board of the Association, in its meeting immediately following, recommended the establishment of a Domestic Poverty Initiative as part of its own programming and support.

Led by Louise Thibodaux, archdeacon in Alabama, by midsummer the Domestic Poverty Task Force was formed. Over the summer, a small group of advisors (deacons from Vermont, Michigan, Arkansas, Atlanta, and Wisconsin) became involved. As a result, a special e-newsletter was developed called "Seeking and Serving." Over the next three years, the single-focus, accessible educational piece would provide teaching tools, practical approaches, personal stories, and advocacy methods, among other things. Specific topics included:

- Making Poverty Visible
- Web Tools for Growing the Network
- When Disaster Strikes
- Safe and Affordable Housing
- Justice and Daily Bread
- Migration and Domestic Poverty
- The ABCs of Sustainable Advocacy
- Children at Risk
- Literacy: Unlocking the Cycle of Poverty
- Tools for Transforming Communities: The Circle, the Line and the Cross
- Justice, Mercy and Deficit Reduction

Members of the church-wide deacon community continued to advise, promote, provide feedback, and contribute to this important initiative and the e-news for education. At each formation director and archdeacon meeting from 2011 through 2013, Louise Thibodaux presented new tools and interactive exercises addressing domestic poverty so participants could add to their own knowledge and share those resources at home.

In 2012, the deacon community would take its own resolution to General Convention, asking the church to assess her relationships with those living in poverty. While more will be shared about this in our next section on interpreting to the church, it was yet another way for the church-wide deacon community to offer their gifts and insights. In 2013, a significant portion of the Association's triennial assembly was offered by Sarah Eagleheart, the church's missioner for indigenous ministries. Eric Law, priest and well-known author who deals with issues of diversity, also offered part of the program. Katrina Browne, founder of the nonprofit center called the "Tracing Center on Histories and Legacies of Slavery," was also invited. These three individuals were asked to help participants weave "a new worldview."

Communities of deacons are important. Other lessons to consider, however, have to do with the importance of networks and the fact that things don't have to cost hundreds of thousands of dollars to be effective. Simply by assessing who we are locally, what our gifts and assets are, and how they can be used to meet the challenges of the community, are very important ways to start. Learning who our neighbors really are, and assessing our relationships with them is another place to start.

Deacons learn from each other in community as they build trust and relationships. Whether it's in designing new fieldwork experiences, or in struggling with how to develop competency-based education programs, many of them have learned to make space for each other.

During one of the bleakest and most divisive times the church has faced after the approval of an openly gay bishop in New Hampshire in 2003, deacons from different dioceses and perspectives still maintained their membership in the Association. Deacons agreed and disagreed on the 500-member listserv maintained by Ormonde Plater. But when a group looks together through diaconal lenses, sees together the authority of the basin and the towel, remembers that they, like Stephen, are heralds and messengers, it's difficult to break the spirit of that community.

My purpose here is not only to talk about the value of deacon communities exclusively, though they are important. However, it is also important to acknowledge the ways in which good partnerships in an ordered church can make us ever richer.

For example, in 2011, the Association for Episcopal Deacons established a program called "The Seven." The church has known for years that the average age of her members has been steadily rising. Also for several years—more than a decade—she has worked to encourage younger people to attend seminary to become priests, and to involve youth and young adults in leadership development programs, and encourage their attendance at official church gatherings. However, there had not been that same emphasis on identifying younger deacons.

Over a decade ago, I had the privilege of working with a young deacon who had the idea of involving young people in diaconal ministry. Kyle Pedersen, now serving as a deacon in New Haven, Connecticut, envisioned a program that would encourage young people to "shadow" deacons and others involved in diaconal ministry, to reflect on that experience, and to consider vocation.

It took nearly ten years until the timing was right, but eventually Kyle's idea was brought to the Association for Episcopal Deacons. After a successful season of fundraising, the Association was able to provide a modest amount of seed money to start "The Seven." The name of the program was based on the story of the first seven deacons as told in the sixth chapter of Acts. The story tells of a rapidly expanding, mixed community of Christians and of the complaints that widows were being overlooked and not being cared for in the daily distribution of food. The twelve apostles were concerned that they couldn't take care of this work and still pray and serve the Word. The young Christian community was expanding so rapidly that it was important that individuals be appointed who could help maintain unity between the different cultures represented, as well as to ensure that all were cared for.

We felt that the story, so often used to highlight the qualities and characteristics of the ministry of deacons, also pointed to a profound responsibility to identify deacons in our own day.[11] As a result, we designed a part-time, hands-on spiritual experience for young adults. Participants were able to serve where they lived, worked, or attended school, while engaging in their communities and reflecting on the needs, concerns, and hopes of their own communities.

We proposed that some young adults might well be deacons in our midst and that we would gain rich and helpful new perspectives from them. However, the program never assumed that all participants would become deacons. It was enough to engage the *diakonia* of those believers, with the possibility that the experience could lead to equipping young adults in unique ways for service in their lives.

The program pointed to the importance of community on many levels. Each participant required a sponsoring community. In addition, each had a deacon mentor. Sometimes the sponsoring community was a congregation, other times a diocese. The point was to make sure there was local support for the ways in which each participant would be involved in diaconal ministry locally.

Foundational parts of the program included: meeting regularly with a deacon mentor, sharing common readings with the community of other young adults, and engaging in online discussion. After several weeks, each young adult was asked to develop a project. The format included the following components:

- **Who am I and why am I here?** This was a statement about why the project was personally meaningful, what gifts and experiences the participant brought to the project, and how it might relate to the joys and challenges they had experienced in their faith journeys.
- **What is my community?** This was a description of where the project would take place and what tools were used to learn about the community.

It asked where the participant saw the needs, concerns, and hopes, as well as the poor, the sick, the weak, and the lonely in their communities. Finally participants were asked to address some of the community's resources and assets.

- **How am I being called to serve?** This was a section in which the details of the project were described: partners; materials or resources needed; timeline; hopes and expectations; and how this project might help the participant and the community understand the ministry of deacons and the *diakonia* of all believers.

What riches we discovered! Words of wisdom from some of the participants will be shared elsewhere. However, some of the things we discovered included that the participants taught us that one of the primary values of The Seven was the creation of a *free space* for serious conversation and reflection that was not directly tied to a formal discernment process. In this *free space* they could explore their own identities and vocations while trying on different theological and ministry ideas with their peers and in relationships with their mentors. Participants ran the gamut in terms of background and experience. A law school student, a social worker, two seminary graduates, a staff member from church-wide offices, a high school senior, a professional working in pregnancy prevention, a librarian, a young mom with responsibilities for extended family—the list goes on. Without exception there was a deep longing to be present to those affected by the unjust structures of society. There was also a common feeling that the church has much to learn about how to be in those situations.

The projects mattered. They weren't all completed by the end of our time together, but they served as a real centerpiece for each young adult to do vocational and theological reflection. For example, one young adult invited members of the congregation to put together small "care packages" for people who were homeless. In that way, she suggested, when people on the street asked for help, there would be something to give them. This was not just about a handout, however. She invited people to come back and talk about their experiences, to reflect on them theologically, to reflect on the people that they met, and where God was in each instance.

The church has much to learn from the wisdom of young adults. Rather than just wishing for them to populate the congregation, young adults long to be taken seriously, accepted for who they are, affirmed for their gifts. For example, one participant developed a young-adult group in his congregation. One of the things that they talked about was not having money to give to the church. They made it clear that while they didn't have the same resources as many in the parish, they loved the church and could still be contributing members. They offered to facilitate events that would make money. They cooked dinners as fundraisers, and looked for other creative ways to be actively contributing members.

It doesn't take a million bucks to start a program. We were able to run the program for an average of about $10,000 per year. This included the small stipend for the coordinator, the cost of conference calls, the use of educational software, and travel expenses for the coordinator. As of this writing the actual program is in its final stage—that being to document our learnings, and offer resources for how this kind of program can be done in parishes and dioceses. Deacons almost always have limited resources, and while we wouldn't advocate for always having to make it on a shoestring budget, we might have something to bring to the church about creativity in the midst of limited resources.

Young adults want to be deacons. Not every participant will become a deacon. But some of the participants are in diocesan discernment processes, and two have entered the formal ordination process.

The program came into being because of the larger deacon community. It was successful because of the help of many others: laypeople, bishops, and priests. It is testimony to how we can be good partners in ministry. For so many years, deacons felt misunderstood, especially by parish priests. Clearly we need the whole community in order to engage *diakonia* well, and we are grateful every time we discover those partnerships.

In fact, when I asked one of the young priests, who was an advisor for the program, for some of his thoughts about deacons, he responded:

> I long to see a diocesan community of deacons let loose in their vocations, not tethered to existing congregations. Wildly seeking God in the world, exercising their ministry of interpretation with sophistication and skill, discovering new forms of Christian community, responding nimbly to changing needs and opportunities. . . .
>
> I know SO MANY people who would make good deacons. They are folks already living the life and doing the work of deacons. In the diocese, congregations were identifying people left and right but the canonical process, formation requirements, and expectation of being involuntarily "moved" deterred people from even starting. . . .
>
> For me the issue isn't about who would make a good deacon; it's about why the good deacons already in our midst aren't being ordained.[12]

We need the whole community in order to engage *diakonia* well.

Unexpected but Critical—The Charge to Be Interpreters

We know that by 2005 deacons in leadership were asking about the relevance of the church, and the importance of prophetic voice. We also know that in 2008 many deacons felt that the charge at ordination to interpret to the church the needs, concerns, and hopes of the world was the one for which they felt least prepared.

That certainly doesn't mean that deacons were unaware of those needs, concerns, and hopes, but interpreting takes clear skills. Combined with the idea that the church sometimes forgets that she wants to hear about these needs, concerns, and hopes, the process can be challenging. Nevertheless, it has emerged—sometimes unspoken or unwritten, but emerged nonetheless—as a critical skill and an expectation for deacons today. It is vital to this wave of integration and, I believe, will continue to serve as a mark of clarity of call for the would-be deacons in our midst.

This charge speaks directly to the relationship between the church and the world. Obvious? Perhaps at first glance. However, it is a charge that has taken us years to plumb, both as deacons, and as the larger church. During that time, I've heard many people describe the diaconate as a bridge between the church and the world—and the world and the church. That is true. However, the focus in this charge is very clear. "You are to interpret *to the Church* the needs, concerns, and hopes *of the world*." The words are clear and directive. They are directed one way—from the world to the church. While I am not opposed to the idea of deacons as bridge builders, we must not oversimplify what this means.

When we hear that phrase, "being a bridge from the world to the church and the church to the world," it has a touch of "warm fuzzies," and an implied relationship that doesn't always exist. The world has been telling us for decades that we are not important. Saying that our average Sunday attendance is not the only measure of our success is true. But it is a measure. Dwindling resources and aging parishioners may not be the case for every congregation, but it is for many. Saying that the church is dying evokes strong responses, both in agreement and disagreement, but there is no denying that we have changed. I find that a useful question is simply, "Who would miss us if we were gone?"

One of the church's current concerns is "mission." We want missional congregations and dioceses. This does not mean (as in earlier centuries) that we have, as our focus, converting others to Christianity. I think that in today's world it means "living our faith." It means something about meeting people where they are and having a presence outside our church walls. It's about building new relationships and entering into new partnerships.

Perhaps deacons have something to bring to this. Interpreting to the church has everything to do with relationships and why we enter into them. It has to do with explaining the cost of reaching out, but offering hope and transformation in taking the risk.

This charge to interpret, for all its strength, can also be a point of tension. While deacons can point the way toward mission and the witness of the church, it is also deacons who sometimes ask the church to dismantle the things that get in the way of mission and caring for others. When I use the term "dismantle," I do not mean a thoughtless tearing down. I do not mean an emphasis on the negative. I do mean that, at the very least, we can name things that get in the way of doing justice, loving mercy, and walking humbly with our God (Micah 6:8). In that way, we can clear out what is unhelpful, and know what assets and attributes we can bring as gifts to address the challenges in mission.

A caution about how we interpret what it means to interpret. Over the years, many deacons have described themselves as thorns in the church's side, or as troublemakers. What I think that really means is that asking the church to look at, and engage in the world around it, is not always easy. Asking the church to tend to the things in its own life that get in the way of that can be difficult. It can be a lonely place. However, I've wondered whether calling ourselves by these names can sometimes lead to an unintended and self-imposed exile. Likewise, it may serve to discourage or isolate prophetic voices in our congregations. While these descriptions are often meant to be just that, we might do well to think of descriptions that remind us that while challenging, interpretation and prophetic voice are part of the church's tradition. In addition, when we do need to reckon with the role of saying difficult things, or inviting difficult actions, it's important to recognize that while critical, the prophet energizes with hope.

Interpreters smooth the way toward understanding differences and building relationships. Imagine two children who do not know each other's language. One points to an object and says, "soccer ball." The other points to the object and says, "futbol." However, the real understanding comes when they juggle the ball back and forth, dribble it to each other, and kick at targets.

To be able to interpret, we must be able to understand the concepts, feelings, customs, and cultural norms that go beyond the mere translation of words. We must be able to understand, and help others understand that when some of us say we are hungry, we can go to the cupboard for a snack. When others say they are hungry, it is because they have no food. They would (and do) gape at the bounty of our cupboards and refrigerators. We might gape at their empty shelves, but better still that we recognize that they have no food because they have no jobs.

Perhaps they have no food because the job they have does not pay enough for food, medicine, transportation, and housing. Are we in a position to help a family of four understand how it is possible, or just, for them to live on under $20,000 each year? Do we think it's acceptable? How can we help change those conditions?

On the other hand, perhaps they have no food because they are refugees. Neither do they have anything else. If they are refugees, what can be done besides dropping food from the sky, or bringing it in a truck? Do our country's politics and diplomatic policies have anything to do with their status? Do we understand the global economy?

These questions are not new. Nor do they bring new insights. However, the work of interpretation takes important skills. We must be educated, not only in immediate need, but in systemic causes of that need. We must understand the relationships between people and issues, between cultures and appropriate approaches, between who has the power to make a difference, and who does not, and why that power is not balanced.

In today's church, the task of Christian formation must include not only the essentials of our faith, but also an understanding of the world. Inviting a presentation by a human service agency that serves people who are hungry is a start. Participating in a simulation exercise in which people need to feed a family of six on $2.00 takes our understanding farther. Inviting an economics teacher in our midst to provide a forum on "Economics 101" honors her gifts and challenges us to use ours in a way that we can begin to address unjust economic systems.

As deacons have lived more deeply into the charge to interpret, they have asked for help to develop more skills. If one is to be a good interpreter, one needs not only to understand concepts beyond simple words, but also to understand how to facilitate dialogue, engage with others, and reflect theologically. This becomes especially important when we don't agree. I once had a friend who would remind me, "There is no important issue that is simple." But we can talk, and we can act, even when we disagree. That is the hope of reconciliation.

In addition to facilitating dialogue, one needs to understand how to organize people and actions. One needs to understand how to advocate, not just in the sense of political advocacy, but what it means to understand the need, articulate something about it, and speak to different audiences.

The church has much to learn from the service-learning movement around the country and beyond. It is a movement that encourages students in elementary, secondary, and postsecondary education to engage in "service," but then to reflect on what they've learned. Their mentors and teachers help them explore the cause of the condition, the various perspectives around the issue, and what the sustainable responses to that issue or condition might be. Using such a method pushes our theological reflection outside the walls of the church. It strengthens us for mission.

If we are interpreters, grounded in our faith, we must be honest about the cost of engaging the needs, concerns, and hopes of the world. Relationships take work. If we truly wish to serve God by serving the people God loves, it won't always be easy. It might require walking away from comfort and privilege. When we take the risk, we may need to count the cost. When we take the risk, we can rejoice that God delights in us. In order to have healthy communities, indeed to serve the common good, we all give something up, and we all take something away. When we take the risk, however small the step may be, we add a little to the building of God's realm on earth.

Deacons in today's church are as likely to talk about the gifts of those living in poverty as they are about their needs. Deacons in today's church are as likely to ask the church to examine the ways in which she mimics culture as they are to ask her to engage with it. Deacons in today's church are as likely to ask the church to talk about controversial subjects as they are to ask her not to divide herself over them.

Recently I had the privilege of speaking about the diaconate at the Convention of the Diocese of Southern Ohio. In preparing for my visit there, Bishop Breidenthal and I had a helpful conversation about his hopes for my visit, and how he thinks about the diaconate. Following on his article "Exodus from Privilege," in the *Anglican Theological Review*, he shared these words with me: **"Deacons are charged with goading the church into exile—away from privilege."** He went on, "I don't mean to say that deacons are anti-institutional, but they are risk takers and they are leading others to take that risk."[13]

As I shared with the Convention, that was very reassuring to me. The fact is that sometimes when you goad the church away from privilege, she accuses you of being anti-institutional. It is an occupational hazard. Do I love the church and God's people? More importantly, do I do what I do because of my love for God? I surely hope and pray so. Am I interested in propping up an ineffective or dying institution? No. If we ground in the prophetic tradition, we urge change because we love God, we love God's people, and we know that God's vision is different than what we're living.

It is, however, the church, the very people of God, who charge deacons to interpret the needs, concerns, and hopes of the world; and it is the church, the very people of God, who charge us to be living reminders of Christ's presence with those who know no privilege. Because the church does this, we are in this together.

Because we've had thirty-five years to live into this vision of the diaconate, the church will continue to hear deacons ask, "Who lives in your neighborhood?" The church will continue to hear about the percentage of people who live in poverty, and about people who do not have access to basic needs, whether they be education, health care, employment, or housing. The church will continue to hear deacons ask, "Why do you think that is? What difference does it make to us?"

That is why the church-wide community of deacons brought a resolution before the 2012 General Convention of The Episcopal Church. It was a resolution that urged the church to pledge to ask one question at every one of her meetings. That question: "How does what we are doing here affect or involve those living in poverty?" We weren't advocating for handouts. We weren't prescribing systemic change—albeit those things are both important. We were asking the church to evaluate her relationships. Some people balked because we were singling out people who live in poverty when there are so many other issues. "Well then," we replied, "at another time, ask yourselves about those issues. Another time ask how what we are doing here affects people who _____. You fill in the blank." Some people balked because they felt this was more about talk and less about action, or more about talk and less about systemic change. But all we wanted was for the church to ask how this affects or involves real people.

Goading the church into exile is no easy thing. Moving God's people from one place to another is a challenge—in both good times and bad.

It was not easy for Moses. It was not easy for Jeremiah. It was surely not easy for Jesus.

Our church today is reevaluating its institutional structure. And in our church today I believe it is the deacon's role, along with those who long for the church to move away from privilege—those who long for the church to make a big difference to this world—to ask the church how she is getting in the way of herself.

This isn't just an Episcopal Church problem—or hope. Our full communion partners in the ELCA have deaconesses and diaconal ministers asking the same thing. Our hopefully soon-to-be partners in the United Methodist Church have deacons asking the same thing. In our young adult program with the Association for Episcopal Deacons we heard these questions all the time. In fact, one of our young adult participants, Aaron Scott, when talking to us about how to attract young deacons, and about her idea of what it means to be a deacon shared this:

> A deacon's job (among other things) is to say to the church, "It's not all about you. It's about God's liberation of this entire broken and beautiful world." At the same time the church's tools of ritual, remembrance, ancient tradition, and prayerful

discipline are indispensable for building a world-changing social movement led by the poor. . . . And Jesus is not waiting for the Episcopal Church to show up before he makes his next move. Diaconal calls are already being lived out by young people everywhere—our job is to see if we can help the church keep up with them, to see if we can do a better job of recognizing them as they arise in unexpected places.[14]

Where is it, in our own lives, that we see people moving away from privilege? Moving toward the common good? Following Jesus, as Verna Dozier has written, instead of just worshipping him.

Indeed being a goader carries real occupational hazards. I'd like to think that deacons are question-askers, lovers of the people of God, and lovers of God who ask those people to live God's dream. Isn't that what the prophets did? Isn't that what Jesus did? They articulated God's vision for what Aaron calls this "entire broken and beautiful world."

Indeed deacons will goad the church away from privilege, but they will also share skills and equip saints. They will affirm those in our congregations who are doing that same goading. They will, with God's help, be good companions in walking away from all that is comfortable.

But deacons will continue faithfully to goad the church away from privilege, and to interpret what's up ahead. And when people become upset with us for doing what the church has asked, perhaps the church can remember that, deep down, what we're really asking is, "Who will live God's dream?"

Who Will Live God's Dream?

They say the prophets are the ones
   who did God's dreaming
Listen to what God is saying, they pleaded
   Who will hear
God does not want your burnt offerings
   or your oil or any other riches
   as much as God asks for your life
   and your partnership
You are what is most precious to God
   they said
They lamented and prayed
   and sang hymns and songs
They spoke in parables and
   gave reproaches
Prophetic voices making poetry

Who will live this vision
Who will be part of my dream
   God asks
And in the voice of the Word made Flesh
   God tells the dream
Blessed are those who long for me
   who know me in the aching
They are poor and they are grieving
   they are reaching for a newness
   that comes only from My imagination
   Not just those who are without
   but those who know their need
   those who see the gifts I give
   to all who turn from principalities
and powers and economics and consumption
   blessed are the simple ones whose wisdom
keeps the riches of the world at bay
and the riches of God's holy people at heart
Who will sing a new song
Could it be we know the ones
   who live the dream of God
Does God's dream emerge still
   through smallish bands of holy people
Looking for a new way
Those who carry justice and mercy
   courageously forward in response to God's love
   and promise
   and joy
   and delight
Those who dare the powers to
   travel to life's edges
bringing the margins gently to the center
   in the riches of the poor
   the wisdom of the grieving
   the blessing of the overlooked
Who will live God's dream[15]

CHAPTER 9

Are We There Yet?

Our praying will always shape our believing. How grateful I am for Louis Weil's insight about living into a "new" prayer book. According to his calculations, it could still take us another fifteen years to live into the implications of the one we're using now. I suspect we might well have the makings of a new Book of Common Prayer by that time. Yet I believe it's helpful to remember that even with our understanding of historical and scriptural precedent, we've only been at living this adapted vision of the diaconate since 1979.

A lot has happened in thirty-five years. It is my prayer that we will see even more. So are we there yet? I think not.

I've written much about where I think we are. People will have their agreements or disagreements with my perspectives. The experience of one deacon is not exactly like another's. The understanding of the diaconate in one diocese is not exactly the same as another. Yet I think a clear vision has emerged. I believe that many deacons and friends of deacons have worked to make that a reality. Living in a more integrative "seventh wave" doesn't mean we're there yet. We still have among us, as friends and colleagues, laypeople, priests, deacons, and bishops who have more experience with the third wave, or the fourth. Or perhaps they are thinking that the sixth wave of interpretation is only beginning to happen where they live—or they wish that it would go away. The differences in thinking can be a frustration, or they can continue to be an opportunity to integrate and educate. By and large, deacons are very clear about who they are.

Are we there yet? No. God is never finished with us.

Indeed there are new possibilities emerging even as we seek to hone our skills and ground more deeply in prayer and action. The reflections that follow are clearly from my point of view alone. These might be next steps that will deepen the roots of a seventh wave. Perhaps they will even lead us into new roles or waves: perhaps as leaders in new areas of education;

or partners in starting new churches; perhaps as contributors to new liturgies; or visionaries in area ministry. Indeed, God is never finished with us.
Here are things to ponder.

Thoughts about Educational Content and Process . . .

In preordination education, as well as continuing education, there are areas
that can always be improved. However, one area I believe is becoming ever
more important is contextual theology. While the idea of contextual theology is not new, it is increasingly important as the world becomes smaller
and flatter. By that I mean that through modern technology, we now have
access—almost instant access—to individuals and situations worldwide.
Traditional political, economic, and social systems are undergoing tremendous change. What are the implications for the church when young people
in Syria can communicate, via social media, with young people in the
American South about social issues? While the cultural contexts are vastly
different, injustice is understood at many levels by many people. Clearly
this points to more understanding in the positive use, or sometimes negative potential, of social media. What insights does theology bring?

In my work with the Anglican Communion Delegation to the United
Nations Commission on the Status of Women, I saw firsthand how young
women from many countries were able to link with each other before and
after meetings in New York advocating for the girl child.

In working with the Anglican Communion task force on theological
education, I learned from colleagues that the word "Anglican" carried
imperialist and colonialist connotations that could be detrimental to the
church being seen as a place of welcome and hope.

In learning about the "emergent" church, I heard Musa Dube (an African
scholar) ask, "Is it possible to be a Christian without the Scriptures?" In
Dube's work, she shows how the interpretation of Scripture by primarily
Western, white men and women has served to justify Western domination.

I have been challenged and enlightened by many African women who
are doing their own scholarly work. There are many other places in the
world where the same thing is occurring, including the Philippines, where
a theology of struggle is emerging.

I am convinced that more work in contextual theology will put us in
closer touch with the legacy of colonialism and what we must do to understand it, just as we are trying to understand and overcome racism. This was
confirmed for me recently when I had an e-mail exchange with Deacon
Patricia Ross of the Diocese of California. Trish is one of two deacons

devoted to MOMS (Midwives on Missions of Service). She and Deacon Christie McManus work with others to provide education and training in maternal health to women in Western Africa. Through their work and the support of many others, many African women have been trained in how to maintain maternal and child health. As she reflected on their work, Trish wrote:

> Although the Church would like to think that colonialism and racism are past, too many church projects rest on that foundation. Many people still cannot see how racism forms the fundamentals of their assumptions—it is like air, invisible. Few understand the realities of the imbalance of power in most kinds of charitable work. Poor people will do just about anything to feed their families. Changing clothes, language, and religion are a small price to pay when you are watching your kids die.[1]

Trish and Chris understand firsthand how the vestiges of colonialism can get in the way of service, or that understanding context can make all the difference in how effectively women are able to understand and implement good methods in maternal and child wellness. They are both members of the Post-Colonial Network.

People in parishes in which they've served have been astounded to learn that as many as 1,000 women were dying each day in childbirth without this education. Trish reports that the number has dropped to about 700 per day.

As of this writing, their work has been hampered by the Ebola outbreak. Their most recent trip was cancelled, and some of the women they trained have died. It has been difficult, if not impossible, to get simple supplies to those who so desperately need them. In the meantime, they share the story, interpret the needs, concerns, and hopes of women and children in Western Africa, and pray for the day they can return with supplies and love.

Underneath the obvious and acute health needs, we see a bigger picture. We see it more clearly through the study of context and cultural reality. While deacons are deeply aware of local context, further study in linking that to theological contexts can strengthen their skills in teaching and interpretation.

As for educational process, I admit that I bring a strong personal bias for competency-based education. However, as we see more ways to identify young adults and people in ethnic communities to serve as deacons, *how* we structure our educational programs deserves another look. This has implications far beyond the preordination education of deacons.

Competency-based education is not new. Over thirty years ago I had the privilege of taking part in a program at the University of Minnesota known as "University without Walls (UWW)." I was working full-time in a community-based agency serving adults with developmental disabilities. It was a period when people were being "deinstitutionalized" and returned to the community. While a background in special education was helpful, it was oriented toward school-based education, primarily for children. In UWW, it was my privilege to work with an advisor and a team who helped me create my own courses, recruit my own faculty, articulate my own learning plan, and incorporate ways to measure my learning and be accountable for it. In that way, I was able to use many professionals in the community—doctors, nurses, psychologists, groundbreakers in community-based programs. While we defined outcomes and standards required for assessment, the program was learner-centered.

Individuals have different learning styles. They have life experience and educational experience that count for something. So many times I have seen situations in which people have to repeat training because they move from one diocese to another. In fact, I've also seen times when seminary graduates have had to repeat training in local programs. Clearly there are some types of "diaconal formation" that are important to experience, especially mentored practice and reflection on ordination vows and charges. However, what prevents us from simply asking of each person in an ordination process to present a portfolio that demonstrates competence in required areas? Answering questions on a written test is one measure of knowledge, but it doesn't ensure competence.

This approach requires that we start with assessment first. While a traditional grading system for a course in Scripture tells us that a student has remembered content, do we know if that individual can facilitate a meaningful Bible study? In a competency-based program portfolio, a person might well include a paper on some aspect of Scripture study, but she might also include a video of a Bible study group, along with feedback from participants.

Competency-based programs allow for a variety of learning experiences to achieve learning outcomes. The Association for Episcopal Deacons currently has a task force on Vocational Development and Lifelong Learning that is working on creating some templates and guidelines for competency-based learning. I would advocate for taking this a step further. Even while dioceses are restructuring programs, creating regional schools as alternatives to seminary, looking for new online programs and other innovative means in education, I believe it would be helpful to develop an alliance of dioceses who will commit to creating and testing a competency-based model. In that way, people who have not had access to traditional programs can have access to a more flexible and learner-centered option. Those who have had access, time, and money for residential or multiweekend training will have the added challenge of demonstrating practical competence. Since there are no church-wide resources to help in this endeavor, sharing resources between dioceses, not only financial and material, but with Christian educators and social media specialists, might well bring innovative approaches for deacons and others.

Promotion of Both the Diaconate and the *Diakonia* of All Believers

One of the reasons we can still say that some parishioners do not understand the diaconate is because they have never been part of a church that has a deacon. Likewise, one of the reasons we continue to distribute the theological statement "On Engaging the *Diakonia* of All Believers" is that it is important to understand the difference between outreach programs, and the call that comes at baptism to serve God by serving others—to make it part of our lives all the time—to orient us toward the needs, concerns, and hopes of others in daily life.

Recently I heard from Deacon Martha Seaman and Archdeacon Veronica Ritson about a pastoral letter sent to congregations in the Diocese of Arizona by Bishop Kirk Smith. In the letter, Bishop Smith reminds the diocese that they are marking the twentieth anniversary of the diocese's commitment to the formation of deacons. I have, with his permission, included excerpts from his letter (which he reminded me he wrote in extensive consultation with Seaman and Ritson). He writes:

> This is a time to celebrate the ministry of deacons in our midst, to envision for the 21st century the role of deacon in this diocese, and to recommit ourselves to the universal call to *diakonia*. . . .
>
> Deacons take the Good News into the community, inviting us to share the love of Christ across boundaries of wealth, religion, age, ethnicity, and language. While engaging the community, the deacon hears the stories and aspirations of the poor, the rejected, the sick and lonely, and the disenfranchised. In a ministry of petition and advocacy, the deacon gathers these "prayers of the people" and proclaims them in church meetings, corporate board rooms, and legislative hearings, everywhere the cry of God's people needs to be heard.
>
> Deacons ask challenging questions: Who is not at the table? How does God ask us to care for others? Are the decisions of government, business, civic groups, and the church consistent with Scriptural tradition? This is prophetic ministry.

The deacon serves with us, people, priest and bishop, at the Lord's Table, as a sign of our baptismal promise "to seek and serve Christ in all persons." This is a ministry of sharing responsibility. The work of the deacon is building capacity and commissioning: helping us recognize God's gifts to us and sending us out to act. . . .

The commitment of this diocese to diaconal formation has borne great fruit. Currently the diocese has one of the largest contingents of deacons (64) in The Episcopal Church, and deacons serve in about half of our parishes and missions. From my years as Bishop, I have seen that deacons bring deep community connections and extraordinary talent to the diocese, to the parishes to which they are assigned, and the communities in which they serve. Deacons are a creative force in readying us to participate in what God is doing in the world.

Dear friends, I invite you to share with me this vision for the 21st century:

First that we all seek and work for a day when every parish and mission in this diocese has at least one deacon, and that we encourage our diocesan Community of Deacons to grow spiritually, to enhance their skills, and to communicate and collaborate with us and the broader church.

The second part of the vision I offer you is interrelated and as important as the first: that we all recommit to our individual and communal call to *diakonia*, that we pray, study, and discern what our diaconal vision asks of us, and that we ultimately act "to seek and serve Christ in all persons."[2]

In a conversation with Deacon Martha Seaman, she indicated that the deacon community is in dialogue about their plans for responding to the letter. Thoughts and plans of action that have surfaced include continued attention to domestic poverty, particularly in the communities of indigenous people in Arizona; attention to how to engage many others in the diocese about the meaning of the *diakonia* of all believers, thus building more partnerships in mission; the importance of aligning with existing initiatives in the church (both in the diocese and beyond) that equip deacons and others for engaging with those in need. For example, JustFaith is a program they are exploring for use in congregations and in formation. JustFaith is a program that equips congregations to engage in social ministry[3] and continues to work on helping people understand the difference between charity and justice.

What a wonderful way to encourage deacons, as well as the *diakonia* of all believers. If this ministry is important to us, let us speak of it regularly and celebrate it. Let us be proactive in offering opportunities and seeking people who will make good deacons and other leaders in diaconal ministry.

New Models of Ministry

Traditionally when dioceses have considered planting new churches, they have considered demographics very seriously. Is this a location that can sustain a new church in numbers of members and in financial resources? Is the area growing? How many people in the area are unchurched or former members of churches who no longer attend? Can we draw from existing congregations to help seed this new church start?

Seldom when we consider planting new churches do we consider things like:

- Barely 30 percent of the people who live in this neighborhood earn enough to cover the costs of food, housing, transportation, and health care. Most parents are working more than one job. That is leaving a lot of kids home alone. The number of violent crimes is on the rise. Can we start a church here?
- Our community has an increasing number of immigrants who are undocumented. They so often have to be looking over their shoulder to make sure that they will not be discovered and deported. Is it possible for us to find or establish a safe space where both physical and spiritual needs can be addressed?
- So many people are using our food pantry, but there has to be more that we can do. We hardly know the folks who are coming for food. Could we add a time for sitting down and eating together?

Some of these situations will be familiar. Perhaps there's an Ecclesia ministry in the community that holds worship services for people who are homeless. It's a good way to get to know people, learn about their challenges, and learn about the gifts they have to offer to the community.

What I'm getting at here is that instead of asking about sustainability for the church as we've always known it, can we ask where the Good News is going unheard? Rather than turning that into an outreach project, perhaps we can see it as a place for continuing to build God's realm, for being God's presence in the midst of difficulty, even as we are blessed with the gifts of those who are struggling.

In a previous chapter I mentioned that years ago when Katharine Jefferts Schori was still bishop in the Diocese of Nevada, we were at the same 20/20 meeting, considering ways to reinvigorate The Episcopal Church. It was time for the committee working on new church starts to make its report to the larger group. At one point, the reporter suggested that one idea was to ask deacons about new church starts. The crowd didn't understand why. As the member of the committee who made the suggestion, Bishop Jefferts Schori stood and suggested that it is deacons who know where the church is needed, and that perhaps we should consider going into those places.

While in some cases, our buildings can be tremendous assets, it is my hope that we move steadily away from thinking they are centers of the Christian universe. Jesus is that Center. What glorious things might happen if we venture into a new neighborhood and look to see how he will show up. Glorious.

Diaconal Spirituality

I would have loved to include "diaconal spirituality" as a characteristic of several of the waves. I think there is one. However, I think we have work to do in reflecting on where we are and what sustains us. Understand that I realize there is probably not a deacon formation program anywhere that does not include something about spiritual practices. I believe that the diaconate has a distinctive and lively spirituality.

In "A Working Paper of Guidelines for Diaconal Formation," published by the North American Association for the Diaconate in 1999 and updated in 2001, there is a section on deacon spirituality. I believe this is a start. It is also time for an update and joyous sharing of what calls us to, and sustains us in, diaconal ministry. What part does the Spirit play, and how are we growing in that Spirit as we fulfill our ordination vows and charges?

The guidelines suggest:

Deacon Spirituality

The vocation of a deacon is to dance on the edge:

- To bear light in the midst of darkness.
- To proclaim truth in the midst of dishonesty and indifference.
- To blur the boundaries between sacred and profane.

The spirituality of a deacon is marked by:

- Compassion for oneself and others.
- Belief that Christ [the divine] is to be found in the depths of humanness.

- Conviction that unity overcomes estrangement.
- Hope that joy conquers despair.

The spirituality of *diakonia* may be enlivened by:

- Calling forth the servant ministry from the community of the baptized.
- Discovering Christ in the outsider or the outcast.
- Experiencing Christ in those on the periphery.
- Encountering Christ in one's deepest self.
- Embracing Christ in the exile.

The spirituality of *diakonia* may be informed by:

- Theology of ministry rooted in baptism.
- Our life in the community of the People of God.
- Being surprised by joy.
- Reading scripture and the lives of the saints.
- Communing with Christ as encountered apart from Word and Sacraments.
- Remembering and interpreting the story of God's people.

The Spiritual Formation of Deacons Includes:

- Developing a Disciplined Prayer Life. This includes experiencing a variety of liturgical expressions and traditions of prayer to aid the deacons in finding places of restoration.
- Broadening definitions of "Prayer" to include:
  - O Humor and laughter.
  - O Body movement.
  - O Singing and making music.
  - O Simplifying one's lifestyle.
  - O Re-creation and creativity.

Programs and Deacons need to Develop and Attend to Support Structures through:

- Work with a spiritual director.
- Colleagues.
- Friends and family.
- Learning techniques for time and stress management [stress is not the same as distress]

- Field work and theological reflection in community
- Increased self-awareness
- Utilizing twelve-step or other appropriate models
- Enabling each other to bring to light and make friends with shadow.
- Recognizing and articulating one's own encounters with the Holy.
- Reflecting on what one's experiences say about one's relationship with God[4]

These helpful suggestions might well provide the basis for helpful retreats where deacons can reflect on the importance of spirituality. Many years ago, I remember hearing Deacon Sarah Tracy talk about deacons as "mystics in action." May it be so.

Attention to Youth and Young Adults

It was a joy, while serving as director of the Association for Episcopal Deacons, to be a part of the program we called The Seven. The young adults who participated in that program have never been far from my mind in writing this book. It has been important to record history for their sake and for the church. It has been important to magnify the importance of how we pray, what was articulated in the prayer book we use, and how we've reached where we are. I close with the conviction that we simply must be more intentional about identifying young people in our midst who are actively engaged in diaconal ministry and those who would make good deacons. Then we must affirm and bless them. We must celebrate and give thanks for what they teach us.

At the gathering of formation directors and archdeacons in 2013, one of the participants was invited to address the gathering. With her permission, I share her remarks:

> Hi. My name is Aaron Scott. I'm a recovering Methodist preacher's kid. At age fifteen, I was a rural, gay, teenage church dropout with a substance abuse problem. At age twenty, I started coming back to faith through liberation theology, in communities living it out from New York City to Managua. I might have become a Catholic had I not, as a student at Union Theological Seminary, met and fallen in love with my partner who was seeking ordination to the priesthood in The Episcopal Church. That worked out well on multiple fronts, so here I am. I'm

twenty-seven now, and an aspirant to Holy Orders in the Diocese of Olympia. I'm discerning a call to the diaconate, participating in The Seven, and taking full advantage of the resources and mentoring that program has offered me. I want to thank each of you for the work this group has done to make **The Seven** possible. I especially want to thank Kyle, Susanne, and Gen for bringing me out to Baltimore so I can eavesdrop on so many good conversations.

So first, I have some questions and reflections for you all. Just shout your answers out.

First: **Why** do you want young deacons?

Second: What have been your **successes** in engaging young leaders in diaconal formation so far?

Third: What have been your **challenges**?

Thank you. It's helpful for me to hear from you, especially as a young discerner standing on the shoulders of so many people who have come before me. So here are some of my thoughts.

One of the great blessings of my life in general (and of my discernment process in particular) is that I got involved young in the grassroots movement to end poverty in this country. When I say "grassroots" I mean: a movement led by the poor themselves, the poor fighting for themselves on their own terms. And even as I came into that work young myself, in my late teens and early twenties, I felt old compared to a lot of the leaders I met. I met public high school students in Philadelphia who had unionized themselves to resist the privatization of their struggling school system. I met teenage mothers in Washington State working together to teach their communities and their legislators that they were human beings who deserved to be treated with support and respect, instead of being treated like statistics of moral decay.

The most talented leaders I've met have been young.

The most talented leaders I've met have been poor.

If you want to engage the leadership of the young, you are going to have to engage the leadership of the poor.

Let me say that one more time: If you want to engage the leadership of the young, you are going to have to engage the leadership of the poor.

The young *are* the poor. The young are disproportionately poor—disproportionately and increasingly locked out of the basic support systems that offer people a chance of thriving. Every day, the outreach worker at my church receives more calls from young families with children who have lost their housing and are living in their cars. Last week in Philadelphia, in a closed-door meeting, twenty-three public schools were shut down. Permanently. The dream of college and continuing education—even at public institutions—is rapidly falling out of reach for all young people except those from well-off families. This is personal for me; my cousin turned eighteen on Sunday. He is enlisting in the military and will ship out in August because he got the "talk" this year, that there is no money for him to go to college. On top of praying for his safety abroad during his deployment, I will continually be praying for his safety when he returns home to this nation, which has gutted its services for veterans. I see his future when I look into the eyes of every homeless vet lining the sidewalks and overpasses near the VA hospital in Vancouver, where I live.

So here is the greatest piece of advice I think I can offer you, when it comes to young diaconal leadership development: if you want to find young leaders with diaconal spirit, go to the shelters. Go to the tent cities. Recruit them at the welfare office, at the VA. Recruit them as you are out in the community, organizing with low-wage workers or labor unions. Leaders are people who both know how to make a stand on their own, and also know they can't do it all on their own. Both of these points are old news to poor folks engaged in the struggle to defend their basic human rights. Daily survival requires a poor person to stand up for her own life in both big and small ways, and also requires her to lean into the goodness of others. Some people might call this an unasked-for spiritual discipline—or, more condescendingly, "a blessing in disguise." But I think Johnnie Tillmon, former head of the National Welfare Rights Union, said it best when she talked about what she learned about poverty as a welfare mother. She said, "There's one good thing about welfare. It kills your illusions about yourself, and about where this society is really at. It's laid out for you straight. You have to learn to fight, to be aggressive, or you just don't make it. If you can survive long enough on welfare, you can survive anything. It gives you a kind of freedom, a sense of your own power and togetherness with other women."

Don't we need deacons who can survive anything? Don't we need deacons who share this sense of freedom and power— not the kind that makes you act like a lone ranger but the kind that radically deepens your sense of accountability to, and togetherness with, the rest of God's children? For too long, those of us in the church who care about justice have believed and perpetuated the lie that we must become "a voice for the voiceless." That's a lie. When you start to take the leadership and talent of the poor seriously—of the young seriously—you will be forced to confront and up-end this lie. It's like Arundhati Roy said, "We know, of course, there's really no such thing as the 'voiceless.' There are only the deliberately silenced, or the preferably unheard." In a living, spirit-filled diaconal ministry, you do not get to speak "for" anybody. You get to 1) speak for yourself, and 2) amplify the voices of others in the world whom the powers and principalities seek to silence. Even when the church itself acts as one of those silencers.

So: how? How can we pull this off? Ther's always that tension, when we talk about the diaconate as an ordained "labor of love" (which is the nicest, churchiest, most insidious way of saying "unpaid"). I struggle with this myself, as a young discerner working full-time with a crushing burden of student debt that I will be paying off for the next twenty years. A full-time volunteer ministry sounds lovely—if you are retired with a comfortable pension. But one of the gifts given to me by my mentor Gen, archdeacon of the Diocese of Olympia, has been the consistent reminder that a deacon's ministry is whatever work the deacon is doing out in the world. I wrestled with that for a long time. Given my own experience and training, my first thought was, "Well, what does that mean for someone who feels a diaconal calling and works at McDonald's? What does it mean for someone who is called and is living on a disability income?" And as I wrestled with that a bit longer, I was reminded of the countless places like McDonalds and like the DHS office where I've seen leaders step up—unpaid, but choosing to lead and choosing to fight for a better world because their lives and families and communities depend on them fighting. And I realized then that our diaconate might just be a key place where the very best of the church can intersect with the courageous, resurrection-inspiring, empire-leveling spirit of the organized poor.

A deacon's job (among other things) is to say to the church, "It's not all about you. It's about God's liberation of this entire broken and beautiful world." At the same time, the church's tools of ritual, remembrance, ancient tradition, and prayerful discipline are indispensible for building a world-changing social movement led by the poor. I know this is true because I have witnessed it again and again. People who have gathered together to face down death (from hunger, from homelessness, from violence) have usually caught the Spirit regardless of whether they've ever set foot in a church. In my experience, sharing even basic theological tools with those folks catches fire every time. It is often a slow start, if you're just starting out—we do a thorough job of grinding down the spirits of the poor. But once people have arrived at the collective decision to stand and defend their God-given right to survive and thrive, there is a profound spiritual shift that occurs. I don't even know what to call it, but I think that's the shift that Christ was referring to when he said, "Where two or three are gathered in my name, I am with them." Where poor youth have gathered, even under threat of arrest and police brutality, to protest the erasure of public education in their communities; where the homeless have collectively and illegally taken over abandoned buildings rather than freeze to death in the streets; where undocumented immigrant nannies have rallied outside the home of an employer who has beaten one of their fellow workers—Jesus is there. And Jesus is not waiting for The Episcopal Church to show up before he makes his next move. Diaconal calls are already being lived out by young people everywhere—our job is to see if we can help the church keep up with all of them, to see if we can do a better job of recognizing and supporting them as they arise in these "unexpected" places (and seriously—CHECK YOUR BIBLES, THESE PLACES SHOULD NOT BE UNEXPECTED).

If you're looking for young deacons, it's time to stop waiting for them to show up at church and eagerly tell you, "I'm interested in becoming an aspirant to Holy Orders." One thing we all know about young people is that they are overwhelmingly NOT in church. Which is great for potential future deacons—they shouldn't be spending too much time there anyway! Go instead out into your communities, find the places where young people are making a stand. Find the places where young people are asking the hardest, most unsettling questions, like: "Why does this society think I am disposable? Why do I work so hard and still struggle to survive? Where the hell is God in this terrible mess?" That agitation, that dissatisfaction, that love-fueled anger is precisely one of the things we should be looking for as we discern the presence of a diaconal calling. Think back to the Exodus, to the moment things really kicked off:

> After a long time the king of Egypt died. The Israelites groaned under their slavery, and cried out. Out of the slavery their cry for help rose up to God. God heard their groaning, and God remembered his covenant with Abraham, Isaac, and Jacob. God looked upon the Israelites, and God took notice of them. (Exod. 2:23–25).

If you want young deacons, find the groaners. Find the young people crying out around you and crying out to one another in their suffering. God is working there. Church is already happening there. If we want this church to matter, we need to be there, too—not just handing out food and blankets and prayers. We need to be there looking for leaders—not just for the future of our church, but for the future of a free world for all God's children.

Who will live God's Dream?

Postscript

Several weeks after the manuscript for this book had gone to my editor, I received an e-mail from Aaron. She wrote, "Well, I quit the ordination process. Here's the letter I sent to the bishop."

In that letter, she outlined, with clarity and passion, why and how she had reached her decision.

"I know this news is sudden, and probably unexpected," she wrote. "It's not a decision I've made in a state of crisis, nor is it based on anything I've kept bottled up for a long time. It's a realization that was catalyzed by external stuff (mainly by the way I've felt called to shift my priorities in this historic moment of action for racial justice). But it's a decision that's grounded in deeper, ongoing questions I've brought to prayer and spiritual direction, and I've had a lot of clarity on those fronts recently.

I'm not called to obedience in the institutional church. I have absolutely no desire to be under Holy Orders. I am not interested in wearing a collar, and I'm even less interested in the leash that comes with it. If it ever came down to conflicting orders between you and the long-time agitators who've raised me in faith, I wouldn't think twice. I genuinely like and respect you, but you're nowhere near the top of my chain of command.

. . . I've been extraordinarily supported through most of this. I loved doing my field education . . . I couldn't have asked for a better placement. Part of what took me so long in coming to this realization is that I was having a really good time with the people surrounding me. In particular worshipping with the San Lucas folks radically transformed my understanding of the role of the laity. Along with God, they really do run their own show . . . they don't wait for him [the priest] or anyone else to tell them what to do. They are already leaders, and they know it, and it's beautiful.

Inside the church, I just want to copycat them. I want more lay people laying claim to their own power and fully exercising it. My understanding of institutional leadership is that it has to be driven by the bottom in order to be most relevant. In being set apart from the laity, my leadership would lose relevance. I'm not the kind of leader who gets more done by virtue of having greater access to institutional power. I'm the kind of leader who gets more done by virtue of having greater access to deep relationships with the base."[1]

Aaron reported that she'd met with her Commission on Ministry liaison. She went on, "When I told her this, she said a true and useful thing: 'Some of us are called to lonely battles. Some aren't.' I'm not. The clergy I trust most . . . really do strike me as having the ability to grow in authority from a lonely place. I don't understand that because I'm not wired that way, but I see them doing good work through that lens, so I know it's real. It's a real and particular calling. It's also not mine. At all."[2]

When Aaron shared this, one thing immediately popped into my mind. "Unexpected Consequences." I had just finished teaching an online course in which I had told participants that Aaron keeps me honest. Indeed. If I have hoped for anything in this book, it has been to call the church around the font in claiming the total ministry of all its members. Aaron now leads the way again. In her vision of a movement led by the poor, and her unrelenting passion for justice, she is an ally of every one of us who longs to engage the diakonia of all believers. In her clarity of call, she helps to clarify that of others, urging deacons and presbyters and bishops to be good partners in ministry.

No, the diaconate does not exist for the sake of having deacons, but for the sake of reaching out in the wholesome humility of Christ, making the church relevant, making the world whole. Nor does the presbyterate exist for the sake of immovable altars and fonts, but for the sake of breaking the bread in daily life, and of keeping the community together as we move away from privilege. Nor does the episcopate exist for the sake of churchly order, but for the sake of a deeper unity that is unafraid to question its effectiveness, insisting that it be a unity that undergirds the mission and ministry of the whole people of God.

Aaron's is a reminder to us all that as the people of God we are blessed with gifts beyond measure and that in our common Christian vocation, we are called *together* to bring God's realm to our world. Right now.

Acknowledgments

During the eight years that I was working toward ordination to the diaconate, I went to graduate school. I took part in the four-year Education for Ministry program. I worked at a university chaplaincy and at a free medical clinic. It took a long time. My youngest son was just fifteen months old when I attended the meeting at Notre Dame on the diaconate that would "launch me." After several years, perhaps he was in kindergarten, he asked one day, "Mom, when will you ever get to be a dinkin?" It was a temptation to call this book, "Dinkin Thinkin." He and his brother both expressed appreciation when the busiest times were behind us and they didn't have to eat so much frozen pizza. Thanks to my family—all my family.

In 1988 a new bishop came to town. Bishop C. Christopher Epting had been providing education and formation opportunities for deacons in the Diocese of Central Florida from 1972 on. He took a chance. When people in the diocese still weren't clear about this new thing, he took a chance. I was ordained at Diocesan Convention in 1989. At the end of his sermon, Bishop Epting said, "Susanne, my sister, you have been through a long and sometimes painful process for this day. You have my respect and gratitude—both for your patience and tenacity. But I think you're being ordained at the right time.

"You will be a sign—a sacrament—of the servanthood we are all called to share. You may also be a sign of much more—of shared ministry, of total ministry, of new directions, and of risk. In short, of the kind of thing we prayed for in the collect for this day.

'Things which were cast down are being raised up, and things which had grown old are being made new, and all things are being brought to their perfection. . . .'

"Welcome aboard! Welcome to a new day in the Diocese of Iowa."

I know that I told my bishop thank you for taking a chance. Without his willingness to take a risk, I might still be in the ordination process.

Little did I know that many years later, he would be the bishop in my living room—the spouse that would cook dinner, mind the menagerie, protect me from interruption—in order to write a book. Thank you to Christopher.

For years I had the privilege of serving as director of a deacons' association. I was entrusted to be an advocate, spokesperson, resource-finder, visionary, coordinator, even a pusher of possibilities. Thank you to the church-wide community of deacons for that trust.

Thank you too to the colleagues who have had a part in the writing of this book.

And thank you to the colleagues who have graciously and helpfully read the manuscript as I've written, sometimes more than once! To my deacon colleagues, Frederick Erickson, Maureen Elizabeth Hagen, and Louise Thibodaux, thank you. To Steve Kelsey, thanks, not only for reading, but for being a presbyter, friend, and colleague who has always supported deacons. Thank you to Jane Root, a layperson who exemplifies what it means to carry out the call to diaconal ministry that comes with baptism. The whole deacon community owes you a debt of gratitude.

Appendix One
Deacons *Are* in the Picture

A Keynote in Two Parts by Deacon Josephine Borgeson June 4, 1987, at the Biennial Conference of the North American Association for the Diaconate[1]

Part I

When I accepted the invitation to make this address I had to ask, "Why me?" I'm guessing that it's because I represent a sort of vanguard of the new wave, a deacon who has worked on the renewal of the diaconate and ministry in general for over a decade. There certainly are deacons who have been ordained decades longer than I have—but I suspect that most of you have been ordained since that day in late June thirteen years ago when I became a deacon with only a beginning experience of what I was getting myself into.

Along these lines, I had a good meeting last week with a woman from a diocese neighboring Nevada who is trying to discern whether or not her vocation is to the diaconate. On our first greeting one another face to face she exclaimed, "I'd heard so much about you, I thought you must be at least sixty." I suspect she was affirming another reason I've been asked to speak—I have not been a silent servant, but very vocal about this office of deacon—and God willing will continue to be so until my age catches up with my reputation!

What I hope to do tonight is give a review of where we as deacons in North America have been in the last decade or so, which will of necessity be highly anecdotal, and then to pose some questions for the future of the diaconate, the *ongoing* renewal of our office of servanthood. I am, as you can tell, addressing the deacons here. It is a pleasure to be able increasingly to talk *with* deacons, rather than just about the diaconate.

I had this photo blown up, because it illustrates so well where I feel we are with the renewal of the diaconate in the church. When you first look at it, it appears to be just another picture of just another presider at just another invitation to communion. If you're into playing ecclesiastical who's who, you may recognize the presider as Stewart Zabriskie, the new bishop of Nevada. If you are from the Diocese of Nevada or receive our newspaper, *The Desert Church*, you will know that the photo was taken at Stewart's ordination liturgy in September.

What does this have to do with deacons? If you look closely, you will see four hands in the picture—the other pair of hands, holding the chalice, belong to Deacon Virginia Ferguson. Virginia, our diocesan treasurer, was one of two deacons serving at table and attending the new bishop.

Deacons *are* in the picture. Though sometimes faceless, though often unnamed (the original caption of the photo would've left close observers believing that Stewart has what all bishops covet—an extra pair of hands), we are present in the church—serving with the other ordained leaders at the community table, and reminding all the faithful, by gesture and example, as much as by word, that the gifts of God are for them—the gifts of God for the people of God in service to the world.

When I was at Church Divinity School of the Pacific—I think in the spring of my middle year when I'd felt called to the diaconate but had yet to test that call in a community context—a woman deacon came to visit and speak with seminarians on the subject of women's ordination to the presbyterate and the episcopate. Over coffee in the refectory I confided that I really felt called to be a deacon. She said, "Why would you want to be a deacon? The only *power* in the church is as a priest or a bishop—or an influential layperson, preferably with money." Over the years I have come to realize what a non-question she asked! A power motive is certainly inappropriate to any vocation—and I do mean *any*, since *any* work understood as a Christian vocation doesn't have power as an ultimate goal. There was, though, a grain of truth in what she said, since deacons were at that time invisible in the church's decision-making bodies. Since that time, the Episcopal Church and many of its several dioceses have labored to reform their canons and other guidelines so that deacons may vote, be members of commissions and committees, and be General Convention deputies. Though there is now some negative reaction to this enfranchisement from deacons themselves—and I gather some of that coming from one of our host dioceses—I frankly must say that I applaud the changes. To me, being a part of the decision-making processes of the church is basic to adult membership in the church—and I wonder how ordination can take that away. In any event, the point is not how it is done—"how" meaning including deacons as part of the church's deliberations. The point is *that* it is done. I recall one General Convention—Minneapolis, Denver, it's rather a blur—when the bishops were questioning how deacons could be in the House of Deputies when deacons are really the Bishop's People. I suggested to another deacon, Frances Zielinski, with whom I was watching the debate, that we get our respective bishops to propose returning to the ancient custom that deacons may represent bishops in their absence; then our bishops could head for the men's room and ask that we be seated. Actually, I still would prefer this solution. But what I want to celebrate is that we *are* trying a *variety* of solutions and that deacons are in the picture as the church takes council.

In Nevada in 1976 Wes Frensdorff called for a symposium on the diaconate in celebration of the twenty-fifth anniversary of his first ordination. I think this was shocking to many people for two reasons. First, who'd want to talk about the diaconate anyway? And second, two of the four speakers were actually deacons! Since that time there has been a lot more—sometimes from my perspective too much—talk about the diaconate. And it is no longer uncommon for *deacons* to speak about the diaconate to commissions on ministry and other such bodies. Deacons coordinate deacon programs, mentor deacons-to-be, and preach at ordinations to the diaconate. A few years ago a deacon friend remarked somewhat sarcastically that she was no longer going to read anything written about the diaconate by priests. One can do a lot of reading today that is both about deacons and *diakonia* and *by* deacons. Thanks be to God! We *are* in the picture—and sometimes we're the photographer as well.

After the last national gathering at Notre Dame, Ormonde Plater said he was never again going to say anything in public about titles and uniforms. I go against his caveat, as I can't resist saying that I see slow but positive growth in this area. At our best we have gone from worrying about how we should be addressed and what should be our insignia to recognizing that these are practical, culturally relative questions that really don't matter very much. I was reminded a few weeks ago that it was in 1979 that I began to wage my battle—with a little help from Betty Fuller—to use "deacon" as a title. Even though it's been a matter of weeks since I had to correct *another deacon* who introduced me as *The Reverend*, I have seen progress in our attempts through appropriate titles and distinctive dress to resist the clericalization of the diaconate. Best of all, I've concluded that if you keep questioning the titles people want to hang on you, they eventually are worn down, give up, and call you by your Christian name—which is the best of all! Whether we've figured out the appropriate caption and costume or not, we *are* in the picture.

Let me swing a bit in the direction of a far less tangible change I've seen, one in the area of theologizing or reflecting on the diaconate. When I first became a deacon, it seemed as though most attempts to define and describe the office were done negatively, and with reference to the offices of presbyter and bishop. You know the sort of thing, "What can a priest do that you can't? Is the parish priest or the bishop in charge of the deacon?"

etc. More and more the arguments and the questions have shifted so that we speak of the diaconate positively, and with the entire body of Christ, not other ordained folk, as the reference point. We have come to see that the relationship we must understand and articulate is the relationship of deacons to the ministry which all Christians share by virtue of their baptism, the ministry of Christ.

While at some level I knew this shift was going on in my own thinking, it was really brought home to me at the 1986 Sindicators conference when my colleague, Jim Kelsey, pointed out how refreshing the shift was. We need to be sensitive to those who have still not made this shift—but we also need to forge ahead and build from our new perspective. We *are* in the picture—and unlike my photo, the picture is not just of assorted clergy, but of all God's people, called and baptized to share in the servanthood of the church.

Next to last, in my review of renewal and change, I want to talk about attitudes and hope. At the gathering analogous to this one in 1979, where there were many more people being quizzical about the diaconate than there were deacons, and when a number of dioceses had imposed moratoria on diaconate ordinations, "until we understand it"—(had they succeeded most of us still wouldn't be here as deacons)—at that gathering one of our senior (pre-1970) women deacons said to me, "I get so discouraged. I sometimes feel like I'm a member of an endangered species."

In my travels around the church—which lately seem more extensive than even I would like—I have been privileged to meet many deacons. And I have seen this attitude of discouragement slowly dissipate, so that even in the most discouraged and discouraging dioceses, there is a good deal more hope among deacons and deacons-to-be that we are a vital office, that our vocation is understood, even if dimly and only by some, and that there is real hope in the vision and ministry we offer the church. The community among deacons is extremely important to this hope—and as we blaze new trails for the diaconate we mustn't lose sight of this—from several different ecclesiastical generations, trained in a variety of diocesan programs as well as residential schools and seminaries, women and men, with various ethnic and racial roots, we share this office, and we share a vision of the importance of servanthood for the church in our time. We are, in our diversity, part of a picture that is hopeful.

This was to have been the wrap up of Part I. But my writing was interrupted by attending the ordination of a young Lutheran friend to the ministry of Word and Sacrament, so I want to underscore a more general change I have seen in the last decade or so—that is a deepening understanding of what it means to have three distinct offices in the church, and within those offices great plurality in the gifts and styles people bring to them. My friend doubtless will be—in fact already is—a good pastor and liturgist. But I despair for anyone who has so many roles and icons laid on him at once. Preacher, prophet, pastor, person of prayer, servant, shepherd, sacramental leader, counselor, community activist—to name a few. The renewal of the diaconate has been part of the action of unpacking the one-man or one-woman band, freeing the leadership of the church to move from gifts and strengths, giving people permission to say, "That's not my job," recognizing the distinctiveness of three offices (someday we'll talk about the perpetual presbyterate and the distinctive episcopate), and celebrating the many faces of ministry among all Christ's people. I really ought to have a series of pictures, taken at altars and in workplaces and marketplaces all over the continent.

Part II

The Ongoing Renewal of the Office of Servanthood

My greatest fear, as I review the progress we have made in the renewal of the diaconate, is that our success will be our downfall. How do we, as our numbers and acceptance grow, preserve the marginal status that has helped us in our ministry and enablement of ministry with the marginalized? Or is it inevitable, as with so many renewal movements, that we will lose our edge and our marginality and that new movements will need to spring up to remind the church of its role on the margins of society? I don't have any facile answers, or even beginnings of one. I'd like to think that our literally eccentric role in the liturgy will remind us of the eccentricity necessary to a life of servanthood—but it's all too easy to get routinized and rigidified in our eccentricity.

In the same vein, at the last of these meetings before this one, I read in one diocese's handout on the diaconate that deacons are called to serve, not to lead. I don't believe that for a minute. We are called to be *servant leaders*—leaders among Christ's servants, leaders in the church's work of servanthood, leaders whose style is servant-like. Many temptations beset those of us who would attempt to live out that vision. We must pay very careful attention to the words and deeds of Jesus Christ read every Sunday, allowing them to judge *us*, and our uses and abuses of power and authority. And we must be open to seeing icons of the Servant Christ that are not of our own designing—in the people whom we think *we* are *serving*, in the laypeople in our parishes and dioceses, and yes, even in the presbyters and bishops.

As we take our place as advocates of the diaconate and *diakonia*, we need to beware of a couple of pitfalls. First, we must always conduct ourselves as servants in the liturgy. I may be sinking to the level of pet peeve here, but I have become aware in my travels that many deacons, while fulfilling certain rubrical duties and expectations, do a lousy job of being generally attentive and helpful in the liturgy. There is no reason for a deacon to have his or her nose stuck in a prayer book or hymnal while the bishop fumbles with the altar book, for example. All that we advocate about servanthood as a Christian lifestyle will be hollow if we don't model it when most of the gathered community sees us in action!

Also—and perhaps here I am speaking to myself, though I expect it affects some of the rest of you as well—I sometimes get rather peevish about going square one on the diaconate again and again. But if we are servant leaders, that is exactly what we must do, no matter how tedious. There are those struggling to understand the diaconate and those testing a vocation to the diaconate who need our help.

We are forging a renewed theology of the diaconate as well as proliferating deacons—and that theology is well-related to the servanthood of all believers. I do see, though, in some quarters, a tendency to create another rung on the ladder of hierarchy—rather than efforts to do away with the ladder altogether. The antidote to the ladder—if I can be allowed to mix metaphors that way—lies, I think, in two things. First, each of us deacons must take responsibility for sharing our particular tasks and foci in ministry with the laity wherever and whenever possible. And those of us who bear some responsibility for the education in ministry of deacons must see that educational opportunities are shared among deacons, deacons-to-be, and lay members of the church. In my experience, the best insurance against creating another caste of ministers is to *share* our learning and opportunities for reflection. This is simply putting into practice a theology of the diaconate rooted in baptismal ministry.

And speaking of theology, it seems important to me that we take not just a theology of the diaconate, but diaconal theologizing seriously. Our charge to interpret to the church the needs, concerns, and hopes of the world is essentially a theological one. Deacons tend to be activists. But we neglect making time for reflection, the kind of reflection that can make of our leadership interpretation, rather than merely reporting, at our peril. We need not do all that interpretation alone, but we must take our leadership of it seriously. I have talked with or heard of more than one bishop who felt that deacons, the institution's official vanguard, needed at least as good, if not better, theological education than presbyters. Usually I have written off such remarks as attempts to block a voluntary diaconate—but I think there's some truth in them. We probably do not need all the academic baggage—but we need theological models and methods which will help us reflect on the world's brokenness and aspirations. We need to continue to stretch ourselves in our reflection and to take our ongoing education in ministry seriously.

A year and a half ago I did some research for a strange and radical ministry renewal network I belong to called Sindicators. We were exploring the question of how the church's *diakonia* is enabled, and how deacons focus or help that process along. I was in touch with many of you at that time, and the correspondence I conducted brought me a great deal of joy in seeing how varied and creative the ministries of deacons were. . . .

But I also had two great disappointments in reviewing my research. First of all, I was surprised at how few deacons were actively supporting what I call bona fide lay ministry—that is, the ministry of Christian people in their work and community involvements beyond the gathered ecclesial community. I suspect part of the reason as few deacons reported such ministry is that we tend to think programmatically. If we can't put a name on it and announce it in bulletins or newsletters, it isn't happening—and much of the support of laypeople in their vocations is done informally. Nevertheless, we need to do more of it—for profound renewal in ministry will only come when we live out, as well as talk about, baptismal ministry, and recover the meaning of the word "vocation," for all Christians.

My second disappointment was in the letters I received where people apologized to me for their ministries! One person—and I suspect other senior or proto-deacons in their dioceses will recognize themselves in this—said all he seemed to do was sit on boards and committees! This reminded me of one board (and you can spell that both ways) experience I had, where I suddenly discovered that I was the ordained member most accessible to the lay members. They came to me with questions they were afraid a presbyter or bishop would judge stupid. They came to me to complain about the underrepresentation of various groups and constituencies. Board and committee membership *is* ministry, and often gives us an opportunity to enable the ministry of others who serve with us. Another memorable apology was from a woman who said she loved being the deacon in the Sunday liturgy, but spent most of her intentional ministry time just visiting the shut-in and the lonely and listening and drinking endless cups of tea. That's ministry to apologize for? Would that every community had such a person! I also suspect that such a ministry does more than that deacon realized to enable laypeople in their vocations—for surely a sense that we are loved and heard as members of the Christian community is basic to anyone's commitment to living out a Christian life.

So let us return to the point with which I concluded the first half of this address. I rejoice to be part of a communion that has three vital offices. And I hope we won't fall into the trap which our sisters and brothers who are presbyters have in the past—the myth of omnicompetence. There is only one deacon in the photograph—but one deacon, or even a handful, can't do it all—and except for the rubrics which cover our role in the liturgy, there is no one way to be a deacon. We need deacons who sit on boards and committees, and deacons who listen over cups of tea. We need the tradition of our elder women deacons—and the enthusiasm of young men. We need deacons in prisons and hospices and soup kitchens. We need deacons who strengthen the laity in their ministry and witness—from tiny congregations in rural communities to corporate-style parishes in the suburbs. Most of all we need deacons who have that true humility which allows them to be honest about what their gifts are and are not—and deacons who are attuned to opportunities to serve and to help others into service.

This has really been more of a pep rally speech than a theological address. The bibliography is my experience—and yours. Some of you may have recognized yourself in my anecdotes and examples. A few of you may have been offended or challenged by something I said—at least I hope a few of you were! And I hope most of you found something in my remarks that brought a smile or an "aha." The real program here is our coming together to challenge and celebrate both our diversity of gifts and experience and our common calling and vision.

Appendix Two
Citizens of the World— Servants of Christ

A Keynote Address by Deacon Maylanne Maybee[1] June 1, 1989, at the Biennial Conference of the North American Association for the Diaconate[2]

We have all been travelling long distances to get here, and I'd like to begin my remarks with a journey image, a reflection by Dom Helder Camara:

> Setting out is first of all getting out of oneself. Breaking through the shell of selfishness hardening us within our own ego.
>
> To stop revolving round oneself as if we were the center of everything.
>
> Refusing to be ringed in by the problems of our own small world. However important these may be, humanity is more important and our task is to serve humanity.
>
> Setting out is not covering miles of land or sea, or travelling faster than the speed of sound. It is first and foremost opening ourselves to other people, trying to get to know them, going out to meet them.
>
> Opening ourselves to ideas, including those with which we disagree, this is what the good traveler should do. Happy are they who understand the words, "If you disagree with me, you have something to give me."
>
> If those who are with you always agree with you before you open your mouth, they are not companions but shadows. When disagreement is not a form of systematic blocking, when it rises from a different vision, it can only enrich us.
>
> It is possible to travel alone. But the good traveler knows that the journey is human life and life needs company. "Companion" means the one who eats the same bread. Happy are

they who feel they are always on the road and that everyone
they meet is their chosen companion. Good travelers take care
of their weary companions. They guess when they lose heart.
They take them as they find them, listen to them. Intelligently,
gently, above all lovingly, they encourage them to go on and
recover their joy in the journey.

To travel for the sake of travelling is not the true journey.
We must seek a goal, envisage an end to the journey, an arrival.

But there are journeys and journeys. For the oppressed minor-
ities, setting out means to get moving and help many others get
moving to make the world more just and more human.[3]

As deacons, we are on a journey. The theme of this conference, "Citizens
of the World—Servants of Christ," is a signpost of where we are on that
journey. For many good reasons, as individuals and as an organization, we
have been concerned with our identity and status, with internal questions
of canons, of the difference between deacons and priests, of title and dress,
with the transitional diaconate and *per saltum* ordination.

But our journey does have a goal, reflected in our theme and workshop
topics. We are not primarily members of an institution. We are also members of the Body of Christ, members of a society, citizens of the world, and
creatures of planet earth. And as such, we go with a clear vision. We recall
it every time we say the Lord's Prayer: "Thy Kingdom come . . . on earth
as it is in heaven." Our goal, our point of arrival, is to build the kingdom
of heaven on earth.

I have been reflecting on a much loved New Testament story as a model
of servanthood. It's the one John the Evangelist uses to describe the beginning of Jesus' earthly ministry—an ordinary event, a wedding where the
wine runs out. I like the story because deacons, "diakonoi," or servants,
figure in it so prominently. And I think that story of the wedding in Cana
has something important to tell us about what it means to be servants,
what our job is, and how we relate to people.

You know the story. It begins with the arrival of Jesus and the disciples
at a wedding, and Mary, who was apparently there already, observes a
very serious need: "They have no wine." Jesus says to her, "Woman, what
have I to do with you? My hour is not yet come." The tone would be more
like, "Mother, don't worry just yet. The moment isn't right." But she isn't
put off. She tells the servants, "Whatever he tells you to do, do it." And
Jesus tells them what to do—to draw water from the water jars. So they
pour out the water and bring it to the governor of the feast . . . who then
goes on to commend the groom for the quality of the wine! And the disciples believe. And the guests have their party.

John gives an important hint to help us understand the story. He begins by saying that it happened "on the third day." If you read the chapter before, it was probably at least the fifth day, so it was probably not referring to actual time. Clearly the third day refers to when Jesus rose from the dead, and what John is really talking about is the resurrection, and this is a resurrection story. We have lots of examples, especially in Luke, of the wedding feast as an image of the Kingdom. It's as if John were writing his gospel backwards: it begins with the kingdom and ends with the cross and resurrection. So what we're looking at here is a resurrection community, a community of new life, transformed from the old order to the new, and the servants here are the agents or enablers of transformation—transformation of water into wine, of guests who are drunk and somewhat chaotic into a community of celebration, of unbelief into belief, and ultimately of slavery, suffering, and death into new life. That's our story, and that's our journey.

For where we fit in, the details of the story are interesting. It's a short drama, but there are lots of actors, and where do the servants fit in? Mary is the one who notices the need ("They have no wine"), and she is the first to speak to the servants ("Whatever he tells you to do, do it"). Jesus gives a practical, short-term order ("Draw the water from the jars"), and the servants obey. The governor of the feast is delighted, but not curious—the servants are the ones who know the source of the wine. The bridegroom is the one who gets the credit ("But you have kept the best wine until now"). The disciples observe, and believe. And the guests get to celebrate.

What does this tell us about being a servant? It tells us we may get our orders from unexpected places . . . not always the obvious ones. It was not the governor of the feast who gave the orders in this instance, but Mary, who was part of the community and saw the need. It's not necessarily the bishop or the rector of our parish who is going to be the one to give us our orders. It tells us that by listening to others, we become receptive to what Jesus asks of us. It tells us that we may not always have the full picture of what we do, we may not always understand or see the consequences of our action. It also tells us that we might not necessarily get credit for what we do; and that as servants, we might not even get noticed by those who benefit by what we do.

But servants, by their attentiveness, responsiveness, by their faith and obedience, are the ones who enable transformation to happen. They know their business, and that knowledge is the source of their influence and their power.

Robert Greenleaf begins his book on Servant Leadership by recalling the theme of Herman Hesse's *Journey to the East*. "In this story," he writes, "we see a band of men on a mythical journey. . . ." The central figure of the story is Leo, who accompanies the party as the servant who does their menial chores, but who also sustains them with his spirit and with his song. He is a person of extraordinary presence. All goes well until Leo disappears. Then the group falls into disarray and the journey is abandoned. The narrator, one of the party, after some years of wandering, finds Leo and is taken into the Order that had sponsored the journey. There he discovers that Leo, whom he had known first as servant, was in fact that titular head of the Order, its guiding spirit, a great and noble *leader*.

Greenleaf concludes that the story clearly tells us that the great leader is seen first as servant—and that applies to us as deacons! We too are part of an Order that calls us to do menial chores and to sustain people with our spirit and our song. For us to be preoccupied with our appearance as leaders in the church is to get things wrong.

Greenleaf goes on to describe some of the qualities of servanthood. Servants are people who search, who listen, and who expect. They are attentive to the moment, striving always to see clearly, to hear the voice of prophecy.

Servants are able to see the disparity between what is possible and what is actual, to see the possibilities of the wine of fellowship and community. They are able to see the disparity because they are the ones who pour out the water of the old order in acts of service. Our discipleship is to see beyond what is expected, to combine the analysis of the need that we see in our work ("They have no wine") with a creative and artistic response ("You have kept the good wine until now").

Servants are not primarily critics or complainers, but are affirmative builders of a better society. That's a difficult and challenging task, and certainly likely to make us the subjects of others' criticisms and complaints.

The leadership of servants comes from making sure that people's highest priority needs are being served. We must always ask ourselves if those we serve, no matter how destitute or seemingly self-sufficient they seem, grow as persons, whether they are more likely themselves to become servants.

Above all, servants know the goal, the vision, and command trust both by their competence and spirit. Servants, by definition, are fully human. They are closer to the ground. They're in touch with reality, and can see and hear things that others don't. They know things by virtue of their position.

Our job as servants is to make the people of God a more serving people, to make the organized church a more serving church. As deacons, we are like trustees, whose influence is from knowing, and asking questions—hard questions, searching questions, ones that can't be answered superficially. We take our orders not primarily from the institution, but from the human context where there is need, and brokenness, and suffering. This is where being "citizens of the world" comes in and takes priority. Just as the servants at Cana listened to Mary so Jesus could act, we too must listen where others don't so the Body of Christ can be effective.

So we have to ask ourselves, "What *is* our context? What *are* the prophetic voices we listen to?" These are questions for reflection and discernment that are the substance of this conference, and not ones which I would presume to answer for you. But let me lay out some guidelines, some caveats, and some illustrations that come out of my experience.

To be attentive to our context, I think, requires three things. First, we attend to our context by listening where others don't—to children, to old people, to women, to street people, to indigenous people, to people of color, to the voice of emerging nations. And listening to people we don't agree with, for they have the ability to enrich our vision. This is especially hard for us as North Americans because we are blinded by the power and affluence that is associated with our culture. It corrupts our thinking and makes us assume that our abundance and our power and our prosperity are what qualify us to be servants. Words like "pity" and "charity," which once had a rich meaning, now have a bad name. I think this is because people who are poor, or handicapped, or oppressed, associate pity and charity with domination and control, and the use of power over rather than with them.

In our culture and context, we have to be particularly attentive to what drives us and how we come across to those with whom we work. Once about three years ago, in preparation for the work I now do, I was involved in making a "plunge"—an experience of taking five dollars and surviving in the streets for three or four days. It's a quick, effective way of getting some sense of the perception of our services and attitudes for people who are in the streets. The first thing I needed was something to eat for lunch, and I went to a mission. And I guess that sandwich will always make me think of what "charity" is: it was dry, with the lowest quality meat imaginable, no butter, no mayonnaise, but an insulting blob of mustard in the middle. That's what "charity" felt like to me.

Servanthood is not the product of prosperity. It is just the other way around. It's what *leads* to fullness of life. The abundant life, healing, and wholeness are the result, the outcome of transforming service and not the point of departure. The first thing we have to do then, in being attentive to our context, is to listen.

And I think that kind of listening is what calls us out from where we are, from what is comfortable and normal for us. So a second guideline is what Henri Nouwen and other authors of the book *Compassion* call "voluntary displacement."

The network that I'm involved with in Toronto has called itself the Single Displaced Persons Project—it was partly taking postwar language in recognition that the people most oppressed by our social system were people who were not just poor, but who were also without community—who were displaced. Their displacement is not voluntary. But in order to be with them, we can choose to displace ourselves from that which is comfortable, familiar, and normal. It's a characteristic of service to take on other people's agenda and to make them our own. But even as we do this, we must realize that we can easily be tempted to listen and to talk about the people whom we serve, but not to trust them.

Another illustration that is powerful to me: in Toronto there is a group that is trying to attend to the health needs of people in the street which are not being met by hospital emergency wards or by traditional medical services. One of the exciting things about this ministry is that the people who are involved in running the service, who are on the board and who are the decision-makers, are not primarily doctors and nurses, but people who are using the services themselves. It's been an amazing lesson for volunteer nurses who give their time to this clinic. They have found that what's probably even more important than medical care is the beginning of building trust.

One story that really struck me is about a nurse who was speaking with a man who came to the clinic and who had a very visible and ugly cut in his ankle—a festering wound in which his sock had become embedded. She was quite concerned and appalled by that, but that's not what he wanted treated. He wanted something else to be treated—a headache. That was what he wanted, and that was what he came for. And she said, "I have a real need to attend to this wound." He said, "No, that's not what I'm here for." And she had to pull back all of her professional expertise and inclinations in order that trust could be built. Now there's more to the story . . . I think eventually the man did come back and have his wound treated, but this first visit was a testing of trust.

And then in a workshop we had recently, some of the participants in the Street Health Clinic were involved in some long-range planning. I had them draw visions of what they liked about the service and what was unique about it and special to them. I divided them into groups of nurses and AIDS workers and actual users. And the most wonderful drawing came out of the users of the service themselves. It showed a great circle—an image, they said, of the continuation of this program—surrounded with faces of everyone they knew from the streets and from their society who was involved in the system. At the center of the circle was a kind of cartoon dialogue between a nurse and a street person. The nurse was saying to a person who had come to the door, "What can I do to help?" And the street person's answer was, "I don't know." And the nurse said the second time around, "What can I do to help? I care." And the answer of the street person in the second frame was, "At last, someone who cares for me. But why?" So clearly the image of the Street Health Clinic was above all an image where people felt trust. But in order to build that trust, we have to displace ourselves, and put ourselves into situations of discomfort, of unfamiliarity.

The third guideline for attending to our context is the ability, the strength, the willingness, to make ourselves inconspicuous, to leave room for God to act, to avoid creating dependency, to recognize our self-interest, our need as well as those we serve, to be healed. Being inconspicuous doesn't mean to disappear. If we think that we're not there, we're not taking into account our own power in the relationship. It means that we put ourselves into a minus situation, so that others might grow and God can act.

There are, in our tradition and culture, and in the life of our church, some very significant blocks that I want to address, that prevent us from listening, from displacing ourselves, and from putting ourselves in inconspicuous or minus situations.

One is that we live in a culture of social segregation. When I go to work every day on the bus, I sit and I look at the ads on the top part of the bus, and all of them show white, healthy, middle-class people doing various things to advertise the product. And when I lower my eyes to see who's sharing the seats on that bus, there are people who are black, people who come from India or Pakistan, there are people from Asian backgrounds, there are people who are poor, there are people who are of native origin. Our dominant culture does not reflect the reality of the people who make up our community. Another disparity is that when I go to church on Sunday, the faces are almost all like mine. And everything in our culture contributes to that. Our housing, our neighborhoods, are designed for privacy and segregation. So that's a block we need to be aware of. If we are part of communities that are made up of people just like us, we have to ask ourselves what we are being called to.

Another block is the emphasis that is very predominant in our pastoral care education on individual care, on one-to-one counseling, on a therapeutic and case-management approach. These are important responses, but they are not enough. They do not heed the root cause of people's condition. I was very struck by a colleague of mine who had her training in social work and who began work in a group home for psychiatric patients. She said she was interested in Jungian psychology. The question she put to her first client was, "How do you feel," and the person's response was "I feel hungry."

That was the beginning of an amazing transformation process for this person because she realized that by offering care to someone whose systemic problem was not having enough food to eat, was somewhat like asking someone how they feel and offering them pastoral care when they're being pinned down by a truck.

If we're going to make the church a servant church, we have to look at a different emphasis. It's not the emphasis that we all take for granted on the nature and existence of God: this is what theologians occupy themselves with. But another emphasis, and that which is specifically and emphatically ours as deacons, is the realization that the real crisis is the existence and nature of human beings. Through involvement with the poor, with people who are oppressed, with those whom our society and culture are marginalizing, we come to understand God and Jesus the poor servant. We do not flee the world as a mystic community that is cut off from the world, and we don't preach to the world, as if we are the ones who have the answers. As servants of transformation, we take the incarnation seriously, we recognize that here and now has priority, we acknowledge creation as good.

Finally I want to address some of the skills that we need if we are to be servants, if we are to overcome these blocks . . . and I don't think these are skills that you learn at seminary, or even at deacons' schools. They're skills that you take on slowly, in community, as part of your practice. First of all, as I've already said, we need to be critically aware of our context, to start with our world citizenship.

We need, of course, to be skilled in human relations—in communication, in listening, in diagnosing need not apart from, but together with others, not as experts, but in dialogue with those whom we are concerned about, not as rescuing angels, but as partners.

As agents of transformation, we need to be knowledgeable about institutions and organizations. We need to understand how they work; we need to realize that these can be the vehicles of oppression or transformation. But if we don't know how they work, we can't help to make the difference.

As agents of transformation, we need to learn how to do social analysis, to observe systems and structures of the economic, social, political, and religious aspects of our society. We need to be astute politicians. This is a complex and difficult task, but an absolutely vital one if our actions are to be part of a liberating and transformative process, and not merely aspirin solutions which reinforce existing structures.

I want to give you an illustration—one you may have heard of before, but it bears repeating. It has to do with a woman who is standing on the bank of a river, and sees someone drowning. She takes off her jacket, and she jumps in and saves the person. A few minutes later, someone else is drowning, and she does the same thing. A crowd starts to gather. And this happens a few more times. But when the fourth person that she sees comes along, she puts her jacket back on and goes away! Those who were standing by in admiration and fascination said, "Where are you going? You can't leave these people to drown!" And she said, "I'm going up the river to see who's throwing them in."

We have to look beyond the external signs, and see the structures and the cause of what we're doing, and that's where we have to address the problem. But it's a journey that we cannot possibly do alone, in isolation, as individuals. It has to be done with others, in community. So we have to be skilled at building networks, at building links with people who have the same commitments and concerns that we do, and not to worry about people who don't agree with us. They're the ones who are looking on, they're the ones who want to see what we can do. It's scary and it's risky, and it's very challenging. But it can be done, especially if it's done in the context of community.

We have lots of food banks in Canada, and the difficulty about these food banks is they have a way of creating dependency, of digging a bottomless pit, that is not going to resolve the root problem of people who do not have enough money to clothe and house and feed themselves. A very courageous person that I met in Halifax who is head of the food bank there, together with his board, has made an unheard of decision: to set a timeline to close the food bank, in five years' time. And already there's a hue and a cry from the public and from the media. But he's not going to do it alone. He's throwing a challenge to the community of Halifax to say, "This is a disgrace. This is not the way to live with others. And you as a community are both part of the problem and part of the solution." We *can* do it.

And finally, as agents of transformation, we need to deepen our understanding of the Christian concept of transformation. As servants we know the true agent: God-made-human in Jesus Christ, God-in-our-midst in the presence of the Holy Spirit.

I began with a wedding—a small story that is clearly linked with the big story of Jesus' glorification on the cross and resurrection. But in between these stories in John's gospel is the towel and the basin. The fact that Jesus did what only the lowliest of servants was expected to do, by washing his disciples' feet, is a sign that servanthood is not slavery, something that we do against our will, but something that we choose. By taking up the tools of the slave, Jesus was taking the old God and revealing the new, turning in the old social structure and exchanging it for another.

But the towel and the basin was not a single, isolated act. It represented what Jesus' whole life and ministry were about: his willingness to listen, to assert his love, to accept the outcast, to serve. He spoke against the rich who lived off the poor. He allowed himself to be touched and anointed by a prostitute. He healed the sick and blessed the helpless. He talked with women in public. He talked with Samaritans and entered the homes of pagans. He cleansed the temple and stirred up crowds.

As servants, by choosing the basin and towel, we also choose the cross. It is not imposed, it is not involuntary. To take up the cross is to live in this world with towel and basin in hand. It is not to gloss over pain or to live a band-aid faith. It is to live in a world where people are oppressed by governments, by employers, by spouses. A world where people do get sick, where people die, where people despair.

It's only when we realize the old wine has run out that we can roll up our sleeves, pour out the water of service, and take up the towel, the basin, and ultimately the cross, knowing they are the instruments of transformation for building a new, resurrection community.

Sources

Dom Helder Camara, *The Desert Is Fertile* (Maryknoll, NY: Orbis Books, 1980), 15.

Robert Greenleaf, *Servant Leadership* (New York: Paulist Press, 1977), 7.

Donald McNeill, Douglas Morrison, and Henri Nouwen, *Compassion: A Reflection on the Christian Life* (New York: Image Books, 1983).

Letty Russell, *The Future of Partnership* (Philadelphia: Westminster Press, 1979).

A. Hope, S. Timmel, and C. Hodzi, *Training for Transformation* (Guweru, Zimbabwe: Mambo Press, 1984).

Mike Wood Daily, "A Basin, a Cross, and a Tomb" (sermon preached by the minister of Martin Grove Baptist Church, Etobicoke, Ontario, Canada, on Good Friday, March 24, 1989).

Barbara Paleczny, SSND, and Michael Côté, OP, *Becoming Followers of Jesus* (Burlington, Canada: Trinity Press, 1983).

Appendix Three
Principles of Orderly Exchange[1]

Seeking to promote greater understanding among the participants in *Called to Common Mission*, representatives of the EC and ELCA offer the following adapted principles to the exchange of leaders in diaconal ministries.

1. *Called to Common Mission* intends an interaction of structures of leadership between our two churches for the sake of God's mission in Christ. As full communion partners, the ELCA and the EC may develop common mission plans in order to be able to use resources more effectively and to promote more fruitful outreach ministry. These principles aim to assist the two churches to develop a process that encourages this common mission.
2. The orderly exchange of deacons and diaconal ministers is understood to be at the discretion of the inviting church and subject to that church's polity and procedures.
3. Diaconal ministers or deacons may be eligible to engage in temporary, i.e., occasional or extended, service in any position open to them in the inviting church except as noted otherwise in the policies of either church.
4. It is important to the faithful and orderly exchange that one who would serve in any ministry setting of the other church first be formed and educated for ministry in one's own tradition and have experience in serving in that church's ministry. Such experience and grounding in one's own tradition are seen to be essential prior to serving in a setting of another tradition; therefore, such service is not intended for a first placement.
5. To be eligible for extended service in the other church, a deacon or diaconal minister will demonstrate to the appropriate synod, diocese, or

churchwide office of the inviting church knowledge of and an appreciation for the history, polity, theological, and liturgical identity, practices of ministry, and discipline of that church. They will be expected to minister in the church in a manner consistent with that knowledge and appreciation.

6. Placement, review of credentials and background, authorization/licensing, supervision, and evaluation procedures of the inviting church shall be observed for temporary service, i.e., occasional and extended.

7. Approval for extended service shall occur only in consultation with, and concurrence of, the sending body.

8. Any deacon or diaconal minister serving in the other church in a stipended position will continue to participate in the pension and benefits program of the sending church, as applicable. The inviting church should therefore be expected to participate fully in that stipended minister's pension and benefits program.

9. Responsibility for pastoral care of deacons and diaconal ministers is shared by the inviting and sending bodies: in the ELCA, the synod; in the EC, the diocese. The primary responsibility for pastoral care rests with the inviting church.

10. The inviting diocese or synod will be responsible for assessment of an individual's suitability for service. However, the deacon or diaconal minister remains accountable to the sending body for continuation of ministerial status.

11. In an ecclesiastical disciplinary review or judicial process, the deacon or diaconal minister remains under the jurisdiction of the sending body, but the inviting body may be asked to participate as appropriate.

12. Dioceses and synods are encouraged to consider how deacons and diaconal ministers in extended service might best participate in the relevant decision-making bodies of the two churches (e.g., granting of voice, vote in judicatory assemblies).

Notes

1 Creating a New Vision; Setting the Stage for a Renewed Order

1. John W. Gardner, *No Easy Victories* (New York: Joanna Cotler Books, 1968), 169.
2. It should be noted here that while the diaconate had been around since the earliest church, it had gone through various stages. Without rehearsing a long history here—one that can be found in many other places—this new incarnation refers specifically to the way in which the Episcopal Church (and others around the same time) articulated new possibilities for a distinctive order, rather than a transitional one.
3. *Can the Diaconate Be Distinctive? A Research Report on the 1978 Survey Study of the Episcopal Permanent Diaconate*, study conducted by the Coordinating Committee, Study on the Diaconate, June 1979, Council for the Development of Ministry, Part III, "Recommendations to the House of Bishops," 1–2.
4. *Consultation on the Diaconate: The Next Step in the Re-examination of the Diaconate in the Life of the Episcopal Church*, a consultation called by the Council for the Development of Ministry, May 7–8, 1980, in Chicago, Illinois, 8.
5. Ibid, 8–9. In the report *"Christ's presence and activity of making whole"* was intended by the members of the consultation to imply the way in which our servanthood to those in need would allow us to share in the healing and transforming action of Christ's presence, allowing us to become whole.
6. Ibid.
7. *Raising Up Servant Ministry: Eight Dioceses Work Toward the Future of the Diaconate and the Enablement of Servant Ministry*, a study presented by The Permanent Diaconate Evaluation Committee, Research Coordinator: Adair T Lummis, PhD; Chair of the Committee was D. Barry Menuez; Education for Mission and Ministry Unit with help from The Rev. John T. Docker, Field Officer, Council for the Development of Ministry. Spring 1985 © Episcopal Church Center.
8. Ibid., foreword, 1–4.
9. The Diaconate . . . a unique place in a total ministry, sponsored by the National Centre for the Diaconate and Associated Parishes, Inc., May 31–June 2, 1979. 171.
10. Ibid. Deacon Phina Borgeson's keynote address, 131.

11. No date other than 1984 provided on the copy of the address Dean McDonald gave at the Conference at Notre Dame. "Deacons in the Total Ministry of the Church," a conference sponsored by the National Center for the Diaconate, May 24–26, 1984, Notre Dame University.
12. Ibid.
13. Richard Nolan, ed., *The Diaconate Now* (Washington, DC: Corus Publishing, 1968), 5–6.
14. James Barnett, *The Diaconate: A Full and Equal Order* (New York: Seabury Press, 1981), 3. Citation from 1 Peter 2:9, Revised Standard Version.
15. Ibid. Barnett uses Reginald Fuller's "Early Catholicism in the New Testament" (lecture, Graduate School of Theology, Sewanee, TN, 1970). Cf., Ernst Kasemann, *Essays on New Testament Themes,* Studies in Biblical Theology 41 (London: SCM Press, 1964), 63–87.
16. Barnett, *Diaconate,* 3.
17. Urban T. Holmes, III, "Education for Liturgy," in *Worship Points the Way,* ed. Malcolm C. Burson (New York: Seabury Press, 1981), 139.
18. Rev. Dr. Louis Weil, e-mail to author, December 4, 2013.

2   Waves and Ways of Being

1. Ormonde Plater, *Many Servants* (Cambridge, MA: Cowley Publications, 2004), 31.
2. Nolan, *Diaconate Now,* 159ff.
3. Ibid., 161.
4. Rev. Phina Borgeson, "Sister Priscilla Celebrates 45 Years of Diaconal Ministry," Episcopal News Service Article, June 19, 2004.
5. Book of Common Prayer 1928 (New York: Seabury Press), 533.
6. Ibid., 534–35.
7. Plater, *Many Servants,* 44
8. From the minute book of the Central House of Deaconesses, previously from files kept with the Association for Episcopal Deacons and now maintained at the Episcopal Church Archives in Austin, Texas.
9. Ibid . . . Nearly forty-five years later, the situation is the same. Prospective deacons at seminaries are looked on more as potential sources of income, and educated in a presbyteral model. There is little or no teaching of presbyters-to-be about the life and work of deacons, effective ways to be partners in ministry, or how to share leadership together.
10. Ibid. Minutes of November 2, 1970.
11. Ibid.
12. Ibid. Minutes of April 16, 1974.
13. Plater, *Many Servants,*.46.
14. Deacon Edward Horton, e-mail message to author, April 6, 2014.
15. Frederick Erickson, e-mail message to author, April 11, 2014.
16. Bishop William Folwell, e-mail message to author, April 24, 2014.
17. http://www.cfdiocese.org/ics/brief-overview.

3   Shaped by a New Prayer Book

1. The name of the newsletter of the National Centre for the Diaconate. The first issue was sent from the Boston office in the fall of 1978.
2. Bloy House series, "Claiming the Vision." Located on the school's website: www.bloyhouse.org/vision.html and released in late 2011.
3. Theodore Eastman, *The Baptizing Community* (Minneapolis, MN: Seabury Press, Winston Press, 1982), 5.
4. Ibid., 4.
5. Ibid.
6. Bloy House video at about the 11:14 minute mark.
7. General Convention, *Journal of the General Convention, cf . . . The Episcopal Church, Minneapolis 1976* (New York: General Convention, 1977), C-118
8. Ibid.
9. "Total Ministry Development Explored," Episcopal News Service release, September 25, 1980.
10. "Total Ministry Explored in Berkeley," Episcopal News Service release, January 15, 1981.
11. Ibid.
12. David Sumner, "Total Ministry Means Everybody's Ministry," Episcopal News Service release, February 3, 1983.
13. Ibid.
14. "Dozier, Film, Higlight Total Ministry Conference," Episcopal News Service release February 28, 1985.
15. Ibid.
16. "Verna Dozier Dies at 88," Episcopal News Service release September 2, 2006.
17. Ibid.

4   Shaped by Living—The Fifth Wave as a Decade of Definition

1. *DIAKONEO* 5, no. 3 (Fall 1983): 3. Published by the National Centre for the Diaconate in Boston, MA.
2. *DIAKONEO* 4, no. 2 (Spring 1982): 3. Published by the National Centre for the Diaconate in Boston, MA.
3. Ibid.
4. Ormonde Plater, "Deacons at General Convention," *DIAKONEO* 7, no. 3 (Fall 1985): 2–3. Published by the National Centre for the Diaconate
5. "Sindicators: Laos and the Diaconate," *DIAKONEO* 7, no. 1 (Spring 1986): 1ff. First published by the National Centre for the Diaconate. Later republished in 1999 as a monograph by the North American Association for the Diaconate.
6. Ibid.
7. Ibid.
8. Ibid.
9. Ibid.

10. Diocese of Central Florida newsletters (September 1985).
11. "The Primate's Challenge to Deacons," *DIAKONEO* 9, no. 2 (Summer 1987): 1. Published by the North American Association for the Diaconate, sent from New Orleans, LA.
12. Ibid., 14.
13. Ibid., 8ff.
14. Ibid.

5 Living in the Fifth Wave—Wading into a Sixth

1. Personal interview with Madelyn Busse, June 20, 2014, and included with her permission.
2. "Yearend: More than 1000 Deacons," *DIAKONEO* 10, no. 2 (March 1988): 1. Published by the North American Association for the Diaconate, sent from New Orleans, Ormonde Plater, Editor.
3. Plater, *Many Servants*, 70
4. Ibid.
5. Ibid.
6. Ibid.
7. Ibid., xiii.
8. "Signs of Service" was produced as a joint effort between the Office for Ministry Development and the Office of Communications at the Episcopal Church. The production effort is described by Deacon Josephine Borgeson in the September 1990 issue of *DIAKONEO*. Phina Borgeson, "Making a National Videotape about Deacons," *DIAKONEO* 12, no. 4, 1.
9. The Rev. Donald Thompson, "A Community for Deacons," *DIAKONEO* 13, no. 5 (November 1991): 1–2. Published by the North American Association for the Diaconate, sent from New Orleans.
10. Ibid.
11. Edwin F. Hallenbeck, ed., *Guidelines for Deacon Programs*, 2nd ed. (Providence, RI: North American Association for the Diaconate Working Papers, no. 277, 2002).
12. A group facilitation process developed by Harrison Owen when he realized that at many conferences, the most important conversations happen at the water cooler, or over meals, or near the pool.
13. Edwin F. Hallenbeck, ed., *Guidelines for Deacon Programs*, 1st ed. (Providence, RI: North American Association for the Diaconate Working Papers, 1999).
14. Ibid.
15. "The Rev. Canon H. Boone Porter Dies at 76," *The Living Church* 218, no. 26 (June 27, 1999): 6.
16. From my personal copy of minutes of the 1999 Conference Committee, November 28–30, 1997, Burnsville, Minnesota. Recorded by the late Bishop George Harris.
17. Ibid.

18. From the keynote address by Timothy F. Sedgwick, PhD, at Living the Covenant—later adapted as an article for the *Anglican Theological Review* 82, no. 1, 155–71.

6 The Sixth Wave—Interpretation and Prophetic Voice

1. Deacon Dutton Morehouse, e-mail message to author, late summer, 1999.
2. Ormonde Plater, e-mail to author, summer, 1999.
3. Elizabeth O'Connor, *Servant Leaders, Servant Structures* (Washington, DC: Servant Leadership School, 1991), 86.
4. Taken from a speech shared in Michigan in November 1999 and adapted for print in *DIAKONEO* 22, no. 2 (Easter 2000): "Parakaleo" column, 16.ff.
5. Further material added for a speech given at the Boone Porter Institute, Nashotah House, Summer 2000.
6. Plater, *Many Servants*, 70.
7. http://www.deathpenaltyinfo.org/documents/FactSheet.pdf. Death Penalty Information Center, Washington, DC, update issued July 24, 2014.
8. Ormonde Plater, "Through the Dust," *DIAKONEO* 24, no. 2 (Eastertide 2002): 18. Published by the North American Association for the Diaconate.
9. Much of the content on canonical changes is summarized from The Ven. Theodore Nitz, "Commentary on New Deacon Canons," *DIAKONEO* 25, no. 6 (Advent 2003). Additional information was provided by Deacon Joyce Hardy in personal conversation and correspondence, August 4, 2014.
10. Walter Brueggemann, *Prophetic Imagination* (Minneapolis: Fortress Press, 1978).
11. This story has been shared in many places, perhaps most recently in an article I wrote, "Common Vows and Common Mission," for *The Anglican Theological Review*, 92, no. 1 (Winter 2010): 71–88. Used with permission from Jacqueline Winter.
12. Bishop Duncan M. Gray Jr., e-mail to author, May 14, 2014.

7 Wading More Deeply into the Seventh Wave—Up to Our Waists Integrating All We've Learned

1. Excerpts of "A Report on TEAC" I provided for the House of Bishops in March of 2007.
2. Participants were: Deacon Maggie Dawson, formation director, Diocese of Louisiana; The Ven. Eugenia Dowdeswell, archdeacon, Diocese of Western North Carolina; Mr. Rod Dugliss, PhD, dean, School for Deacons, Berkeley, California; Deacon John Harper, PhD, Diocese of Iowa, teacher in program for local formation of deacons and priests; Ms. Jane Root, PhD, codirector of

deacon formation, Diocese of Indianapolis; Deacon Robert Snow, missionary and canon to the ordinary, Diocese of the Dominican Republic; Deacon Carol Stewart, assistant to the bishop for outreach and community development, Diocese of Mississippi; The Rev. Margaret Thomas, coordinator, deacon formation program, Diocese of Maine, member of the NAAD Board; The Ven. James Visger, archdeacon, Diocese of Nebraska; Deacon Susanne Watson Epting, executive director of NAAD and cofacilitator of the Consultation; The Ven. Lauren Welch, archdeacon, Diocese of Maryland; Deacon John Willets, PhD, retired professor in DePaul University's School for New Learning and cofacilitator of the Consultation, from the Diocese of Chicago; Deacon Dutton Morehouse, editor of *DIAKONEO* and Deacon Update (online news), observer and reporter.

3. Dutton Morehouse, "Notes on the Consultation on Deacon Formation," *DIAKONEO* 30, no. 4 (2008): 8–9.
4. As listed in the Title III Ministry Canons: academic studies, *diakonia* and the diaconate, human awareness and understanding, spiritual development and discipline, practical training and experience.
5. The full summary and report—some seventy pages—is available from the Association for Episcopal Deacons. The website with appropriate contact information is: www.episcopaldeacons.org. In addition, I have sent the full report to the Episcopal Archives in Austin, Texas: www.episcopalarchives.org.
6. "A Look at the Diaconate in 2008, a summary of research conducted on the Diaconate," © 2009, Episcopal Church Center and North American Association for the Diaconate, 7.
7. Ibid., 16.
8. The full text of the agreement can be read on the Episcopal Church website at: http://www.episcopalchurch.org/page/agreement-full-communion-called-common-mission or from the Ecumenical and Interreligious Office of the Episcopal Church.
9. *"The Diaconate as Ecumenical Opportunity," The Hanover Report of the Anglican-Lutheran International Commission* (London, England: Anglican Consultative Council and the Lutheran World Federation by Anglican Communion Publications, 1996). The report is an excellent synopsis of conversations and recommendations made by the Anglican-Lutheran International Commission, and the place of the diaconate ecumenically. This is a "must read" for anyone preparing for the diaconate.
10. Madelyn Busse, ELCA diaconal minister, and Susanne Watson Epting, Episcopal deacon, "The Diaconate and Called to Common Mission—Continuing Exploration of the Diaconate as Full Communion Partners" (report to the Lutheran Episcopal Coordinating Committee 2005). Available from www.episcopalarchives.org.
11. "An Epistle from the Lutheran World Federation Consultation on Diakonia," November 7, 2002. Further studies would follow from the Lutheran World Federation, resulting in a 100-page document: "Diakonia in Context: Transformation, Reconciliation, Empowerment," published in 2009 in several languages by the Lutheran World Federation, Geneva, Switzerland.
12. Busse and Epting, "The Diaconate and Called to Common Mission," 19.

8   Seven Waves and Room for More

1. Thomas Breidenthal, "Exodus from Privilege: Reflections on the Diaconate in Acts," *The Anglican Theological Review* 95, no. 2 (Spring 2013): 275.
2. Ibid., 277.
3. The statement is not copyrighted, but I do acknowledge and extend gratitude to the Association for Episcopal Deacons, and particularly the small group that worked on it, including: Deacons Lauren Welch (convener), Ernestina Campbell, William Joyner, Pamela Nesbit, James Visger, Susanne Watson Epting, and Mr. Rod Dugliss. Again, the Lutheran World Federation Document was published as a letter from the global consultation in Johannesburg, "Prophetic Diakonia: For the Healing of the World," November 7, 2002.
4. Breidenthal, "Exodus from Privilege," 292.
5. Robert Brooks, "Post-Baptismal Catechesis," in *The Baptismal Ministry and the Catechumenate*, ed. Michael Merriman (New York: Church Hymnal Corp., 1990), 145 ff.
6. Plater, *Many Servants*, 62,
7. Ormonde Plater, e-mail to author, December 7, 2012.
8. Elaine Clements's posting on anglodeacons listserv, April 25, 2014. Used with permission.
9. Deacon Elaine Clements, e-mail to author, July 15, 2014.
10. General Convention, *Journal of the General Convention of the Episcopal Church, Anaheim, CA, 2009* (New York: General Convention, 2009), 649.
11. Much of this description is taken from the project proposal and brochures Kyle and I worked on together. I offer him my thanks here as the author of the program and its coordinator.
12. Rev. Josh Thomas, director of Kids for Peace, e-mail to author, July 7, 2014.
13. Bishop Thomas Breidenthal, phone conversation with author, July 16, 2013.
14. Excerpt from remarks shared at an archdeacon and formation director gathering of the Association for Episcopal Deacons in 2013; used with Aaron Scott's permission.
15. "Who Will Live God's Dream?" © Susanne Watson Epting.

9   Are We There Yet?

1. Patricia Ross, e-mail to author, June 17, 2014.
2. Rt. Rev Kirk Stevan Smith, pastoral letter of June 14, 2014, written to the people of God in the Diocese of Arizona.
3. http://justfaith.org/about/.
4. Edwin F. Hallenbeck, ed., *A Working Paper of Guidelines for Diaconal Formation* (North American Association for the Diaconate, 1999), 13–14.

Postscript

1. Aaron Scott, e-mail to author, December 17, 2014.
2. Ibid.

Appendix One: Deacons *Are* in the Picture

1. © Deacon Josephine Borgeson, used with permission.

Appendix Two: Citizens of the World—Servants of Christ

1. At the time of the conference, Maylanne Whitall.
2. © Deacon Maylanne Maybee, used with permission.
3. Dom Helder Camara, *The Desert Is Fertile* (Maryknoll, NY: Orbis Books, 1980), 15.

Appendix Three: Principles of Orderly Exchange

1. Author's Note: This document was a part of a proposal made in 2005 and included in the paper "The Diaconate and Called to Common Mission." As of this writing, there is no official document like this in our full communion agreement with the Evangelical Lutheran Church in America. However, it is offered here as a suggestion for a model, should there be communities in which it would be helpful.